The Joy of
MICROWAVING

MICROWAVE
COOKING
INSTITUTE

Prentice Hall Press • New York

This unique cookbook, especially designed for microwave cooking, gives you two feasts — one for your eyes and one for your palate. Hundreds of beautiful photos of finished dishes will appeal to your tastebuds; and the meals you prepare will taste as good as you imagined they would.

Step-by-step photo sequences will show you *exactly* how to prepare recipes successfully. So even if you're just starting to cook with a microwave, you can feel confident with these recipes. Consumer-tested by people like you, they combine imaginative ingredients with foolproof techniques. You'll have a winner every time.

The Joy of Microwaving will quickly become your essential reference for all kinds of microwave cooking, from simple to elegant. The diet conscious will appreciate the nutritional value charts following many healthy, tasty but slenderizing recipes. Other charts present detailed information you'll refer to again and again. The general tips section will give you ideas for making your microwave even more useful, such as household hints, tips on how to microwave convenience foods, and recipes for baby foods and snacks kids can make. We know you'll reach for this indispensable book again and again — so bon appetit!

MICROWAVE
COOKING
INSTITUTE

CREDITS:
Design, Photography & Production: Cy DeCosse Incorporated

Material in *The Joy of Microwaving* is compiled from the following books, authored by Barbara Methven and available from the publisher:

- Basic Microwaving
- Recipe Conversion for Microwave
- Microwaving Meats
- Microwave Baking & Desserts
- Microwaving Meals in 30 Minutes
- Microwaving on a Diet
- Microwaving Fruits & Vegetables
- Microwaving Convenience Foods
- Microwaving for Holidays & Parties
- Microwaving for One & Two
- The Microwave & Freezer
- 101 Microwaving Secrets
- Microwaving Light & Healthy
- Microwaving Poultry & Seafood

CY DE COSSE INCORPORATED
Chairman: Cy DeCosse
President: James B. Maus
Executive Vice President: William B. Jones

Library of Congress Cataloging-in-Publication Data

The Joy of Microwaving.

A compilation of several books from the Microwave Cooking Library.
Includes index. 1. Microwave Cookery. I. Microwave Cooking Institute.
TX832.J69 1986   641.5'882   86-12276
ISBN 0-13-511551-5

Published by Prentice Hall Press
A Division of Simon & Schuster, Inc.
Gulf + Western Building
One Gulf + Western Plaza
New York, NY 10023
PRENTICE HALL PRESS is a trademark of Simon & Schuster, Inc.
ISBN 0-13-511551-5
Manufactured in the United States of America
10 9 8 7 6 5 4 3 2
Printed in U.S.A.

Contents

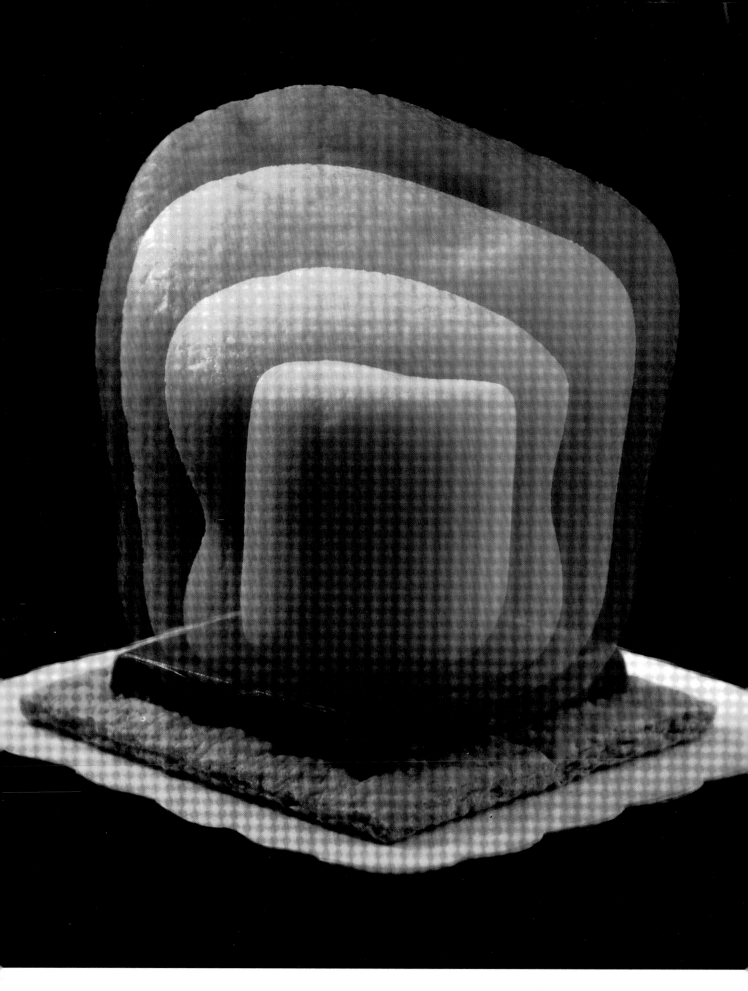

Multiple Exposure of Marshmallow S'mores through oven door at four second intervals demonstrates microwave speed.

Microwaving: What you Should Know before You Start

A wide variety of microwave ovens is available today to make almost all food preparation faster and easier. The directions in this book have been tested in all major brands of ovens, so you can use them with confidence in your oven.

All Ovens Do Not Cook Alike

Like conventional ranges, microwave ovens differ in their rate and evenness of cooking. House power differs from one part of the country to another. If you live in a small farming community, your appliance may cook faster than the same model in a large city. Voltage fluctuates and is lower during periods of peak consumption. An appliance will cook slower on extremely hot or cold days when more electricity is being used.

You Control the Cooking

A microwave oven is a cooking appliance. It may be faster and easier to use than a conventional appliance, but it still needs a cook to control it. Personal preferences differ. Food which is undercooked for one person may be overcooked for another.

To allow for differences in equipment, house power and personal tastes, both microwave and conventional recipes provide a time span during which food may be done, and a test by which you may determine doneness. Unless you have a fast oven and live in a high voltage area, the minimum time suggested in these directions will probably be too short. However, checking food at the minimum time will allow you to judge how much more time is needed.

The amount of attention (stirring, turning, etc.) suggested in our directions is based on the minimum needed for satisfactory results. No matter what type of oven you have, the more attention you give the food, the better the results will be. If you feel that food is not cooking evenly, you can usually correct this by stirring or turning more often, or by allowing a longer standing time.

Look While You Cook

Don't be afraid to watch your food through the oven door. The diffused light inside a microwave oven is due to the finely perforated metal screen imbedded in the door. This screen prevents the escape of microwave energy, while it allows you to look as you cook.

If food is ready to boil over, or is overcooking in one area, you can stop cooking immediately by opening the oven door or by pushing the stop button. This has the same effect as removing a pan from the range but it also stops microwave energy immediately. The oven cannot operate while the door is open.

Microwave Ovens are Safe

Microwave ovens are built for safety. They must be thoroughly tested to meet the standards of several regulating agencies.

Since a microwave oven is a miniature broadcasting system, the Federal Communications Commission makes sure that it does not broadcast on the wrong frequency.

Underwriters Laboratory assures that the oven is electrically safe when properly grounded and operated.

The Department of Health, Education and Welfare must approve the design of the oven, especially the door's safety interlock system.

Government regulations are strict and allow a wide margin for safety. In addition, the government requires that all oven manufacturers publish the following precautions. They assure that the oven, which is safe when you buy it, will remain safe while you use it.

Precautions to Avoid Possible Exposure to Excessive Microwave Energy

Do not attempt to operate the oven with the door open since open door operation can result in harmful exposure to microwave energy. It is important not to defeat or tamper with the safety interlocks.

Do not place any object between the oven front face and the door or allow soil or cleaner residue to accumulate on sealing surfaces.

Do not operate the oven if it is damaged. It is particularly important that the oven door close properly and that there is no damage to the (1) door (bent), (2) hinges and latches (broken or loosened), (3) door seals and sealing surfaces.

The oven should not be adjusted or repaired by anyone except properly qualified service personnel.

What are Microwaves?

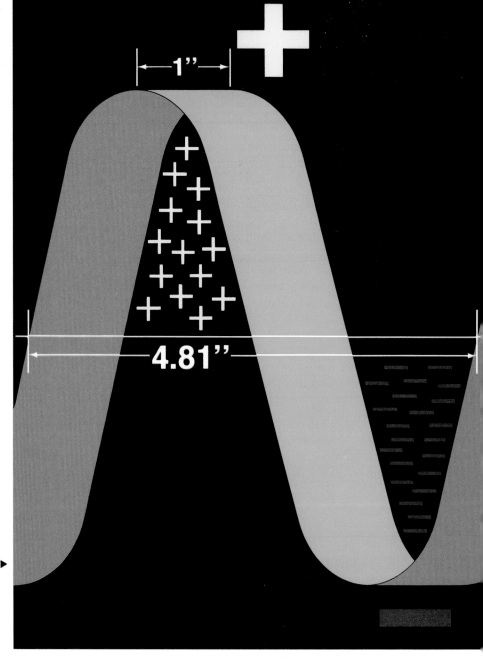

Microwaves are high frequency electromagnetic waves, like ordinary daylight and radio waves. Microwaves used in ovens are very short, less than 5 inches long, while radio waves vary in length from 3 feet to many miles.

Radio waves are in the air around us all the time. Radio energy can be broadcast from great distances, even from the moon, and is converted to sound in your radio. The microwave "broadcasting system" is contained within the oven, where the energy is converted to heat in food.

The microwave is an energy ▶ field which alternates in positive and negative directions, and acts like a magnet on the positive and negative particles in food molecules.

How Microwaves are Broadcast into the Oven

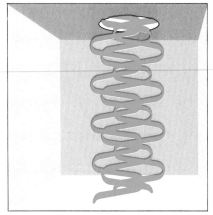

Energy enters the oven cavity through an opening in the metal case, usually at the top. Hot spots occur if it is not distributed in the oven or the food.

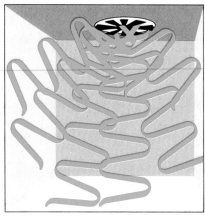

A Stirrer, similar to a fan blade, deflects microwaves to different parts of the oven so all do not follow the same path. Some ovens move food through the energy field on a turntable.

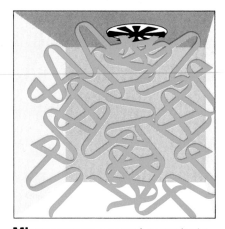

Microwaves cannot penetrate metal. They are reflected off the oven walls at right angles. There must be food in the oven to absorb the energy.

How Microwaves Cause Heat by Friction

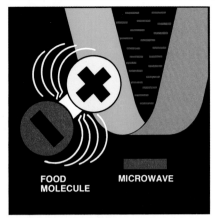

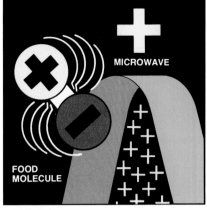

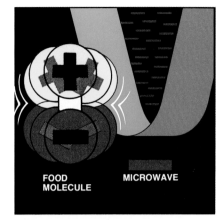

Opposites attract. Plus particles in food molecules are attracted to the negative or minus direction of the microwave.

Positive direction of the microwave attracts minus particles. Microwaves reverse direction 2,450,000,000 times a second.

Friction between molecules vibrating almost 2½ billion times a second produces heat in food.

How Microwaves Cook Food

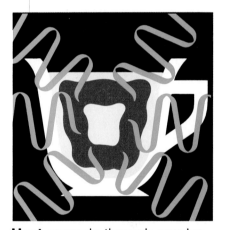

Microwaves penetrate food from all directions to a depth of ¾ to 1½-in. They cause no chemical change in the food.

Vibration of food molecules causes heat in the areas of penetration. These areas begin to cook.

Heat spreads through conduction to other parts of the food, as it does in conventional cooking.

How Microwaves Affect Water, Fat & Sugar Molecules

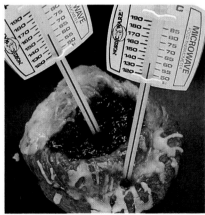

Water is driven to the surface of food during microwaving. This moisture evaporates but surface does not become crisp.

Fat is drawn to the surface, where it browns on long-term foods. Center of roast is cooked by heat conduction.

Sugar attracts microwave energy. Surface temperature of roll equalizes with air. Center becomes very hot and burns.

7

Food Characteristics & Microwaving

These food characteristics affect all cooking, but microwave speed makes the differences more pronounced. Water, fat and sugar attract microwave energy, so foods containing them cook faster. When several foods are cooked at once, microwave-attractive foods may draw energy away from foods which contain less water, fat or sugar and alter their cooking time.

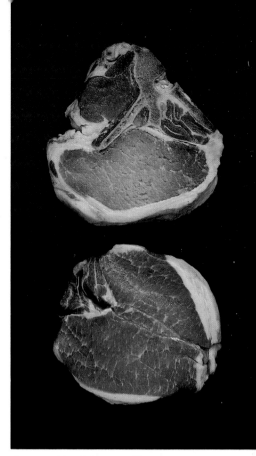

Size. Small pieces cook faster than large ones in both microwave and conventional cooking. Since microwaves penetrate food ¾ to 1½ inches, uniform pieces under 2 inches in diameter cook from all sides.

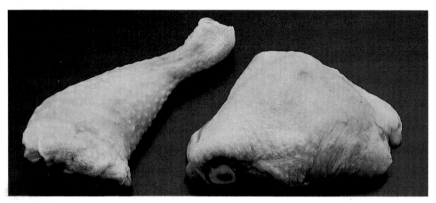

Shape. Thin parts of uneven foods cook faster than thick parts. Uniformly thick foods cook evenly. Place thin parts toward the center of the dish where they receive less microwave energy.

Amount of bone. Bone conducts heat. When bone is on side of meat, that side cooks first. Boneless cuts cook less rapidly but more evenly.

Quantity. Small amounts cook faster than large ones. Microwaving time is always directly related to the amount of food and increases with the quantity. When doubling a recipe, increase time by about ½ and check for doneness.

Quality. Fresh vegetables microwave best. Test by cutting. Moisture should appear on surface rapidly. If it takes more than a minute, add more water.

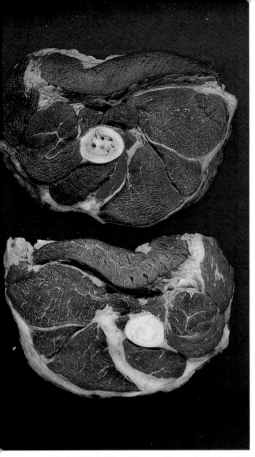

Fat distribution. Evenly distributed fat tenderizes and helps cook meat evenly. Large fatty areas attract energy away from meat and slow cooking.

Density. Dense, heavy foods like brownies take longer to microwave than porous, airy ones like cake. A food changes in density with the way it is prepared. Solid beef is denser than ground; baked potatoes hold their heat longer than mashed.

Starting temperature. Room temperature foods cook faster than refrigerated or frozen ones. Room temperature varies with the season. Cooking times may be longer on a cold winter day.

Moisture content. Add a minimum of water to fresh or frozen vegetables. Extra water slows cooking. Foods with low moisture do not microwave well.

Precooking. Fresh vegetables need time to tenderize. Frozen vegetables have been blanched and may take less time, even though they are frozen. Some brands of frozen vegetables are almost fully cooked and need only defrosting and heating.

Microwave Techniques:
Comparison with Conventional

Start with what you already know. Most techniques used in microwaving are the same ones used when cooking conventionally. There may be differences in application but they are easy to understand once you compare cooking methods.

Range Top. The surface burner on your range becomes hot and transfers heat to the bottom of the pan. This in turn heats the bottom of the food. To cook evenly and prevent burning, you must turn food over or stir cooked portions from the bottom to the top.

Conventional Oven. Heating elements in a conventional oven heat the air. This hot air heats the surfaces of food from all directions. Slowly the heat transfers from the surface to the center of the food. Since air in the oven is hot and dry, the surface of food becomes dry.

Microwave Oven. Microwaves penetrate food from all directions to a depth of ¾ to 1½ inches. Heating takes place beneath the surface; there is no heat in the oven itself. The center of food over 2 inches thick cooks by heat transference, as it does conventionally.

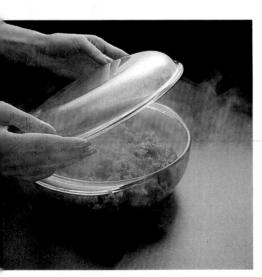

Covering food holds in steam to tenderize it and speed cooking in both microwave and conventional methods.

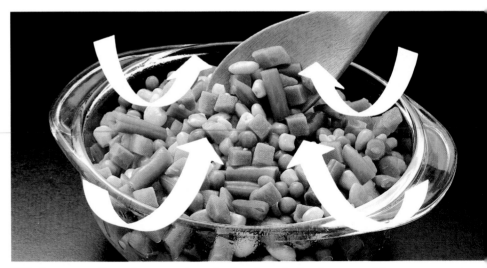

Stirring equalizes temperature in food and shortens cooking time. Since microwaves cook from all directions, you should stir from outside to center of dish. Ovens vary in amount of stirring needed, but all cook more evenly with occasional stirring.

Turning Food over is done in both range top and microwave cooking to help it heat evenly. When microwaving, turn over large, dense foods such as whole vegetables or roasts, which might cook more near the top of the oven.

Arranging food in oven when cooking several items is done in both types of cooking. Use ring pattern for microwaving.

Shielding protects sensitive areas from overcooking in both the conventional and microwave oven.

Rearranging food in the dish or on the oven shelf is done conventionally, but is used more often when microwaving. Corners or sides of dish receive more energy. Some places in oven may be warmer than others. Rearranging helps foods cook evenly.

Arranging uneven foods with thinner areas toward the center of dish prevents overcooking. Thicker parts, which take longer to cook conventionally, receive more microwave energy and will be done at the same time as thinner or more delicate areas.

Rotating, or turning in the oven, is used with foods which cannot be stirred, rearranged or turned over.

Microwave Techniques:
Covering

Covering serves much the same purpose in microwaving as it does in conventional cooking. While there is little evaporation during microwaving, a cover holds in steam to tenderize food, keep it moist and shorten cooking time.

In general, foods which you cover conventionally should be covered during microwaving. Remove covers carefully; steam can cause burns.

Loose casserole cover allows some steam to escape. In most cases this makes little difference. A sheet of wax paper may be placed between casserole and lid to make it tighter.

Tight cover fits snugly over rim of casserole, leaving no gaps for steam to escape. Use this type of cover when steaming vegetables which do not require added moisture.

Tight cover of plastic wrap can be used with dishes which do not have covers.

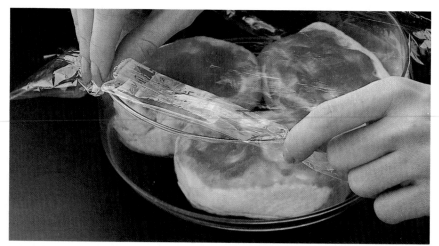

Vent plastic wrap by rolling back one edge to form a narrow slot. A tight cover of plastic wrap may split during microwaving unless you provide an opening for excess steam to escape.

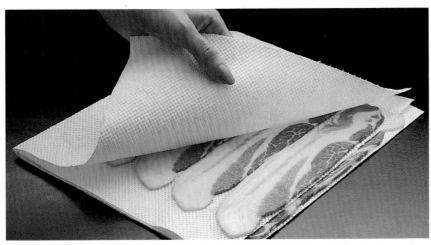

Dry paper towel allows steam to escape while it prevents spatters and absorbs excess moisture. Use to cover bacon, or foods which are cooked uncovered but tend to spatter.

Wax paper forms a loose cover similar to "partial covering" in conventional cooking. Use it to hold in heat, speed cooking and prevent spatters with foods which do not need steam to tenderize.

Cooking bag holds in steam to tenderize meat. Before microwaving, remove any foil from bag and discard metal twist tie. Tie loosely with string or strip of plastic cut from end of bag; leave small space for steam to escape. Place bag in cooking dish.

Paper towels absorb moisture trapped between food and oven floor, and keep bread surfaces dry.

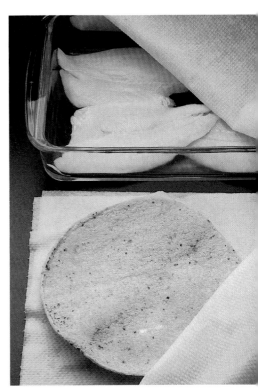

Damp towel steams scallops or fish fillets. To soften tortillas, heat 4 at a time between moist towels; 10 to 20 seconds at High.

13

Microwave Techniques:
Dish Shapes, Shielding, Standing

Using the right dish or casserole is important in microwaving. Both size and shape affect the way foods cook, the attention needed and microwaving time. Get to know your casserole sizes.

Depth of the container is as important as capacity. Both of these casseroles hold 1½ quarts of food, but the deeper one takes longer to microwave. A shallow casserole exposes more food surface to microwave energy.

Round shapes microwave more evenly than squares or rectangles. More energy penetrates corners, which may overcook.

◄ **Avoid** casseroles with sloping sides. Food is less deep in the areas which receive most energy and can overcook. A straight sided casserole keeps the depth of food uniform.

Ring shapes are excellent for foods which cannot be stirred during microwaving. Energy penetrates food from the center as well as the sides, top and bottom for faster, more even cooking.

14

Dramatic experiment demonstrates the affect of shielding. Wrap ice cube in foil and place in oven with a glass of water. Microwave until water boils.

Unwrap ice cube; it will still be ▶ frozen because microwave energy cannot penetrate metal. Note, water continues to boil.

Shield foods which attract mi- ▶ crowave energy with a sauce to keep them moist. When microwaving casseroles, bury pieces of meat in sauce or vegetables. Use small strips of foil on thin areas to prevent overcooking.

Reduce power level when microwaving dense foods, such as roasts, or delicate foods like custard. The lower power level protects foods from a high concentration of energy and helps them cook evenly.

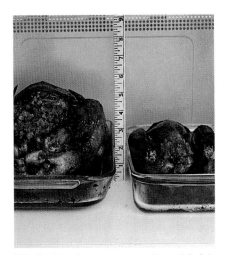

High foods may require shielding or turning over. Areas close to the top of the oven receive more energy.

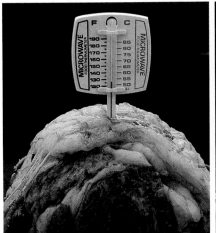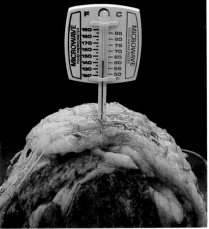

Standing time allows microwaved foods to finish cooking by internal heat after they are removed from the oven. The internal temperature of this roast rose from 125° to 140° during 15 minutes standing. Roast is also easier to carve after standing.

Microwave Techniques:
Testing for Doneness

Start with what you already know. The appearance of some microwaved foods may be different from conventionally cooked, but many tests for doneness are the same. The final test is your own preference. Some people like food crisp; others prefer it very soft. Adjust cooking times to suit yourself.

The directions in this book tell you when to test for doneness and what to look for. Standing is part of the microwaving process. Wait until after standing time before taste-testing food. You can always microwave a little longer, but nothing can save food which is overcooked. Standing is especially important for foods which need time to tenderize or which toughen when overcooked.

Wooden pick inserted in center of cake comes out clean. Moist spots on surface will dry on standing. Do not insert pick in moist spot.

Cake pulls away from sides of pan when done. Top will not be brown, but cake will be higher and lighter than conventionally baked.

Knife inserted halfway between center and edge of custard comes out clean. Center appears soft but will set on standing.

Raw shellfish are gray and translucent. They turn pink and opaque when cooked. To avoid toughening, undercook slightly and let stand.

Fish flakes easily with fork. Center is slightly translucent but cooks on standing. Fish toughens and dries if overcooked.

Meat is done when fork tender. Less tender cuts split at fibers. Allow standing time to tenderize them.

Drumstick of chicken moves freely at joint and is soft when pinched. Last juices drained from cavity run clear yellow.

Most testing techniques are the same as the ones you learned for conventional cooking, but there are a few which are unique to microwaving.

When food is brought to a boil on an electric burner, it continues to cook after the burner is turned off. Manufacturers call this "coasting time" and advise you to use it to save energy. Few cooks do; they take the pan off the stove.

With microwaving, heat is inside the food. You can't stop cooking by removing food from the oven. Use the heat to finish cooking and save energy.

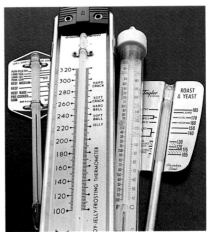

Feel the bottom when reheating a plate of food. It will be warm when food is hot enough to transfer heat to the dish.

Remove some foods from the oven while they still look partially cooked. This is the hardest thing to learn about microwaving, although standing time is also used conventionally to allow foods to settle.

Be patient and let the food stand. If it isn't done to your taste after standing, you can microwave a little longer, but there's no remedy for overcooking.

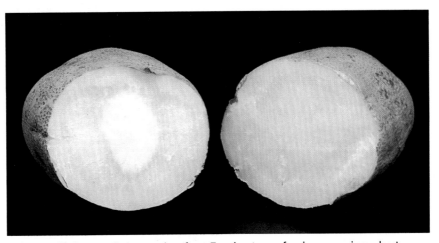

Potato is heated through after 5 minutes of microwaving, but when cut it reveals an uncooked center. After standing 5 minutes the center is completely cooked. Potatoes hold their heat up to 45 minutes when wrapped in foil.

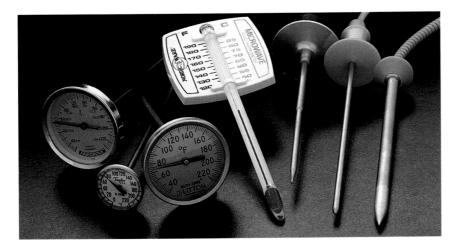

Probes and microwave thermometers register the internal temperature of meat. Insert them as you would a conventional meat thermometer. A probe shuts the oven off automatically when the meat reaches a pre-set internal temperature. It is not accurate for poultry because the fat becomes hot rapidly and a probe may turn the oven off before the meat is fully cooked.

Do not use conventional meat or candy thermometers. They may be used to check temperatures outside the oven, but only microwave thermometers can be used during cooking.

Microwave Techniques:
Browning

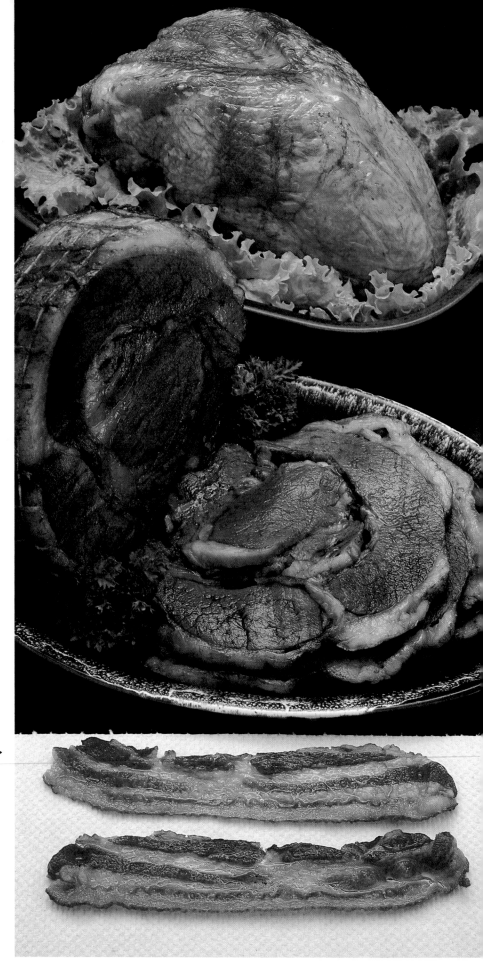

People who have never used a microwave oven before are sometimes concerned about browning because they don't know what to expect. Once they become familiar with microwaving, many cooks feel that browning is unimportant.

The appearance of some foods may be slightly different from conventionally cooked, but microwaved foods look cooked, not raw.

Some foods do brown. Examples are roasts with a good fat covering, bacon, whole chickens and turkey breasts. These foods have a high fat content which comes to the surface quickly and browns.

With the exception of bacon, these browned foods will not be crisp. Chicken pieces take less time to microwave than a whole chicken and do not have time to brown.

Browning Utensils

These utensils, designed specifically for microwaving, sear and brown foods the way a conventional skillet does. They should never be used with a conventional range.

Browning utensils have a special coating on the bottom which absorbs microwave energy and reaches a temperature of 500° to 600°. The sides and handles of the utensils stay cool. Feet or ridges raise the bottom to protect counters, but hot browning utensils should not be placed on plastic mats or table tops.

Browning grill well catches fat and juices so steaks and chops don't steam. Paper towels or wax paper should never be used to reduce spatters. They could catch fire, as they would on a range top, because of high heat generated by dish.

Browning dish sides and cover prevent spatters. When meat is browned, sauces can be added for continued cooking in the same dish.

How To Use Browning Utensils

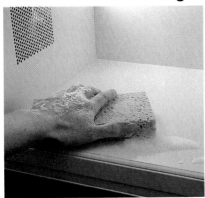

Be sure oven is clean. Grease will bake onto oven floor or shelf when dish is preheated.

Preheat dish as manufacturer directs. Preheat only ½ to ⅔ of time before adding butter.

Do not use non-stick sprays or coatings with browning utensils; they scorch.

Microwave Techniques:
Browning Agents

Some foods do not brown during microwaving. While many cooks find them unnecessary, browning agents can be used to give microwaved foods an appearance similar to conventionally cooked. Many browning agents flavor foods, too.

Plain microwaved hamburger▶ loses its gray color on standing. For browner color and added flavor, sprinkle meat with onion soup mix before microwaving.

Plain microwaved chicken has a light golden color. Piece on the right was brushed with melted butter and sprinkled with paprika before microwaving.

Microwaved cakes do not brown. Top or frost them as you would a conventionally baked cake.

How to Use Browning Agents

Choose a browning agent appropriate for your food from the chart. Browning agents can be savory, sweet or unflavored. Some liquids are applied full strength, but most are diluted with equal parts of water or butter. Dry agents are sprinkled on before or during microwaving.

Brush on liquid browning agents before microwaving. Soy sauce gives meat an oriental flavor. Bouquet sauce colors with little flavoring.

Browning Agent & Coating Chart

Agent	Foods	Comments
Soy or Teriyaki Sauce	Hamburgers, Beef, Lamb, Pork, Poultry	Brush on meat; rub into poultry
Barbecue Sauce	Hamburgers, Beef, Lamb, Pork, Poultry	Brush on or pour over
Melted Butter and Paprika	Poultry	Brush on butter; sprinkle with paprika
Brown Bouquet Sauce and Melted Butter	Hamburgers, Beef, Lamb, Pork, Poultry	Brush on meat; rub into poultry
Worcestershire or Steak Sauce and Water	Hamburgers, Beef, Lamb, Pork	Brush on
Onion Soup or Gravy Mix, Bouillon Granules	Hamburgers, Beef, Lamb	Sprinkle on before microwaving
Taco Seasoning Mix	Hamburgers, Savory Quick Breads	Sprinkle on before microwaving
Bread Crumbs, Bread Crumbs and Parmesan Cheese, Crushed Corn or Potato Chips	Casseroles	Sprinkle on after final stirring
Crushed French Fried Onion Rings, or Crumbled Bacon and Shredded Cheese	Savory Quick Breads, Casseroles	Sprinkle on before microwaving or after final stirring
Brown Sugar, Chopped Nuts, or mixture of both	Cakes, Sweet Quick Breads	Sprinkle on halfway through or after microwaving
Cinnamon-Sugar or Coconut	Sweet Quick Breads	Sprinkle on before microwaving
Powdered Sugar	Cakes	Sprinkle on after microwaving
Jelly, Preserves or Glazes	Ham, Poultry	Glaze ham after microwaving; poultry after ½ cooking time

Dry chicken thoroughly. Rub liquid agents into skin before microwaving. Dilute bouquet sauce with butter.

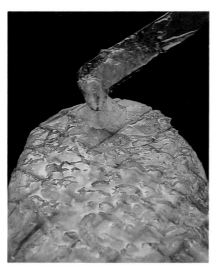

Glaze ham or poultry with jelly, preserves or glazes for sheen and flavor. See chart for methods.

Sprinkle on dry toppings as directed. Casseroles which require stirring should be topped after last stirring.

21

Microwave Techniques:
Combine Microwave with Conventional Cooking

Many foods are prepared most efficiently when you do part of the cooking by microwave and part conventionally. Use microwaving for its speed, easy clean up and unique jobs which cannot be done conventionally.

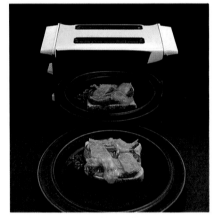

Toast bread conventionally. Prepare sandwiches and microwave to heat fillings and melt cheese.

Brown meats in a pyroceram® casserole on the conventional range. Microwave as directed in this book, but reduce time by ¼ to ⅓.

Microwave fillings and sauces for crepes you prepare with a crepe maker or skillet.

Prepare and fill crepes in advance. Refrigerate until serving time, then microwave until hot.

Warm syrup for pancakes in serving pitcher or uncapped bottle. Reheat leftover pancakes, too.

Soften brown sugar. Place apple slice in bag. Close tightly with string or plastic strip. Microwave ¼ minute at High or until lumps soften.

Shell nuts which are difficult to remove whole. Microwave 8 ounces of nuts in 1 cup water 4 to 5 minutes at High.

Plump raisins. Sprinkle 1 or 2 teaspoons of water over fruit. Cover tightly. Microwave ½ to 1 minute at High.

◄ **Blanch** almonds. Microwave 1 cup water until boiling. Add nuts. Microwave ½ minute at High. Drain and skin.

Make instant mashed potatoes right in the measuring cup. Place water, butter and salt in cup. Microwave until boiling. Add milk to correct measure. Stir in flakes.

Peel tomatoes or peaches easily. Put enough water to cover food in a casserole or measuring cup. Microwave until boiling. Drop in food for a few seconds. Peel strips off quickly.

Melt chocolate in its paper wrapper or a plastic cup you've already used to measure milk or shortening. It won't scorch and you'll save dishwashing. Use 50% power.

Melt butter for blender hollandaise, basting sauces and frostings for conventional cakes.

Microwave sauces while you cook pasta conventionally. Reheat pasta without flavor loss.

Soften gelatin. Measure water into a bowl or 4-cup measure. Microwave until boiling, stir in gelatin and cold water.

Microwave chicken or ribs until almost done. Finish on barbecue grill for charcoal flavor. Interior will be fully cooked without overbrowning.

Grill extra hamburgers while the coals are hot. Undercook slightly and freeze. Defrost and finish by microwaving.

Soften cream cheese directly from the refrigerator. For dips and spreads, it can be softened right in the serving dish.

◄ **Get** more juice from lemons. Microwave 20 to 35 seconds at High before cutting and squeezing.

Microwave Utensils

Some materials are transparent to microwaves. Energy passes through them as light passes through a window, and heats the food inside.

Metal reflects microwaves. The metal does not get hot, but reflected energy can overheat materials next to it.

Microwave utensils can become hot, but the heat comes from food, not microwave energy. Heat sensitive materials can be used for warming but not cooking foods.

Paper products can be used for heating and serving foods, or as light covers to absorb moisture and spatters during cooking.

Plastic, such as foam dishes and dishwasher safe containers can be used for heating, but melt or distort at cooking temperatures.

Plastic Films and cooking bags hold in steam to tenderize foods and speed cooking.

Packages, such as wax-coated freezer wrap and plastic-coated boxes, can be placed in the oven for defrosting.

Microwave Plastics are designed especially for microwave cooking. Use them as the manufacturer recommends.

Look for labels reading "Microwave Oven Safe" or "Suitable for Microwave". Check the warranty for heating and cooking information.

Oven glass and glass ceramic (pyroceram) are among the most versatile microwave utensils. Make sure they have no metal trim or screws in lids or handles.

Stoneware, which is safe for use at low and medium conventional temperatures, is excellent for microwave cooking and serving.

Pottery, porcelain and china, which cannot be used for conventional cooking, can be used for microwaving.

Metal Rims and signatures on dishes will darken and may cause the dish to crack.

Foil Trays under ¾-in. deep can be used, although heating will occur only on exposed top surface. Deeper pans take too long to heat. Keep foil at least 1-in. away from oven walls.

Metal Pans reflect energy and slow cooking so much that all microwave advantage is lost.

Foil Lined packages, used for some dairy products, dry foods and take-home foods, shield the food from microwave energy. Do not attempt to defrost or reheat foods in these packages.

Microwave Utensils continued

You don't need a cupboardful of new equipment to use with your microwave oven. Many utensils you already have are suitable for microwaving, including some things you never before thought of as cooking utensils.

Some utensils are designed especially for microwaving. Browning dishes and grills are discussed on page 19.

Many of the new microwave utensils do double duty and can be used in a conventional oven, too. Before using any plastic utensil, read the manufacturer's instructions. While plastics are transparent to microwave energy, some of them are sensitive to heat from food and will melt or distort when used to cook foods which reach high temperatures.

Microwave Utensils You May Already Have

Oven glass custard and measuring cups, pie and baking dishes, casseroles and mixing bowls are all suitable for microwaving. You can measure, mix and cook in one utensil.

Pyroceram®casseroles and skillets can be used with microwave and conventional ovens as well as on the range. They're good for combination cooking.

Special Microwave Utensils

Test dish if you are not sure it is microwave oven-safe. Place it in oven. Measure ½ to 1 cup water in glass cup. Place on or beside dish. Microwave 1 to 2 minutes at High. If dish remains cool it is suitable for microwaving.

Deep cake pans allow for the greater volume of microwaved cakes. Fluted molds provide a traditional bundt shape.

Muffin makers arrange food in a ring. Some offer ventilation on the bottom to reduce moisture.

Pottery and stoneware serving dishes, cups and plates can be used to cook and serve. Food stays hotter when it's cooked in the serving dish, and you have less clean-up.

Porcelain ramekins, soufflé, quiche and au gratin dishes are both microwave and conventional oven-safe.

Paper and plastic products you use for casual meals, food storage and clean up are useful microwave cooking utensils.

Baking sheets provide a broad surface for large items and foods cooked in quantity.

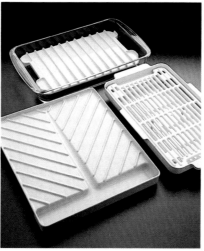

Roasting racks are available as a molded in one piece utensil, or as an insert for a glass utility dish. They elevate meat so it doesn't steam in fat and juices.

Ovenable paper can be used for heating food in any type of oven. It's freezerproof, too, so you can make your own freezer-to-microwave-to-table entreés.

Microwave Techniques:
Defrosting

Defrosting frozen food is one of the benefits of a microwave oven. Most ovens have a Defrost setting, but the power level assigned to it may vary from 70% to 30%. In this book, defrosting times are given for 50% and 30% because one of these settings is found on most ovens, although neither may correspond to the Defrost setting.

The final quality of the food you defrost depends on two factors. The first is good freezer management. Food should be properly packaged and not stored too long. The second is attention to the food while microwave-defrosting.

Lower power levels reduce the amount of attention needed during defrosting. At lower levels, the oven cycles on and off. During the "off" periods, heat has time to equalize. The photograph below shows what happens when 1-lb. of hamburger is defrosted without attention at various power levels.

Microwaves are attracted to water, not ice. As soon as some ice crystals melt, they draw energy away from frozen areas. This heated water melts channels through the block of frozen food.

High Power **50% (Medium)** **30% (Low)**

At High power hamburger has started to cook on the outside by the time the center is defrosted. At 50% power fewer areas have begun to cook. At 30% cooked areas are minimal, even without attention. Breaking up and removing defrosted parts improves defrosting at any power.

Flex pouches and packages which cannot be broken up or stirred. This distributes heat.

Defrosted areas begin to cook and change color before frozen parts are thawed unless the block is broken up and redistributed.

Cover meat with wax paper. It will hold warmth around food as it begins to defrost.

Tips to Speed Defrosting

Remove styrofoam tray as soon as possible when defrosting meat. It insulates bottom of meat like an ice chest. The paper liner used to absorb meat juices will draw energy from meat unless removed.

Pour off liquid from poultry frozen in plastic bag. It absorbs energy and slows defrosting.

29

Microwave Techniques:
Reheating

How to Reheat Meats

Most foods reheat in the microwave oven without loss of quality or texture. They taste freshly cooked, not warmed-over. Main dishes reheat especially well; some even improve in flavor if they are made in advance. Care must be taken to avoid additional cooking; rare meat should never be heated beyond its original doneness temperature, or it will cook to medium or well done.

Never reheat meats at High power. Refrigerated main dishes should be reheated at 50% power. Individual plates of food heat best at a lower power setting.

Thin slices of meat reheat more evenly than thick slices.

How to Reheat Main Dishes

Always cover main dishes. If they have been refrigerated, reheat at High.

Stir main dishes and casseroles, if possible, to distribute heat.

Rotate main dishes which cannot be stirred and microwave at 50% power (Medium).

How to Reheat Plates of Food

Arrange plate with thick or dense foods to outside and delicate foods to center of plate.

Spread out main dishes to a shallow, even layer for quick, uniform heating.

Cover plate with wax paper or plastic wrap to hold in heat and moisture.

Arrange thick portions of food to outside of dish as you do when cooking.

Add sauce or gravy to dry meats to provide moisture.

Cover with wax paper. When reheating dry meat without sauce, place paper towel under wax paper.

How to Reheat Vegetables

Saucy vegetables, such as scalloped potatoes, reheat well. Stir if possible, or rotate dish.

Moist or starchy vegetables reheat with a fresh taste when well wrapped.

Fibrous vegetables, such as artichokes, asparagus or broccoli lose texture when reheated.

Test by feeling bottom of plate. When food is hot enough to transfer heat to plate, it's ready.

How to Reheat Breads

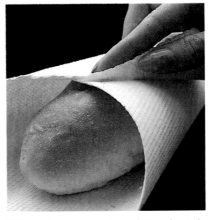

Wrap in paper towel to absorb moisture. Bread toughens if over-heated. One roll takes only 8 to 12 seconds.

How to Reheat Desserts

Reheat carefully. Sugary fillings get very hot, although pastry or cake may remain cool.

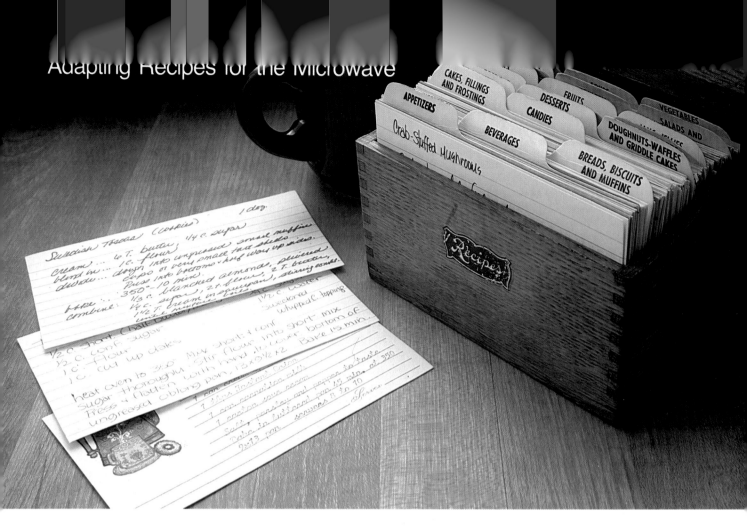

Once you become familiar with microwave cooking, you can make changes in microwave recipes to suit your needs, or adapt many of your favorite conventional recipes for preparation in the microwave oven.

You may want to increase or decrease the yield of a microwave recipe to make it fit your family size or the number of guests you are serving. In microwave cooking, a change in the amount of food cooked usually requires a change in time.

Favorite recipes can be converted for low-calorie or low-salt diets and still be good-tasting. Fat is not required to prevent sticking in microwave cooking, even when you cook lean foods like fish fillets or skinned chicken. Special diet recipes which call for a non-stick frying pan or spray coating adapt well. Microwaving brings out the natural flavor of foods like fresh vegetables, so you can cook without salt; season lightly with herbs and spices.

Whether you want to convert a conventional recipe or adapt a microwave recipe to your needs, the guidelines in this section will point out most of the changes you need to make.

Changing Yield of Microwave Recipes

Microwave time is affected by the amount of food cooked and the depth of food in the container. The same amount of food microwaves faster in a shallow container than it does in a deep one.

Choose a container which will keep the layer of food at the same depth as in the original recipe. The container should be deep enough to prevent boilover, and not so large that the food will be spread thinly on the bottom.

Halve a microwave recipe by using half the amount of all ingredients and microwaving for two-thirds the original time.

Double a microwave recipe by using twice the amount of solid ingredients and 1⅔ to 1¾ the amount of liquid. A doubled recipe will take one-half to two-thirds more time.

How to Convert Regular Recipes to Microwave Recipes

Use the following four guidelines to convert many conventional recipes to microwave, with minor changes to suit microwave cooking techniques and speed.

Step 1: Choose Recipe

Choose recipes which make no more than six to eight servings. Since more food takes more time, you will lose the advantage of microwave speed if you convert larger quantities. Look for conventional recipes which have one or more of the following features.

Cooking techniques similar to those used in microwaving, such as stirring, steaming or covering, indicate that the recipe will adapt well to microwaving.

Moist ingredients, such as poultry pieces, ground meat, vegetables, fruits, or sauces microwave well and are easy to adapt.

Rich foods, like quick-cooking candies, bar cookies, or layer cakes can be adapted.

(continued on next page)

Step 2: Adjust Ingredients & Methods

Foods which are warmed or heated, such as dips, spreads, or casseroles made with precooked ingredients, can be adapted for microwaving without a change in ingredients or preparation for cooking. Other foods may require special microwaving techniques. Check microwave recipes for the type of food you wish to prepare. You'll notice that pie shells are always microwaved before filling; cake dishes are always filled no more than half full; and quick bread loaves are elevated on a saucer to help the bottom cook evenly. Use the following guidelines to make changes in recipes.

Cut smaller pieces of meat and vegetables for stews and casseroles. Smaller, more uniform pieces microwave faster and more evenly.

Reduce liquid by one-third to one-half, then add more if needed for the consistency you want. Exceptions to this rule are recipes containing uncooked rice, pasta or dried beans and peas. These foods need the full amount of water to tenderize.

Reduce seasonings, such as salt. Microwaving enhances the natural flavor of food. Season the food to taste after microwaving is completed.

Add delicate ingredients, like cheese or shellfish, near the end of microwaving to prevent toughening and overcooking.

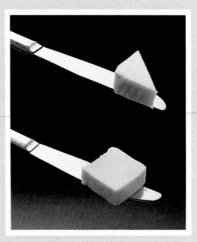

Reduce or omit fats in main dishes. Fats are not needed to prevent sticking. Use a small amount of butter or oil for flavor.

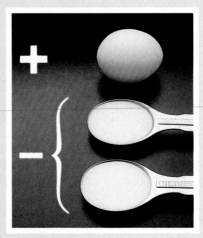

Add an extra egg and reduce liquid by 2 tablespoons to make tender cakes less fragile.

Step 3: Select Power Level

Compare your conventional recipe to a similar microwave recipe to determine the right power level. For example, cakes are microwaved first at 50% (Medium), then finished at High. A few minutes at High gets soups and stews started, then they microwave at 50% (Medium). The following factors influence the choice of power level used.

Type of liquid determines the power setting. Water, tomatoes, broth or wine can be microwaved at High. Delicate sauces containing cream, sour cream or cheese microwave at 50% (Medium) even when they are combined with ingredients normally microwaved at High.

Main ingredients like ground meats, poultry pieces or fish fillets microwave well at High. Pork chops and stew meat need time to tenderize and should be microwaved at 50% (Medium).

Stirring is important. If a casserole, such as lasagna, cannot be stirred during microwaving, reduce the power to 50% (Medium) and rotate the dish, even when all the ingredients are foods that microwave well at High.

Step 4: Estimate Time

The best guide to time is a microwave recipe which calls for similar amounts and types of main ingredients and liquid. If you can't find a similar recipe, try microwaving the food for one-fourth to one-half the conventional time. In either case, watch the food closely, adding more liquid if it is needed, and checking often for doneness.

Beverages

◄ Spiced Coffee

4 cups hot water
1 stick cinnamon
1 teaspoon whole allspice
1 tablespoon sugar
Dash nutmeg
1 tablespoon instant coffee
Lemon twists or cinnamon
sticks, optional

Serves 4
Serving size: 1 cup

Combine water, 1 stick cinnamon, allspice, sugar and nutmeg in 1-qt. mixing bowl. Microwave at High 6 to 8 minutes, or until mixture comes to a full, rolling boil. Immediately remove from oven; strain. Pour mixture over instant coffee in a serving pot. Stir to dissolve.

If desired, serve with a twist of lemon or a cinnamon stick.

Per Serving:
Calories: 8
Sodium: 0
Cholesterol: 0
Exchanges: free

Café au lait

2 cups skim milk
2 cups water
1½ tablespoons instant coffee
4 tablespoons non-dairy
    frozen whipped topping,
    optional
Dash nutmeg

Serves 4
Serving size: 1 cup

In 2-qt. casserole combine milk and water. Cover. Microwave at High 5 to 8 minutes, or until hot but not boiling. Blend in coffee until dissolved. Pour into 4 cups. Garnish with whipped topping, if desired. Sprinkle each serving with nutmeg.

Per Serving:
Calories: 50
Sodium: 78 mg.
Cholesterol: 4 mg.
Exchanges: ½ milk

Hot Chocolate

3 tablespoons unsweetened
    cocoa
2 tablespoons fructose
3 cups skim milk
1 teaspoon vanilla
1 cup water

Serves 4
Serving size: 1 cup

Combine cocoa and fructose in small dish. Set aside. Place remaining ingredients in 2-qt. casserole. Stir in cocoa mixture and beat with a wire whip. Cover. Microwave at High 6 to 8 minutes, or until hot but not boiling, beating with wire whip halfway through cooking.

Per Serving:
Calories: 94
Sodium: 174 mg.
Cholesterol: 5 mg.
Exchanges: 1 milk, ½ fruit

Spiced Tomato Cocktail ▲

1 cup water
1 teaspoon instant beef
   bouillon granules
   Dash cayenne pepper
½ teaspoon summer savory
2 cups tomato juice
   Dash garlic powder
   Celery stalk or green onion

Serves 6
Serving size: ½ cup

Combine all ingredients except
celery in 2-qt. casserole. Cover.
Microwave at High 5 to 10 minutes, or until boiling. Garnish
with celery or green onion.

NOTE: for low sodium diet
substitute low-salt bouillon and
tomato juice.

Per Serving:
  Calories: 16
  Sodium: 481 mg.
  Cholesterol: 0
  Exchanges: ½ vegetable

Hot Bouillon

1 cup water
1 teaspoon instant beef
   bouillon granules
1 stalk celery

Serves 1

Place water in coffee mug.
Microwave at High 1 to 2½
minutes, or until boiling. Stir in
bouillon until dissolved. Serve
hot, garnished with celery stalk.

NOTE: for low sodium diet
substitute low-salt bouillon.

Per Serving:
  Calories: 25
  Sodium: 943 mg.
  Cholesterol: 0
  Exchanges: 1 vegetable

Fresh Cranberry Juice ▲

1 lb. cranberries
6 cups hot water
¼ cup fructose

Serves 12
Serving size: ½ cup

In 5-qt. casserole combine
cranberries and water. Cover.
Microwave at High 20 to 25
minutes, or until cranberries
split. Strain. Stir in fructose and
chill. Serve mixed with orange
juice or use in recipes on
following page.

Per Serving:
  Calories: 27
  Sodium: 0
  Cholesterol: 0
  Exchanges: ¾ fruit

Hot Mulled Cider ▲

½ teaspoon whole allspice
½ teaspoon whole cloves
1 stick cinnamon
½ cup water
1½ cups Fresh Cranberry
    Juice, opposite
1 qt. apple cider

Serves 12
Serving size: ½ cup

In 2-qt. casserole combine all ingredients. Cover. Microwave at High 5 to 8 minutes, or until hot. Strain to remove spices.

Per Serving:
Calories: 45
Sodium: 0
Cholesterol: 0
Exchanges: 1 fruit

Spiced Tea

4 cups hot water
1 tablespoon grated orange
    peel
1 teaspoon grated lemon peel
6 whole cloves
1 stick cinnamon
3 tea bags

Serves 4
Serving size: 1 cup

In 2-qt. casserole combine water, orange peel, lemon peel and spices. Cover. Microwave at High 6 to 10 minutes, or until boiling. Remove from oven; immediately add tea bags and let steep 3 to 5 minutes. Serve hot or chilled.

Per Serving:
Calories: 0
Sodium: 0
Cholesterol: 0
Exchanges: free

Citrus Warmer ▲

2 cups unsweetened orange
    juice
1 cup water
1 cup Fresh Cranberry Juice,
    opposite
½ cup pineapple juice
1 tablespoon lemon juice
2 drops red food coloring,
    optional
Mint leaves

Serves 8
Serving size: ½ cup

In 2-qt. casserole combine the liquids; cover. Microwave at High 10 to 12 minutes, or until boiling. Reduce power to 50% (Medium). Simmer 5 minutes. Serve hot, garnished with mint.

Per Serving:
Calories: 24
Sodium: 0
Cholesterol: 0
Exchanges: 1½ fruit

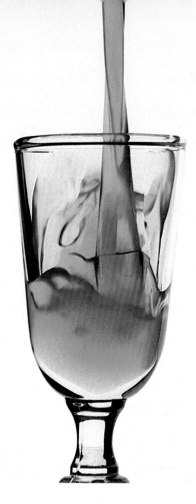

Orange Liqueur

3 oranges
1 cup sugar
1 stick cinnamon
2 cups brandy

Makes about 3 cups

Remove the peel from one orange with vegetable peeler or zester. Do not include white membrane. Cut oranges in half; squeeze juice. (Yields 1 cup.) In 4-cup measure combine orange peel, orange juice, sugar and cinnamon. Microwave at High 3 to 4 minutes, or until boiling, stirring after each minute. Boil 30 seconds. Watch closely; stir if necessary to prevent boilover. Cool to room temperature.

Remove cinnamon stick. Strain cooled juice mixture through cheesecloth. Add brandy to the strained liquid. Pour into bottle; cap. Let stand in a cool, dark place 1 month before serving. Shake bottle occasionally to mix.

Creme de Menthe

1½ cups sugar
1 cup water
1½ cups vodka or gin
1 teaspoon mint flavor
¼ teaspoon green food coloring

Makes about 4 cups

In 4-cup measure or large bowl combine sugar and water. Microwave at High 4 to 5 minutes, or until boiling. Boil 5 minutes. Watch closely; stir if necessary to prevent boilover.

Cool to room temperature. Skim any foam from top. Stir in remaining ingredients.

Pour into bottle; cap. Let stand in a cool, dark place 1 month before serving. Shake bottle occasionally to mix.

Anise Liqueur

1½ cups light corn syrup
½ cup water
¼ teaspoon instant unflavored, unsweetened tea powder
1½ cups vodka
¾ teaspoon anise extract
½ teaspoon vanilla
2 drops yellow food coloring

Makes 3½ cups

In 4-cup measure or large bowl combine corn syrup, water and tea powder. Microwave at High 4 to 5½ minutes, or until boiling. Watch closely; stir if necessary to prevent boilover. Cool to room temperature.

Skim any foam from top. Stir in vodka, anise extract, vanilla and yellow food coloring. Pour into bottle; cap. Let stand in a cool, dark place 1 month before serving. Shake bottle occasionally to mix.

Raspberry Liqueur

  2 pkgs. (10 oz. each) frozen
      raspberries in syrup
1½ cups sugar
1½ cups vodka

Makes 3 cups

Remove raspberries from
packages and place in large
bowl. Microwave at 50%
(Medium) 4 to 5 minutes, or
until partially defrosted. Gently
separate with fork. Let stand to
complete defrosting. Drain juice
into 8-cup measure or large
bowl. Set raspberries aside.

Add sugar to juice. Microwave
at High 3 to 5 minutes, or until
sugar dissolves and mixture
boils, stirring every 2 minutes.
Cool to room temperature. Skim
any foam from top. Add reserved
raspberries and vodka. Pour
into bottle; cap. Let stand in a
cool, dark place 1 month before
serving. Shake bottle occasionally
to mix. Strain through cheesecloth before serving. Serve
raspberries over ice cream.

Coffee Liqueur

1½ cups sugar
  1 cup water
  ¼ cup instant coffee crystals
1½ cups vodka
  1 vanilla bean or 1 teaspoon
      vanilla extract

Makes 2½ cups

In 4-cup measure or large bowl
combine sugar and water.
Microwave at High 4 to 5
minutes, or until boiling. Boil 5
minutes. Watch closely; stir if
necessary to prevent boilover.

Stir in coffee crystals until
dissolved. Cool to room temperature. Skim any foam from
top. Add vodka and vanilla bean.

Pour into bottle; cap. Let stand
in a cool, dark place 1 month
before serving. Shake bottle
occasionally to mix.

Apricot Brandy

  1 pkg. (6 oz.) dried apricots
1½ cups white wine
  1 cup sugar
  1 cup brandy

Makes about 3 cups

If desired, chop apricots. In
4-cup measure combine
apricots, wine and sugar. Cover
with plastic wrap. Microwave at
High 4 to 6 minutes, or until
sugar dissolves and mixture
boils, stirring every 2 minutes.
Cool to room temperature. Skim
any foam from top. Add brandy.

Pour into bottle; cap. Let stand
in a cool, dark place 1 month
before serving. Shake bottle
occasionally to mix. Strain
through cheesecloth before
serving. Serve apricots over
ice cream.

Appetizers

With dips or spreads, offer a selection of crisp, fresh vegetables. Microwaving offers an alternative to strictly raw vegetables. Microwave raw vegetables at High about one minute per cup, or until heated, stirring once. Chill until serving time. This cuts the raw taste without destroying the crispness.

Liver Paté

1 lb. chicken livers, rinsed and drained
2 cloves garlic, minced
1 small onion, chopped
2 tablespoons white wine or water
½ teaspoon parsley flakes
½ teaspoon salt, optional
½ teaspoon pepper
1 hard cooked egg, chopped
1 tablespoon brandy

Serves 16
Serving size: 2 tablespoons

In 2-qt. casserole combine livers, garlic, onion, wine and seasonings; cover. Microwave at High 5 to 8 minutes, or until meat is no longer pink, stirring once. Drain well.

Place cooked livers, egg and brandy in blender or food processor. Puree until smooth. Turn into serving dish and chill.

Pipe or spoon paté on melba toast, cherry tomatoes or celery sticks.

Per Serving:
Calories: 62
Sodium: 82 mg.
Cholesterol: 173 mg.
Exchanges: 1 low fat meat

Clam Dip

½ pkg. (8 oz.) Neufchâtel cheese
1 can (6½ oz.) minced clams, drained
¼ cup plain low fat yogurt
¼ cup chopped onion
1 teaspoon prepared horseradish
1 teaspoon Worcestershire sauce

Serves 10
Serving size: 2 tablespoons

Place cheese in small baking dish. Microwave at 50% (Medium) 45 seconds to 1¼ minutes, stirring after half the time. Stir in remaining ingredients. Microwave at 50% (Medium) 3½ to 5½ minutes, or until heated through, stirring after half the cooking time.

Serve hot or cold with assorted fresh vegetables.

Per Serving:
Calories: 56
Sodium: 16 mg.
Cholesterol: 9 mg.
Exchanges: 1 low fat meat

◄ Marinated Vegetables

1 cup tomato juice
½ cup water
½ cup thinly sliced celery
1 teaspoon onion powder
½ teaspoon basil leaves
½ teaspoon oregano leaves
¼ teaspoon garlic powder
⅛ teaspoon tarragon leaves
1 cup cauliflowerets
1 cup broccoli flowerets
1 cup thin carrot strips

Serves 8

Combine tomato juice, water, celery, onion powder, basil, oregano, garlic powder, and tarragon in 2-qt. casserole. Microwave at High 3 to 5 minutes, or until bubbly.

Stir in vegetables. Microwave at High 3 minutes. Reduce power to (50%) Medium. Microwave 3 to 5 minutes, or until flavors are blended and vegetables are softened. Serve warm or chilled.

NOTE: for low sodium diet, use low sodium tomato juice.

Per Serving:
Calories: 23
Sodium: 65 mg.
Cholesterol: 0
Exchanges: 1 vegetable

Stuffed Celery ▲

2 tablespoons assorted dry
  vegetable flakes
½ teaspoon onion flakes
3 tablespoons water
2 oz. Neufchâtel cheese
4 large celery stalks,
  ends trimmed
  Paprika

Serves 10
Serving size: 2 pieces

In 1-cup measure combine vegetable flakes, onion flakes and water. Cover with plastic wrap. Microwave at High 20 to 45 seconds, or until vegetable flakes are soft. Set aside.

Place cheese in small bowl. Reduce power to 50% (Medium). Microwave 20 to 45 seconds, or until softened. Stir in vegetable flakes.

Stuff celery with cheese mixture. Cut each stalk into 5 pieces. Sprinkle with paprika.

Per Serving:
Calories: 18
Sodium: 1 mg.
Cholesterol: 1 mg.
Exchanges: free

Cheesy Tomato Puffs

¼ to ⅓ lb. bacon, cut into ¼-in.
    widths
8 oz. cream cheese
½ teaspoon minced onion
1 teaspoon baking powder
1 egg yolk
⅓ cup finely chopped green
    pepper
2 to 3 pints firm cherry tomatoes

Makes about 50 puffs

How to Microwave Cheesy Tomato Puffs

Microwave bacon in 2-qt. covered casserole at High 9 minutes, or until crispy, stirring every 3 minutes. Drain well.

Place cream cheese in casserole with bacon; microwave at High 30 seconds to soften. Add onion, baking powder and egg yolk to cheese and bacon. With electric mixer, cream contents of casserole until well blended and fluffy. Stir in green pepper.

Cut tops from tomatoes and scoop out seeds. Fill with cheese mixture. Place 10 to 12 close together in ring on large dinner or pie plate lined with paper towel. Place 3 or 4 in center of ring.

Microwave at 50% (Medium) 1 to 2 minutes, or until cheese is just dry on surface, rotating ¼ turn every 30 seconds. Serve warm.

Sweet & Sour Chicken Wings ▲

2 lbs. chicken wings
¼ cup white wine vinegar
1 tablespoon honey
1 tablespoon soy sauce
1 tablespoon catsup

½ teaspoon ginger
1 can (8 oz.) chunk pineapple,
 packed in own juice
½ teaspoon bouquet sauce

Serves 12
Serving size: 2 wings

Cut chicken wings into 3 pieces, separating at joints. Discard wing tips. Combine remaining ingredients and wing pieces in plastic bag or small bowl. Let stand overnight, turning wings once or twice. Place marinade and chicken wings in 8×8-in. dish. Cover with wax paper. Microwave at High 8 to 12 minutes, or until chicken wings are fork tender, stirring once during cooking.

NOTE: for low sodium diet substitute low-salt soy sauce and catsup.

Per Serving:
Calories:	71	Cholesterol:	58 mg.
Sodium:	105 mg.	Exchanges:	½ fruit, 1 low fat meat

Chicken Kabobs ▲

12 wooden skewers, 6-in. long
1 whole boneless chicken
 breast, skin removed, cut
 into 24 pieces
1 medium green pepper,
 cut into 24 pieces
1 apple, cut into 24 pieces
1 teaspoon lemon juice
1 tablespoon water
1 teaspoon lemon pepper

Serves 4
Serving size: 3 kabobs

On each skewer alternate 1 piece of chicken, green pepper and apple; repeat once. Place on roasting rack. Combine lemon juice with water; brush on kabobs. Sprinkle with lemon pepper. Cover with wax paper. Microwave at 50% (Medium) 8 to 12 minutes, or until chicken is no longer pink, rearranging and basting once or twice.

Per Serving:
Calories:	21
Sodium:	11 mg.
Cholesterol:	13 mg.
Exchanges:	free

Tomato Cucumber Aspic

1 envelope unflavored gelatin
½ cup cold water
1 can (12 oz.) no-salt tomato
    juice
1 tablespoon frozen apple juice
    concentrate
½ teaspoon low-sodium instant
    beef bouillon granules
⅛ teaspoon pepper
1 bay leaf
1 cup peeled, seeded and
    chopped cucumber
2 tablespoons sliced green
    onion

    5 servings, ½ cup each

Per Serving:
Calories: 28
Protein: 1.7 g.
Carbohydrates: 5.6 g.
Fat: —
Cholesterol: —
Sodium: 9.6 mg.
Calcium: —
Exchanges: 1 vegetable

How to Microwave Tomato Cucumber Aspic

Soften gelatin in cold water in 1-cup measure. Set aside. In 4-cup measure, combine tomato juice, apple juice concentrate, bouillon, pepper and bay leaf.

Microwave at High for 2½ to 5 minutes, or until boiling. Remove bay leaf.

Add softened gelatin mixture. Stir until gelatin dissolves. Chill until thickened but not set (about 2 hours).

Fold in cucumber and onion. Spray 3 to 4-cup mold with vegetable cooking spray.

Pour into prepared mold. Chill until set (about 2 hours).

Dip mold into warm water for 30 seconds. Loosen edges and unmold onto serving plate.

Vegetable Kabobs with Lemon Dressing

Lemon Dressing:
 3 tablespoons reconstituted
   natural butter-flavored mix
 1 tablespoon lemon juice
 ¼ teaspoon onion powder
 ⅛ teaspoon dried marjoram
   leaves
   Dash pepper

 8 frozen whole Brussels sprouts
   (about 1 cup)
 8 frozen whole baby carrots
   (about ¾ cup)
 1 small green pepper, cut into
   16 chunks
 8 fresh cauliflowerets, 1-inch
   pieces (about 1 cup)
 8 wooden skewers, 6-inch
 2 tablespoons water

        8 servings, 1 kabob each

In 1-cup measure, blend all
dressing ingredients. Set aside.
In 1-quart casserole, combine
frozen Brussels sprouts and
carrots. Cover. Microwave at
High for 1½ to 3 minutes, or
until defrosted. Let stand,
covered, for 5 minutes.

For each kabob, assemble one
Brussels sprout, carrot, green
pepper chunk, caulifloweret and
another green pepper chunk on
wooden skewer. Repeat to
make 8 kabobs. Arrange on
platter with Brussels sprouts
toward center. Sprinkle with
water. Cover with plastic wrap.
Microwave at High for 3 to 5
minutes, or until tender-crisp,
rotating platter once. Let stand,
covered, for 3 to 4 minutes.
Pour dressing over kabobs.
Serve hot.

Per Serving:
Calories: 21
Protein: 1 g.
Carbohydrates: 5 g.
Fat: —
Cholesterol: —
Sodium: 49 mg.
Calcium: 12 mg.
Exchanges: 1 vegetable

Turkey-on-a-Stick

¼ cup sliced green onions
¼ cup shredded carrot
1 clove garlic, minced
1 lb. ground turkey
2 egg whites
⅓ cup rolled oats
2 tablespoons no-salt ketchup
½ teaspoon chili powder
¼ teaspoon dry mustard
¼ teaspoon paprika
¼ teaspoon liquid smoke
⅛ teaspoon cayenne

10 wooden skewers, 6-inch

Coating:
¼ cup cornflake crumbs
⅛ teaspoon paprika
Dash cayenne

Tangy Mustard Sauce:
¼ cup sour cream
1 tablespoon prepared mustard
1 teaspoon snipped fresh parsley

10 servings

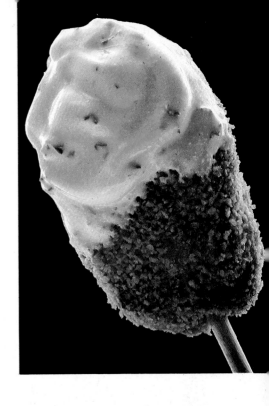

How to Microwave Turkey-on-a-Stick

Mix together onions, carrot and garlic in 1-quart casserole. Cover. Microwave at High for 1½ to 2½ minutes, or until tender-crisp.

Combine remaining ingredients, except coating and Tangy Mustard Sauce, in medium mixing bowl. Mix well.

Divide turkey mixture into 10 equal portions, using ¼ cup for each. Shape into about 3-inch oval loaves. Insert wooden skewer into each loaf.

Blend all coating ingredients on wax paper. Roll each loaf in coating. Arrange on roasting rack, skewers toward center.

Microwave at High for 6 to 9 minutes, or until turkey is firm to touch and cooked through, rotating rack once.

Let turkey stand for 3 to 4 minutes. In small bowl, blend all Tangy Mustard Sauce ingredients. Serve turkey with sauce.

49

Fresh Zucchini Dip

Pictured above, upper left

1½ cups shredded zucchini
   (1 medium)
¼ cup finely chopped onion
¼ cup finely chopped green
   pepper
1 tablespoon butter or
   margarine
¼ cup mayonnaise or salad
   dressing
¾ cup dairy sour cream
1 teaspoon garlic salt
1 teaspoon Worcestershire
   sauce
   Dash cayenne

Makes 2 cups

Place shredded zucchini
between layers of paper towel.
Press to remove excess
moisture. In 1-qt. casserole
combine onion, green pepper
and butter. Microwave at High 1
to 3 minutes, or until onion is
tender. Stir in zucchini and
remaining ingredients. Chill at
least 2 hours.

Chipped Beef Dip

Pictured above, lower left

¼ cup chopped green onion
1 clove garlic, minced
1 tablespoon butter or
   margarine
1 pkg. (8 oz.) cream cheese
½ cup dairy sour cream
¼ cup half and half or milk
1 pkg. (2½ oz.) dried beef,
   chopped
2 tablespoons snipped fresh
   parsley
1 tablespoon prepared
   horseradish
1 tablespoon lemon juice

Makes about 2 cups

In 1-qt. casserole combine
green onion, garlic and butter.
Microwave at High 30 to 60
seconds, or until butter melts.
Add cream cheese. Microwave
at High 45 seconds to 1½
minutes, or until cream cheese
is softened. Mix in remaining
ingredients. Chill at least 2
hours or overnight.

Jalapeño Cheese Dip

Pictured above, upper right

1 medium onion, chopped
1 tablespoon vegetable oil
2 cups shredded Monterey
   Jack cheese
2 cups shredded Cheddar
   cheese
½ cup half and half
2 tablespoons chopped
   jalapeño peppers

Serves 10 to 12

Place onion and oil in 1½-qt.
casserole. Cover. Microwave at
High 2 to 3 minutes, or until
onion is tender. Stir in remaining
ingredients. Reduce power to
50% (Medium). Microwave 3 to
6 minutes, or until heated and
smooth, stirring every 2 minutes.
Serve with taco chips, if desired.

Curry Dip

Pictured opposite, lower right

1 pkg. (8 oz.) cream cheese
3 tablespoons milk
½ teaspoon curry powder
½ teaspoon garlic salt
1 cup dairy sour cream
8 to 10 cups raw vegetables
(carrot and celery sticks,
cauliflowerets, broccoli
flowerets, zucchini strips)

Serves 6 to 8

Place cream cheese in small bowl. Microwave at High 20 to 45 seconds, or until softened. Mix in milk, curry powder and garlic salt. Microwave at High 30 to 60 seconds, or until warm. Stir to blend. Mix in sour cream. Serve with raw vegetables.

Advance preparation: Prepare the day before or the morning of the party. Cover and refrigerate. Before serving, microwave dip at High 45 seconds to 1½ minutes, or until softened, stirring once or twice. Add 1 to 2 teaspoons milk if needed for smoother consistency.

Cheese Ball

Pictured below

¼ cup chopped green pepper
¼ cup chopped green onion
1 teaspoon butter or margarine
1 pkg. (8 oz.) cream cheese
2 cups shredded Cheddar
cheese
1 pkg. (4 oz.) blue cheese,
crumbled
1 tablespoon chopped pimiento
2 teaspoons prepared
horseradish
2 teaspoons Worcestershire
sauce
1 clove garlic, minced
½ cup chopped pecans

Serves 10 to 12

In small bowl combine green pepper, onion and butter; cover. Microwave at High 30 to 45 seconds, or until vegetables are tender-crisp, stirring once. Place cream cheese in large bowl. Reduce power to 50% (Medium). Microwave 1 to 1½ minutes, or until softened. Stir in vegetables and remaining ingredients except pecans. Shape into ball. Wrap in plastic wrap. Chill 2 to 3 hours. Unwrap; roll in pecans. Serve with assorted crackers, if desired.

Miniature Chicken Drumsticks

3 lbs. chicken wings
6 tablespoons butter or
margarine
1 cup finely crushed rich,
round crackers
2 tablespoons sesame seed
1 teaspoon paprika
½ teaspoon onion powder
½ teaspoon salt

Serves 10 to 12

Cut chicken wings at joints into 3 parts each; discard tip. Wash thoroughly; pat dry. Melt butter in pie plate at High 1 to 1½ minutes. Mix remaining ingredients. Dip chicken into butter, then roll in crumbs. Place on baking sheet with meatiest portions to outside of dish. Microwave at High 10 to 16 minutes, or until juices run clear, rearranging 2 or 3 times but do not turn over.

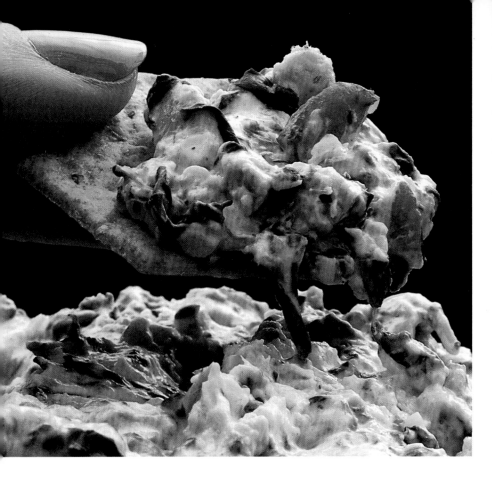

Hot Florentine Dip

8 oz. cream cheese
2 tablespoons milk
1½ tablespoons minced onion
¾ teaspoon garlic salt
½ teaspoon black pepper
1 pkg. (10 oz.) frozen, chopped spinach
1 can (6¾ oz.) chunk ham, drained*
1 cup sour cream
¾ cup (about 3 oz.) chopped pecans, optional

Makes 3 cups

Microwave cream cheese in 2-qt. casserole at High for 30 seconds. Add seasonings and milk to cheese and cream together.

Place package of spinach on plate; microwave at High 5 to 6 minutes, or until defrosted, rotating ½ turn after 3 minutes. Drain spinach thoroughly.

Stir ham and spinach into cheese mixture. Fold in sour cream and pecans. Microwave at High 4 to 6 minutes, or until very hot, stirring gently after 2 minutes, then every minute. Place casserole on candle warmer or warming tray and serve with crackers.

*1 can (8½ oz.) small shrimp, drained, may be substituted for ham.

Rarebit Appetizer

1 can (10¾ oz.) cream of mushroom soup
2 tablespoons milk
½ teaspoon onion powder
½ teaspoon garlic powder
½ cup grated American cheese
2 cups grated, sharp Cheddar cheese
¼ cup white wine
French bread cubes, raw vegetables, or sliced apples

Makes 2½ cups

Combine soup and milk in 2-qt. casserole. Microwave at High 2 to 3 minutes, or until very hot but not boiling, stirring every minute. Stir in seasonings, cheese, and wine. Microwave at High 2 to 6 minutes, or until cheese melts and mixture is hot and smooth, stirring every minute.

Place casserole over candle warmer or on warming plate and serve with French bread cubes, vegetables or sliced apples.

Stuffed Mushrooms

These hot and tasty mouthfuls are the star attraction of any collection of appetizers. Each recipe stuffs 8 ounces of fresh mushrooms.

Spinach Filled
Pictured lower left

- 6 oz. frozen spinach soufflé
- ¼ cup shredded Cheddar cheese
- ¼ cup seasoned bread crumbs
- ¼ teaspoon thyme
- ¼ teaspoon salt

Remove soufflé from foil; divide in half with sharp knife. Return half to freezer. In small bowl, defrost at 50% for 2 to 5 minutes, or until soft. Mix in other ingredients.

Cheese & Walnut

- Chopped mushroom stems
- 3 oz. bleu cheese, crumbled
- ½ cup chopped walnuts
- ¼ cup seasoned bread crumbs

Microwave stems. Stir in cheese. Add walnuts and bread crumbs, reserving 2 to 3 tablespoons of each. Stuff mushrooms, garnish with reserved nuts and crumbs.

Ham & Cream Cheese
Pictured middle left

- Chopped mushroom stems
- 3 oz. cream cheese, softened 15 to 30 seconds on High
- ½ cup finely chopped ham
- ¼ cup finely chopped almonds

Classic
Pictured upper left

- Chopped mushroom stems
- 1 small onion, finely chopped
- 2 tablespoons butter or margarine
- 1 tablespoon parsley
- ⅓ cup seasoned bread crumbs
- ¼ teaspoon salt
- ⅛ teaspoon garlic powder

Smoked Cheese & Salami

- Chopped mushroom stems
- 2 tablespoons onions, finely chopped
- ⅓ cup processed smoked cheese spread
- ¼ cup seasoned bread crumbs
- ¼ cup finely chopped salami

How to Microwave Stuffed Mushrooms

Wash 8-oz. fresh mushrooms. Remove and chop stems. Place stems in small bowl with onion or butter, if included in recipe. Cover with plastic wrap.

Microwave at High 1½ to 2½ minutes, until tender. Stir in remaining ingredients. Mound in mushroom caps.

Arrange caps on paper towel lined plate with larger caps to outside. Microwave 1½ to 3 minutes, until heated, rotating plate once or twice.

53

Meats & Main Dishes

Meats microwave in ⅓ to ½ the time it takes to cook them conventionally. They stay juicy because they are not exposed to hot, dry air. For the same reason, their surface will not become dry and crisp.

The flavor of microwaved meats may be slightly different, due to retention of natural juices and lack of a seared surface. If you wish to sear meats, use a browning dish or grill.

Defrosting meat is an important advantage of a microwave oven. Microwave defrosting is not only faster, it can help retain meat quality. Frozen meat begins to lose its juices as soon as it is thawed. For best results it should be cooked immediately. With a microwave oven you can time defrosting so the meat will be at its best when you are ready to cook it.

Main dishes are another microwaving specialty. They're fast and flavorful. If you use precooked meats, they won't have a leftover taste, and leftover main dishes reheat easily.

Selecting & Storing Meat for Microwaving

Meat is an important part of the menu and a major item in the food budget. Select and store meat carefully for the best flavor and freshness. Place it in the coolest part of the refrigerator as soon as you bring it home, and use within the recommended time.

Well-marbled beef microwaves best. This is true of less tender cuts as well as tender steaks and roasts. Beef should have fine streaks of smooth, white fat distributed throughout the lean. During microwaving, the fat melts and tenderizes the meat.

Chuck roast is well-marbled and usually costs less than leaner cuts of less tender beef. It's a good microwave choice.

Compare the amount of meat juices lost in microwaving with conventionally cooked results. For this demonstration, uniform portions of lean ground beef were placed in cooking bags to prevent evaporation, and cooked to an internal temperature of 180°.

Use ground beef within 24 hours. It spoils more rapidly than solid meat because more surface is exposed to bacteria. Store other meat in the original package up to 2 or 3 days. If you do not plan to use it within that time, place meat in a lemon juice, wine or vinegar marinade as soon as you bring it home. A marinade tenderizes, flavors and preserves meat about 5 days.

Select pork chops which are free of excessive moisture and have firm white fat. Avoid wet looking pork with crumbly, milky colored fat. Use pork within 2 days.

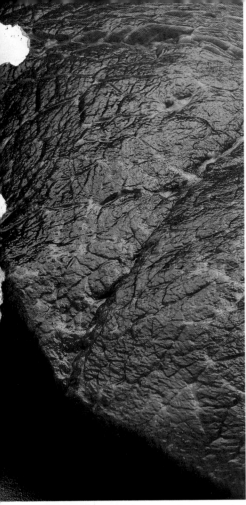

Round roast is very lean and has little marbling. It will be more chewy than chuck roast when microwaved.

Cut a boneless chuck roast into 1-inch cubes for beef stew. Supermarket stewing meat is usually cut from the leaner round, and piece size may be irregular. Small pieces microwave best and you can be sure they are uniform when you cut them yourself.

Fat covering helps tenderize lean roasts. Some markets sell roasts with a fat layer secured by string or mesh. Strips of bacon, held with string or wooden picks, add flavor.

Plain Ground Beef

Lean Ground Beef

Extra Lean Ground Beef

Ground beef is sold in several grades. Since microwaving extracts fat, regular ground beef will shrink and make main dishes fatty. Most of our directions call for lean ground chuck. Extra-lean ground round is an excellent choice for dieters.

Freezing and Defrosting Meat for Microwaving

Meat should be wrapped as air tight as possible before freezing. Air draws moisture from meat and produces ice crystals which cause dry, white areas called "freezer burn". For best quality, freeze meat quickly by placing it next to the wall of the freezer.

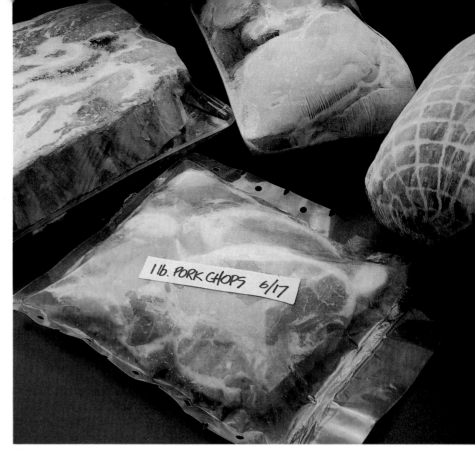

Freezer burn can be discarded easily during microwave-defrosting. Simply pick off the hard, dry areas with a fork.

Freeze meat in original packages for storing 1 to 2 weeks. For longer storage, rewrap meat tightly in wax-coated freezer paper, or package in heat-sealable bags. Press out as much air as possible before sealing. Label with contents, weight and date.

Package bulk ground beef in ▶ convenient, ready-to-use forms.

1. Pre-make hamburger patties. Stack with plastic wrap or doubled wax paper between layers. Wrap tightly in freezer paper. To use, remove as many patties as needed and reseal package. Use this method for chops and steaks.

2. Divide beef into 1 or 1½-lb. packages. Most recipes call for these amounts.

3. Use shallow plastic freezer boxes for freezing and defrosting; follow manufacturer's directions. Deep freezer containers are difficult to defrost.

4. Pre-cooked ground beef keeps longer than raw meat. Microwave meat, with chopped onion or green pepper if you like, until it loses its pink color. Cool quickly and freeze in recipe-sized amounts for casseroles and main dishes.

How to Defrost Ground Beef

Ground beef is easiest to defrost when it is frozen in recipe-size amounts. During the final defrosting period, check meat occasionally. Remove or scrape off softened parts, especially when defrosting amounts over 1 pound.

50% Power (Medium)
3¾-4¾ minutes per lb.

30% Power (Low)
5-7 minutes per lb.

Place paper or plastic wrapped package or freezer box in oven. Defrost for ⅓ of time. Turn over. Defrost for ⅓ of time.

Twist fork in meat to break up. Remove soft pieces. Defrost remaining time. Break up amounts over 1-lb. part way through.

Let stand 5 minutes (1-lb.) to 10 minutes (over 1-lb.). Meat will still contain ice crystals, but will be pliable.

How to Defrost Cubed Meat

50% (Medium) 3-4 min. per lb.; 30% (Low) 7½-9 min. per lb.

Place package in oven. Defrost for ½ the total time. Unwrap and separate cubes.

Spread cubes out in casserole or baking dish. Remove any defrosted pieces.

Defrost for second ½ of time. Let stand 5 minutes, or until they can be pierced with fork.

How to Defrost Chops   50% (Medium) 3-4 min. per lb.; 30% (Low) 5½-7 min. per lb.

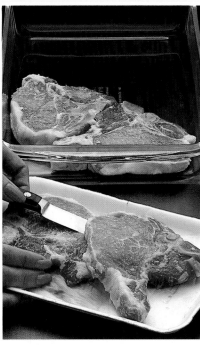

Place package in oven. Defrost for ½ the total time.

Separate chops with table knife. Arrange in baking dish with least defrosted parts to outside of the dish.

Defrost for remaining time. Let stand 5 minutes, or until chops can be pierced with a fork.

How to Defrost Roasts over 2-inches Thick   50% (Medium) 5-6½ min. per lb. 30% (Low) 9½-11½ min. per lb.

Place package in oven. Defrost for ¼ the total time.

Unwrap roast. Remove plastic tray and paper liner, which slow defrosting.

Shield any warm areas with foil. Turn roast over into baking dish.

How to Defrost Steaks & Flat Roasts

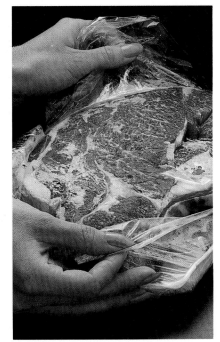

Place package in oven. Defrost for ½ the time. Remove wrapping, plastic tray and paper liner.

Shield any warm areas with foil. Turn meat over into baking dish. Defrost for remaining time.

Let stand 5 minutes. Meat is defrosted when it can be pierced to center with a fork.

Defrost second ¼ of time, or until surface yields to pressure. Let stand 10 minutes.

Defrost for third ¼ of time. Turn roast over; shield warm areas. Defrost remaining time.

Let stand 20 to 30 minutes, or until a skewer can be inserted to the center of roast.

61

How to Microwave Tarragon Beef

Combine all ingredients, except beef, in 2-cup measure. Microwave at High for 2 to 3 minutes, or until mixture boils.

Reduce power to 50% (Medium). Microwave for 1 minute. Cool slightly. Place beef in large plastic food storage bag in baking dish. Pour marinade over beef.

Secure bag. Chill for 4 to 8 hours, turning bag several times.

Beef

Tarragon Beef

1 cup water
3 tablespoons lemon juice
2 tablespoons red wine vinegar
1 tablespoon olive oil
1 teaspoon dried
    tarragon leaves
¼ teaspoon salt*
⅛ teaspoon pepper
1 lb. beef tenderloin

4 servings

*To reduce sodium omit salt.

Per Serving:
Calories: 252
Protein: 23 g.
Carbohydrates: 1 g.
Fat: 17 g.
Cholesterol: 68 mg.
Sodium: 184 mg.
Calcium: 8 mg.
Exchanges: 3 med.-fat meat

Remove beef. Arrange on roasting rack with thinner portion of beef tucked under for an even shape. Secure with string. Discard marinade.

Shield 1½ to 2 inches on each end of beef with foil. Microwave at High for 3 minutes. Remove foil from beef.

Reduce power to 50% (Medium). Microwave for 5 to 8 minutes longer, or until internal temperature registers 135°F, turning beef over once. Let stand for 3 minutes.

◄ Stuffed Flank Steak

1 pkg. (10 oz.) frozen
   asparagus spears
1 tablespoon steak sauce
1 tablespoon water
1½ lbs. flank steak, pounded
   to ¼-in. thickness
¼ teaspoon pepper

Serves 6

Microwave asparagus package
at High 3 to 5 minutes, or until it
flexes easily. Drain. Combine
steak sauce and water. Brush
steak with half of mixture. Place
asparagus on steak. Sprinkle
with pepper. Roll steak jelly-roll
style. Place in 8 × 8-in. baking
dish. Brush with remaining
mixture. Cover with wax paper.
Microwave at High 5 minutes.
Reduce power to 50%
(Medium). Microwave 15 to 20
minutes, or until internal temperature is 150°; rotate dish once.

Per Serving:
  Calories: 186
  Sodium: 102 mg.
  Cholesterol: 77 mg.
  Exchanges: 1 vegetable, 3 low
                fat meat

Roast Tenderloin ▲

¼ teaspoon garlic powder
¼ teaspoon onion powder
2 lb. beef tenderloin roast

Serves 8

Combine garlic and onion
powders. Rub well over surface
of roast. Place tenderloin on
roasting rack in 12 × 8-in.
baking dish. Shield ends and 1
inch down sides of tenderloin
with aluminum foil. Microwave at
High 3 minutes. Reduce power
to 50% (Medium). Microwave 5
minutes. Turn roast over and
rotate dish; remove shielding.
Microwave at 50% (Medium) 8
to 12 minutes longer, or until
internal temperature reaches
125°. (Roast will be medium
rare). Let stand, tented loosely
with foil, 10 minutes.
Temperature will rise 15° to 20°.

Per Serving:
  Calories: 165
  Sodium: 94 mg.
  Cholesterol: 77 mg.
  Exchanges: 3 low fat meat

Liquid provides moisture and a cooking bag holds in steam. Cut a strip of plastic from the top of the bag to use as a closure. Do not slash the bag to vent, as it will be turned over during cooking and juices may escape.

50% Power (Medium)
25-30 minutes per pound

Old-Fashioned Pot Roast

2 to 3½ lb. boneless chuck roast

Sauce:
¼ cup tomato paste
½ cup water
 1 tablespoon instant beef bouillon granules
½ teaspoon thyme
½ teaspoon salt
 1 bay leaf

Vegetables:
 4 medium carrots cut in 1-in. lengths (2 cups), halve thick carrots lengthwise before slicing
 1 medium onion, cut in eighths
 1 large potato, cut in ½-in. cubes (1½ cups)

TIP: Freeze remaining tomato paste in small glass jar. To use, defrost in microwave oven until surface softens and you can scrape off amount needed.

How to Microwave Old-Fashioned Pot Roast

Place roast in cooking bag. Combine sauce ingredients; pour over meat. Close bag as shown on page 13.

Microwave at 50% power (Medium) for ½ the total time. Turn roast over. Open bag carefully; steam can burn.

Add vegetables to bag and reseal. Microwave remaining time. Let stand in closed bag 20 to 25 minutes.

Swiss Steak

Four factors help tenderize this less tender cut. Pounding and cooking in tomato sauce break down fibers. A lower power level allows meat to simmer slowly. Standing time is the most important; meat will not be tender without it.

2 lbs. beef round or chuck, cut in serving size pieces
¼ to ⅓ cup flour
1 envelope onion soup mix
1 can (8-oz.) tomato sauce
2 teaspoons parsley flakes
¼ cup water

Serves 4

How to Microwave Swiss Steak

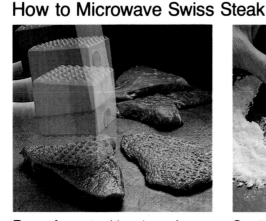

Pound meat with edge of saucer or meat mallet to tenderize and flatten it to ¼ to ½-in. thickness.

Coat meat with flour by shaking in a paper bag or dredging on a sheet of wax paper.

Place meat in 2-qt. baking dish. Sprinkle with soup mix.

Combine remaining ingredients in a 2-cup measure. Pour over meat. Cover with vented plastic wrap.

Microwave at 50% power (Medium) 25 minutes. Rearrange meat. Re-cover. Microwave 25 to 35 minutes longer.

Meat should be fork tender. Let stand, tightly covered, 10 minutes to tenderize further.

Pepper Steak Strips

4 servings rice
1½ lbs. boneless beef round steak, ½-in. thick
¼ cup soy sauce
1 tablespoon paprika
2 tablespoons butter or margarine
1 medium green pepper, cut into thin strips
1 stalk celery, thinly sliced
1 clove garlic, minced or pressed
½ cup water, divided
1½ tablespoons cornstarch
1 cup green onion cut into ½-in. pieces
1 medium tomato, peeled and cut into chunks

Serves 4

How to Microwave Pepper Steak Strips

Cook rice conventionally. Trim fat from steak; pound to ¼-in. thickness with meat mallet. Cut into ¼-in. wide strips. Combine strips, soy sauce and paprika.

Set aside while preparing other ingredients. Preheat browning dish at High 5 minutes. Add butter and drained beef strips.

Microwave at High 2½ to 3½ minutes, or until meat is browned, stirring once. Add green pepper, celery, garlic and ¼ cup water. Cover.

Reduce power to 50% (Medium). Microwave 11 to 14 minutes, or until meat is tender and vegetables are tender-crisp, stirring once during cooking.

Combine cornstarch and remaining water. Add to meat mixture with onions and tomato. Increase power to High.

Microwave uncovered 2½ to 4 minutes, or until sauce is thickened, stirring once during cooking. Serve over rice.

◄ Ginger Beef

2 tablespoons water
2 tablespoons soy sauce
¼ teaspoon bouquet sauce,
  optional
1 tablespoon cornstarch
¼ teaspoon ginger
⅛ teaspoon garlic powder
1 lb. flank steak, thinly sliced
1 medium green pepper,
  cut into thin strips
4 small green onions, chopped
1 tomato, cut into wedges

Serves 6

In 2-qt. casserole blend water,
soy sauce, bouquet sauce,
cornstarch, ginger and garlic
powder. Add flank steak, stirring
to coat. Stir in green pepper
and onion. Microwave at High 8
to 10 minutes, or until meat and
green pepper are tender,
stirring 2 or 3 times. Stir in
tomatoes. Microwave at High 1
to 2 minutes, or until tomatoes
are heated through.

NOTE: if desired, serve over
rice. See Exchange Chart,
page 311.

Per Serving:
Calories: 122
Sodium: 178 mg.
Cholesterol: 51 mg.
Exchanges: ½ vegetable, 2 low
                 fat meat

Beef Burgundy ▲

¼ cup water
¼ cup burgundy wine
1 tablespoon cornstarch
1 lb. boneless sirloin, cut
  into ¾-in. cubes
1 small onion, chopped
8 oz. sliced fresh mushrooms
½ teaspoon salt, optional
¼ teaspoon garlic powder
¼ teaspoon pepper

Serves 4

Blend water, wine and
cornstarch in 3-qt. casserole.
Stir in remaining ingredients;
cover. Microwave at High 3
minutes. Reduce power to 50%
(Medium). Microwave 20 to 30
minutes, or until meat is fork
tender, stirring once or twice.
Let stand, covered, 5 minutes.

NOTE: if desired, serve over
rice. See Exchange Chart,
page 311.

Per Serving:
Calories: 198
Sodium: 322 mg.
Cholesterol: 77 mg.
Exchanges: 1 vegetable,
                 3 low fat meat

Cube Steak With ▲ Fresh Vegetables

4 cube steaks
1 medium onion, cut into
    8 wedges
1 medium zucchini, cut into
    ¼-in. slices
1 medium tomato, cut into
    wedges
2 tablespoons white wine
½ teaspoon dill

Serves 4

Place steaks on roasting rack. Microwave at High 6 to 8 minutes, or until meat is no longer pink, rearranging after half the cooking time. Drain and set aside.

In medium mixing bowl combine onion, zucchini, tomatoes, wine and dill. Cover with plastic wrap. Microwave at High 6 to 9 minutes, or until onions are translucent and zucchini is tender, stirring two or three times during cooking. Place mixture on steaks. Microwave 2 to 3 minutes, or until tomato and steaks are heated thoroughly.

Per Serving:
  Calories: 187
  Sodium: 69 mg.
  Cholesterol: 77 mg.
  Exchanges: 1 vegetable, 3 low
                fat meat

Flank & Tomato Curry ▶

1 to 1½ lbs. flank steak,
    thinly sliced
¼ cup thinly sliced celery
¼ cup chopped onion
¼ cup chopped green pepper
1 tablespoon cornstarch
1 can (16 oz.) whole tomatoes,
    drained, juice reserved
1 teaspoon curry
1 teaspoon salt, optional
¼ teaspoon pepper

Serves 6

In 2-qt. casserole combine flank steak, celery, onion and green pepper. Microwave at High 7 to 11 minutes, or until meat is no longer pink and vegetables are tender, stirring 2 or 3 times during cooking.

Blend cornstarch into reserved tomato juice. Add cornstarch mixture, tomatoes, curry, salt and pepper to meat mixture. Stir to break apart tomatoes. Microwave at High 7 to 12 minutes, or until meat is tender and flavors blended.

NOTE: if desired, serve over rice. See Exchange Chart, page 311.

Per Serving:
  Calories: 194
  Sodium: 282 mg.
  Cholesterol: 118 mg.
  Exchanges: 1 vegetable,
                3 low fat meat

Meatloaf

Meatloaves remain moister when microwaved than they do when baked conventionally, so this mixture contains no milk or water. If you want to adapt a favorite meatloaf for microwaving, reduce the liquid by about half.

Microwave meatloaves by time, rotating them during cooking, and test for doneness with a probe or thermometer. (145° to 155°). They should be firm to the touch on top.

Basic Meatloaf

Mix together thoroughly:

  2 eggs, lightly beaten
1½ lbs. lean ground beef
  ¼ cup fine bread crumbs
   1 small onion, chopped
   2 tablespoons
     Worcestershire sauce
   1 teaspoon seasoned salt
  ½ teaspoon dry mustard
  ¼ teaspoon pepper

Spread over top, if desired:

   2 tablespoons catsup, steak,
     barbecue or chili sauce

Serves 4 to 5

High Power	
Round	12-18 min.
Ring-shaped	8-13 min.
Loaf	13-18 min.
6 Individual	10-13 min.

How to Microwave Meatloaf

Spread mixture evenly in dish. For ring-shaped meatloaves, form mixture into large balls and pack into dish. This reduces cracking.

How to Select Meatloaf Shapes

Microwaved meatloaves come in many shapes. Which one you select depends on your oven's cooking pattern and on your own taste. A different shape can vary the presentation of a popular item on the menu.

Loaf shape is traditional. It tested successfully in all ovens at ▶ High power when rotated after half the cooking time. If your oven overcooks the corners, reduce power level to 50% (Medium) and microwave for twice the time.

Round meatloaves may be pie or ring-shaped. Use a 10-in. pie plate. The ring shape works well in most ovens. The ring is deeper than a pie-shaped meatloaf but energy penetrates from the center for even cooking. If you don't have a ring-shaped dish, place a 6-oz. custard cup in center of a 2-qt. casserole.

Individual meatloaves. Pack mixture into six 6-oz. glass custard cups. Arrange in ring in oven. Rotate after ½ the cooking time.

Top with sauce. For fewer moist spots and browner surface, leave uncovered.

Microwave, rotating dish after half the cooking time.

Let stand 5 to 10 minutes. It will complete cooking and become firm. Use this time to microwave vegetables for dinner.

Hamburgers

Hamburgers microwave easily because of their uniform consistency and even fat distribution. When they are served in buns with condiments, a browning agent is not needed for appearance. Picture shows a hamburger without browning agent. The charts are for ½-in. thick hamburgers, weighing ¼-lb. apiece.

High Power

Medium-Rare

Patties	1st side Minutes	2nd side Minutes
2	1½	¾-1
4	2	1-2
6	3	3¼-3½

Medium-Well

Patties	1st side Minutes	2nd side Minutes
2	2	1½-2½
4	2½	2-3
6	3½	3¼-3½

How to Microwave Hamburgers on a Plate or Roasting Rack

Brush or sprinkle with browning agent, if desired. Soy sauce, onion soup mix, or steak sauce and water or butter add flavor.

Arrange hamburgers on a roasting rack in a baking dish or on a plate lined with paper towel. Rack drains off fat while paper absorbs it; this improves flavor and reduces calories. Cover with wax paper to prevent spatters. Microwave on first side.

Preheated Browning Dish or Griddle Method

Preheat browning dish or griddle as manufacturer directs. Glass cover on browning dish may be used to prevent spatters, but griddle should be used uncovered. Microwave first side. Turn hamburgers over and rearrange them if you are cooking more than four. Microwave second side. Standing time is not needed.

High Power

	Medium-Rare		Medium-Well	
Patties	1st side Minutes	2nd side Minutes	1st side Minutes	2nd side Minutes
2	1	¾-1¼	2	1-2
4	2	1-2	2½	2-3
6	2½	2¼-2¾	3	3-3½

Turn hamburgers over. If you are microwaving more than 4 patties, rearrange them at this time, so those in the center of the dish are moved to the outside. Microwave minimum of remaining time. Check for doneness. They will cook a little more on standing.

Let hamburgers stand, covered with wax paper, 1 to 2 minutes. Gray color will turn brown but surface will not be crusty.

73

Veal

Veal is always roasted well done, but it dries out easily because it contains little fat. Use a microwave thermometer or probe; remove the roast from the oven at 160° and let it stand to complete cooking to 165° to 170°. Orange Marmalade helps seal in juices. For variety, substitute sage for rosemary and currant jelly for the marmalade.

The most common veal roasts are from the leg and shoulder. A shoulder roast should be boned and rolled; the shoulder blade roast is uneven in shape and has a complicated bone structure which makes it difficult to carve.

Approx. Time	Start at High	Finish at 50%
13½-17½ min. per lb.	First 5 min.	160°

How to Insert Probe or Thermometer in a Veal Roast

Rump or Round Roast. Insert sensor into largest muscle, parallel to the bone, so tip is in center of meatiest area.

Rolled Roasts. Insert sensor from end or side so tip is in center of roast.

How to Microwave Veal Roasts

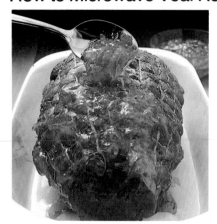

Rub roast with rosemary. Place roast, fat side down, on rack in baking dish. Coat with ½ jar (10-oz.) orange marmalade. Insert thermometer, if used, so tip is in center of meat, not touching bone.

Estimate the total cooking time; divide in half. Microwave at High 5 minutes. Reduce power to 50% (Medium). Microwave remaining part of first half of time. Turn roast over.

Coat with remaining marmalade. Insert probe, if used. Microwave until roast reaches internal temperature of 160°. Let stand 10 minutes, tented with foil. Temperature will rise to 165° to 170°.

Lemon-Dill Veal ▲

½ cup dry seasoned bread
    crumbs
¾ teaspoon dill weed
1 egg, beaten
2 teaspoons lemon juice
4 veal cube steaks (about 1 lb.)
2 tablespoons butter or
    margarine
1 cup sliced fresh mushrooms
¼ cup chopped onions

Serves 4

On waxed paper, combine
bread crumbs and dill weed. Set
aside. Blend egg and lemon
juice in shallow bowl. Dip steaks
into egg mixture and dredge in
bread crumbs.

Preheat 10-in. browning dish at
High 5 minutes. Quickly add
butter and veal. Microwave at
High 45 seconds. Turn. Add
mushrooms and onions. Cover.
Microwave at High 4 to 6 minutes
or until veal and vegetables are
fork tender, rearranging steaks
after 2 minutes.

Veal in Sour Cream ▶

1 tablespoon butter or
    margarine
1 lb. veal cube steaks or cutlets
8 oz. fresh mushrooms, sliced
1 tablespoon grated onion
1 cup (8 oz.) sour cream
¼ cup sherry
1 teaspoon salt*
2 tablespoons flour

Serves 4

Preheat 10-in. browning dish at
High 5 minutes. Add butter and
veal. Let veal stand 15 to 20
seconds. Turn cutlets over. Add
mushrooms and onion.
Microwave at High 1 to 2
minutes, or until mushrooms are
tender, rotating cutlets after half
the cooking time.

In 2-cup measure, mix sour
cream, sherry and salt. Blend in
flour. Stir sour cream mixture into
veal and mushrooms.
Microwave at 50% (Medium) 1 to
2 minutes, or until sauce is hot
and slightly thickened.

*Omit salt if using cooking
sherry.

Veal With Vegetables

1 lb. boneless veal, pounded
    to ¼-in. thickness, cut
    into serving pieces
1 medium onion, thinly sliced
    and separated into rings
1 can (6 oz.) tomato paste
1 tablespoon all-purpose flour
½ teaspoon basil leaves
½ teaspoon oregano leaves
2 teaspoons parsley flakes
¼ teaspoon garlic powder
¼ teaspoon salt, optional
¼ teaspoon black pepper
2 large tomatoes, peeled
    and chopped
1 cup thinly sliced zucchini
1 medium green pepper, cut
    into thin strips

Serves 4

Pound veal well with mallet or saucer edge to flatten and tenderize.

Place veal in 12 × 8-in. baking dish. Top with onion rings. In medium bowl blend tomato paste, flour, basil, oregano, parsley, garlic powder, salt and pepper. Stir in tomatoes, zucchini and green pepper. Spread vegetable mixture over veal. Cover with wax paper. Microwave at High 13 to 18 minutes, or until veal is no longer pink and vegetables are tender, rearranging veal after 8 minutes cooking time.

Per Serving:
    Calories: 231
    Sodium: 210 mg.
    Cholesterol: 86 mg.
    Exchanges: 2½ vegetable, 4
                 low fat meat

Mushroom Veal ▶

1 lb. boneless veal, pounded to
    ¼-in. thickness, cut into
    serving pieces
8 oz. sliced fresh mushrooms
⅓ cup water
2 tablespoons white wine
2 teaspoons all-purpose flour

2 teaspoons dried chives
2 teaspoons lemon juice
½ teaspoon instant beef
    bouillon granules
⅛ teaspoon salt, optional
⅛ teaspoon bouquet sauce,
    optional

Serves 4

Arrange veal in 12 × 8-in. baking dish. Top with sliced mushrooms.
Cover with wax paper. Microwave at 50% (Medium) 7 to 10
minutes, or until veal is tender and no longer pink; rearrange veal
once, leaving mushrooms on top. Set aside.

In small bowl blend remaining ingredients. Increase power to High.
Microwave 1½ to 4 minutes, or until thickened, stirring with wire
whip once or twice. Pour sauce over veal; cover with wax paper.

Reduce power to 50% (Medium). Microwave 1½ to 3½ minutes, or
until heated through.

Per Serving:
Calories: 180   Cholesterol: 86 mg.
Sodium: 262 mg.   Exchanges: ½ vegetable, 3 low fat meat

Veal Mozzarella ▶

1 can (8 oz.) tomato paste
¼ teaspoon oregano leaves
½ teaspoon basil leaves
¼ teaspoon garlic powder
¼ teaspoon salt, optional
¼ teaspoon sugar
⅛ teaspoon pepper

1 lb. boneless veal, pounded
    to ¼-in. thickness, cut into
    serving pieces
¾ cup shredded mozzarella
    cheese
1 tablespoon parsley flakes

Serves 4

Combine all ingredients except veal, cheese and parsley in small
bowl. Microwave at High 2 minutes. Reduce power to 50%
(Medium). Microwave 6 minutes. Set aside.

Place veal in 12 × 8-in. baking dish. Cover with wax paper.
Microwave at 50% (Medium) 6 to 9 minutes, or until veal is no
longer pink, rearranging once. Drain. Cover with sauce. Sprinkle
cheese and parsley on top; cover with wax paper.

Microwave at 50% (Medium) 3 to 7 minutes, or until sauce is hot
and cheese melts, rotating dish once.

Per Serving:
Calories: 280   Cholesterol: 100 mg.
Sodium: 327 mg.   Exchanges: 1½ vegetable, 4 low fat meat, ½ fat

Liver

Calf, beef and pork liver have similar nutritional value, and can be used interchangeably in these recipes. Calves' liver is more tender and has a milder flavor, but it is expensive.

How to Defrost Liver

50% (Medium) 5-7 min. per lb.
30% (Low) 8½-11 min. per lb.

Place package in oven. Defrost for ⅓ the total time. Turn package over.

Defrost for ⅓ of time. Unwrap and separate pieces. Spread out in baking dish.

Defrost remaining time. Let stand 5 minutes, or until pieces can be pierced with a fork.

How to Defrost Chicken Livers

50% (Medium) 4-6 min. per lb.
30% (Low) 7-9½ min. per lb.

Place package in oven. Defrost for half the total time. Unwrap and separate livers.

Remove any defrosted livers. Spread out the rest in baking dish. Defrost remaining time.

Let stand 5 minutes, or until livers can be pierced with a fork.

Chicken Livers in Browning Dish

1 lb. chicken livers
2 tablespoons butter or
  margarine
½ cup chopped green onion
1 teaspoon salt
  Dash pepper

Serves 4

Preheat browning dish according to manufacturers directions.

Add livers and butter. Microwave at High 1 minute.

Stir in remaining ingredients. Microwave 4½ to 7 minutes, or until livers lose their pink color, stirring after half the cooking time.

Oriental Liver

6 slices bacon, cut in eighths
⅓ cup brown sugar
⅓ cup cider vinegar*
1 tablespoon cornstarch
1 teaspoon salt
¼ teaspoon marjoram
⅛ teaspoon pepper
1 lb. pork or beef liver, cut into
  serving size pieces
1 small onion, chopped
½ medium green pepper,
  chopped

 * For sweeter sauce, use ¼ cup
   vinegar

Serves 4

Place bacon in 12×8-in. dish. Cover with wax paper. Microwave at High 5 to 6 minutes. Drain fat from dish.

Stir in brown sugar, vinegar, cornstarch and seasonings. Arrange liver in dish, turning over to coat with sauce. Top with onion and green pepper. Cover with wax paper.

Microwave at High 5 minutes. Reduce power to 50% (Medium). Microwave 12 to 16 minutes, or until liver is fork tender, turning over and rearranging liver after half the cooking time.

Liver, Bacon & Onions ▲

4 slices bacon, cut in sixths
¼ cup flour
1½ teaspoons seasoned salt
1 lb. liver, cut in serving size
  pieces
2 medium onions, thinly sliced
½ cup water

Serves 4

Place bacon in 12×8-in. dish. Cover with plastic wrap. Microwave at High 4 minutes.

While microwaving bacon, combine flour and seasoned salt. Dredge liver in flour. Sprinkle excess flour over pieces. Set aside.

Drain all but 2 tablespoons bacon fat from dish. Place liver in dish. Add remaining ingredients. Cover with plastic wrap. Microwave at High 5 minutes. Reduce power to 50% (Medium). Microwave 11 to 15 minutes, or until liver is fork tender. Turn over and rearrange pieces after half the cooking time.

Liver in Wine Sauce

1 lb. liver, cut in serving size
  pieces
3 tablespoons flour
2 tablespoons butter or
  margarine
1 can (4-oz.) mushroom stems
  and pieces, drained
⅓ cup white wine
1 clove garlic, pressed or
  minced
2 teaspoons parsley flakes
1 teaspoon instant beef bouillon
1 teaspoon salt
  Dash pepper

Serves 4

Preheat browning dish according to manufacturer's directions. While preheating dish, dredge liver in flour.

Place liver and butter in dish. Microwave at High 1½ minutes. Turn liver over; microwave 1½ minutes.

Add remaining ingredients. Reduce power to 50% (Medium). Microwave 11 to 15 minutes, or until liver is fork tender, turning over and rearranging pieces after half the cooking time.

Lamb

Lamb Meatballs
With Dill Sauce

4 servings noodles

Meatballs:

1 lb. ground lamb
⅓ cup quick-cooking oats
1 egg
¼ cup chopped onion
1 teaspoon salt
⅛ teaspoon pepper

Sauce:

2 tablespoons butter or
  margarine
2 tablespoons flour
½ teaspoon dill weed
½ teaspoon paprika, divided
¼ teaspoon salt
⅛ teaspoon pepper
1 cup milk

Serves 4

Cook noodles conventionally
while microwaving meatballs. In
medium bowl combine meatball
ingredients. Shape into 15 to 18
meatballs. Place in 12×8-in.
baking dish. Microwave at High
6 to 8 minutes, or until no longer
pink, turning over and rearranging after half the cooking time.
Drain; remove to serving platter,
if desired. Cover to keep warm.

In 1-qt. measure melt butter at
High 30 to 40 seconds. Stir in
flour, dill weed, ¼ teaspoon
paprika, salt and pepper. Blend
in milk. Microwave at High 4 to 5
minutes, or until thickened,
stirring every minute.

Pour sauce over meatballs.
Sprinkle evenly with remaining
paprika. Microwave at High 1
minute to reheat.

Serve with hot buttered noodles.

Marinated Lamb Kabobs

1 can (8 oz.) pineapple chunks
   in own juice, drained,
   juice reserved
1 tablespoon lemon juice
2 teaspoons soy sauce
¼ teaspoon ground ginger
¼ teaspoon dry mint leaves
1 lb. boneless lamb, cut into
   24 pieces
8 firm cherry tomatoes
½ medium green pepper, cut
   into eighths
4 wooden skewers, 12-in. long

Serves 4

In small bowl combine ⅓ cup
reserved pineapple juice, lemon
juice, soy sauce, ginger and
mint leaves. Stir in meat; cover.
Marinate overnight in
refrigerator. Remove meat;
discard marinade.

Alternate lamb, tomatoes,
green peppers and pineapple
chunks on skewers.

Arrange skewers on roasting
rack. Microwave at 50%
(Medium) 8 to 11 minutes, or
until lamb is desired doneness.

NOTE: for low sodium diet
substitute low-salt soy sauce.

Per Serving:
Calories:	205
Sodium:	234 mg.
Cholesterol:	85 mg.
Exchanges:	1 fruit, 3 low fat meat

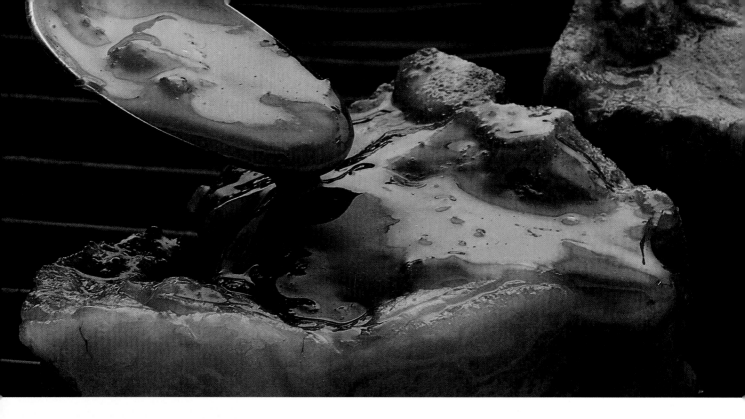

◄ Barbecued Lamb Chops

1 small onion, chopped
1 tablespoon butter or
   margarine
¼ cup chili sauce
¼ cup catsup
3 tablespoons brown sugar
1 teaspoon vinegar
⅛ teaspoon garlic powder
4 lamb chops, 1½-in. thick

Serves 4

In 1-qt. casserole combine onion and butter. Microwave at High 1½ to 2 minutes, or until tender. Stir in remaining ingredients except chops.

Arrange chops on roasting rack with meatiest portions to outside. Spoon half of sauce over chops. Cover with wax paper. Microwave at High 3 minutes. Reduce power to 50% (Medium). Microwave 5 minutes.

Turn over and rearrange chops. Spoon on remaining sauce; re-cover. Microwave 10 to 20 minutes, or until chops are desired doneness.

Orange Glazed ▲ Lamb Chops

⅓ cup orange marmalade
2 tablespoons honey
1 tablespoon prepared mustard
2 teaspoons lemon juice
1 teaspoon Worcestershire
   sauce
4 lamb chops, 1½-in. thick

Serves 2 to 4

Combine all ingredients except chops in 2-cup measure. Microwave at High 30 to 45 seconds, or until marmalade melts. Stir.

Arrange chops on roasting rack with meatiest portions to outside. Spoon half of glaze over chops. Cover with wax paper. Microwave at High 3 minutes. Reduce power to 50% (Medium). Microwave 5 minutes.

Turn over and rearrange chops. Spoon on remaining glaze. Re-cover. Microwave 10 to 20 minutes, or until chops are desired doneness.

Lamb Pilaf

1 cup uncooked long grain rice
2 cups water
1 tablespoon instant chicken bouillon
½ teaspoon salt
½ cup chopped onion
½ cup chopped green pepper
1 clove garlic, minced or pressed
1 tablespoon olive oil
¼ to ½ teaspoon tarragon leaves
1½ to 2 cups cooked lamb, ¾ to 1-in. cubes

Serves 4 to 6

How to Microwave Lamb Pilaf

Combine rice, water, bouillon and salt in 2-qt. casserole; cover. Microwave at High 5 minutes, stir. Re-cover. Reduce power to 50% (Medium). Microwave 10 to 12 minutes. Let stand while preparing vegetables.

Combine onion, green pepper, garlic and oil in 1-qt. measure. Microwave at High 2½ to 5 minutes, or until pepper is tender. Stir in tarragon and lamb.

Fluff rice with fork. Remove half of the rice from casserole and set aside.

Spread lamb mixture over rice in casserole. Top with remaining rice. Cover. Reduce power to 50% (Medium). Microwave 3 to 6 minutes, or until heated through.

Lamb Stew With Italian Green Beans

1 lb. lean lamb shoulder,
    cut into ¾-in. cubes
2 tablespoons all-purpose
    flour
1 teaspoon salt, optional
¼ teaspoon pepper
1 can (16 oz.) whole tomatoes
¾ cup water
8 oz. sliced fresh mushrooms
1 medium onion, quartered
1 teaspoon instant beef
    bouillon granules
½ teaspoon dried basil
¼ teaspoon crushed rosemary
    leaves
1 pkg. (10 oz.) frozen
    Italian green beans

Serves 6

In 3-qt. casserole combine lamb, flour, salt and pepper. Stir to coat lamb. Add tomatoes, water, mushrooms, onion, bouillon, basil and rosemary. Stir to break apart tomatoes; cover.

Microwave at High 5 minutes. Reduce power to 50% (Medium). Microwave 20 minutes; stir and re-cover.

Microwave at 50% (Medium) 20 to 30 minutes longer, or until lamb is fork tender. Add Italian beans; cover.

Microwave at 50% (Medium) 10 minutes, or until beans are hot; stir. Let stand, covered, 5 to 10 minutes.

NOTE: for low sodium diet substitute low-salt bouillon.

Per Serving:
Calories:	156
Sodium:	540 mg.
Cholesterol:	57 mg.
Exchanges:	2 vegetable, 2 low fat meat

84

Lamb Burgers ▲

4 slices bacon
1 lb. ground lamb
⅓ cup chopped green onion
1½ teaspoons Worcestershire
   sauce
½ teaspoon seasoned salt
4 slices Monterey Jack cheese

Serves 4

Place bacon on two layers of paper towels. Cover with paper towel. Microwave at High 3 to 4 minutes, or until slightly under-done. Set aside. Preheat browning grill at High 5 minutes.

While microwaving bacon and preheating grill, prepare lamb burgers. In medium bowl combine lamb, green onion, Worcestershire sauce and salt. Shape into 4 patties.

Place patties in preheated dish. Microwave at High 2 minutes. Turn over. Microwave at High 2 to 3 minutes, or until patties are desired doneness.

Cut bacon slices in half. Place two halves on each patty. Top each with a cheese slice. Cover dish. Microwave at High 1 minute to melt cheese.

Serve on buns or hard rolls.

Lamb Creole ▶

1 medium onion, chopped
1 stalk celery, chopped
½ medium green pepper,
   chopped
1 tablespoon olive oil
1½ cups cooked lamb, cut into
   ¾-in. cubes
1½ cups quick-cooking rice
1 can (8 oz.) tomato sauce
¾ cup water
1 can (4 oz.) mushroom stems
   and pieces, drained
2 teaspoons brown sugar
½ teaspoon basil
½ teaspoon salt
⅛ teaspoon pepper
1 bay leaf
⅛ teaspoon thyme
⅛ teaspoon red pepper

Serves 4

In 2-qt. casserole combine onion, celery, green pepper and oil. Cover; microwave at High 3 to 5 minutes, or until tender.

Stir in remaining ingredients. Cover. Microwave at High 5 minutes. Stir; re-cover.

Reduce power to 50% (Medium). Microwave 5 to 8 minutes, or until rice is tender and all liquid is absorbed, stirring once during cooking.

Pork

Fresh pork should be thoroughly cooked, but not over-cooked. Pork releases moisture quickly, so the dividing line between cooked and over-cooked is critical. Studies show that pork is safe to eat and more juicy and tender when it is served at a finished temperature of 170°. Smaller cuts should be fork-tender with slightly pink juices. Standing time is important because it allows pork to cook completely without drying out.

◄ ## Pork Chops with Bulgur & Bourbon Sauce

1 cup water
¼ cup bulgur or cracked wheat
1 tablespoon chopped almonds
1 tablespoon reduced-calorie
   margarine
⅓ cup chopped celery
⅓ cup chopped apple
¼ cup sliced green onions
1 tablespoon snipped
   fresh parsley
¼ teaspoon ground sage
⅛ teaspoon salt*
⅛ teaspoon pepper

1 teaspoon bourbon
4 butterflied pork chops, about
   ½ inch thick

Sauce:
1 can (10½ oz.) ready-to-serve
   low-sodium cream of
   mushroom soup
1 tablespoon snipped
   fresh parsley
1 tablespoon bourbon
⅛ teaspoon ground sage
⅛ teaspoon pepper

4 servings

Place water in 2-cup measure. Microwave at High for 1½ to 4½ minutes, or until water boils. Place bulgur in small mixing bowl. Add boiling water. Cover and let stand for 30 minutes to soften. Drain and press out excess moisture. Set aside.

In 1-quart casserole, combine almonds and margarine. Microwave at High for 3 to 4 minutes, or just until almonds begin to brown. Add celery, apple, onions, parsley, sage, salt, pepper and bourbon. Mix well. Cover. Microwave at High for 3 to 4 minutes longer, or until vegetables are tender, stirring after half the time. Add bulgur to vegetable mixture. Arrange pork chops in 9-inch square baking dish with thickest portions toward outside of dish. Top each with one-fourth of the bulgur mixture. Set aside.

In medium mixing bowl, combine all sauce ingredients. Mix well. Spoon around chops. Cover with wax paper. Microwave at 70% (Medium High) for 18 to 20 minutes, or until pork is no longer pink, rotating dish after every 5 minutes. Let stand, covered, for 5 minutes.

*To reduce sodium omit salt.

Per Serving:
Calories:	447	Cholesterol:	73 mg.
Protein:	21 g.	Sodium:	156 mg.
Carbohydrates:	17 g.	Calcium:	37 mg.
Fat:	33 g.	Exchanges:	1 bread, 3 high-fat meat, 2 fat

Hungarian Pork Chops

4 pork loin chops, about
   ½ inch thick
1 small onion, thinly sliced
1 can (8 oz.) no-salt
   tomato sauce
1 teaspoon sugar
1 teaspoon paprika
¼ teaspoon caraway seed
¼ teaspoon celery salt*
¼ teaspoon dried
   marjoram leaves
⅛ teaspoon pepper

4 servings

Arrange pork chops in 9-inch square baking dish with thickest portions toward outside of dish. Top with onion. In small mixing bowl, combine remaining ingredients. Mix well. Pour over chops. Cover. Microwave at 70% (Medium High) for 13 to 15 minutes, or until pork is no longer pink, turning chops over and basting with sauce after half the time. Let stand, covered, for 10 minutes.

*To reduce sodium omit celery salt.

Per Serving:
Calories:	331
Protein:	20 g.
Carbohydrates:	6 g.
Fat:	25 g.
Cholesterol:	73 mg.
Sodium:	141 mg.
Calcium:	13 mg.
Exchanges:	1 vegetable, 3 high-fat meat

Microwaved pork chops need to be encased in a crumb crust to hold in juices, or masked with a dense sauce to provide moisture.

You may use the methods photographed here with your favorite coating recipe or other flavors of condensed soup.

Crumb-Coated Pork Chops

4 pork chops, ½-in. thick
1 envelope prepared coating mix

Photo directions below.

Smothered Pork Chops

4 pork chops, ½-in. thick
1 can (10¾-oz.) mushroom soup

Photo directions opposite.

50% Power (Medium)
16½-18½ minutes per pound

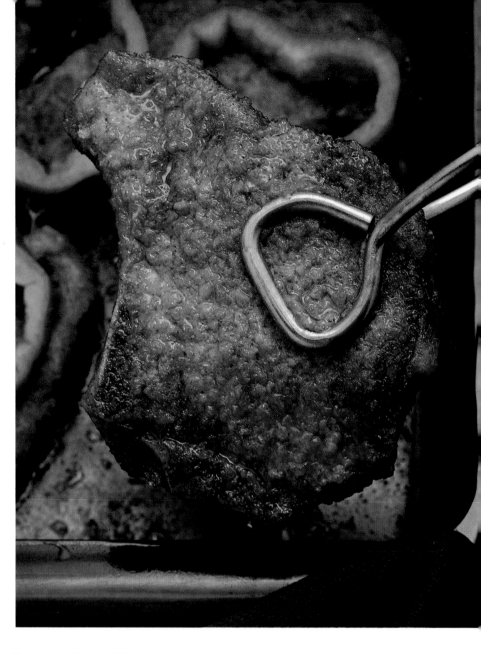

How to Microwave Crumb-Coated Pork Chops

Shake pork chops with coating as directed on package, or toss with crumbs in paper bag.

Arrange chops in 8×8-in. dish with meaty portions to outside. Cover with wax paper. Cook at 50% power for ½ the time.

Rearrange chops so less cooked areas are to outside of dish. Discard wax paper. Microwave for second ½ of time.

How to Microwave Smothered Pork Chops

Arrange chops in 8×8-in. dish with meaty portions to outside. Spread undiluted mushroom soup over chops.

Cover with vented plastic wrap. Microwave at 50% power (Medium) for ½ the cooking time.

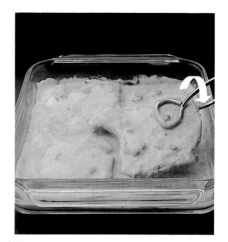

Turn over or rearrange chops. Replace plastic wrap. Microwave for remaining time.

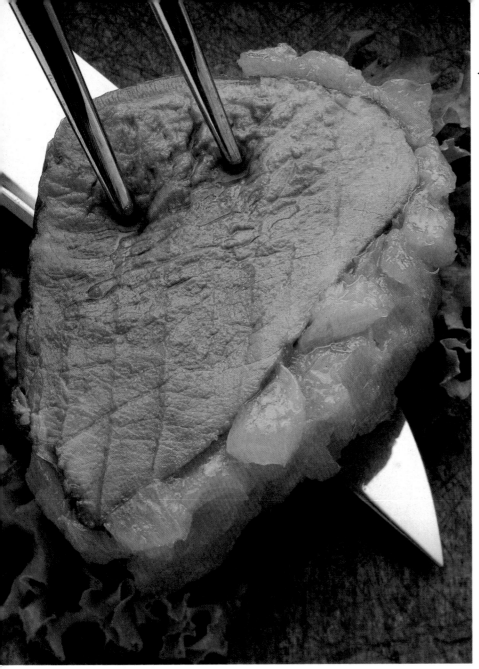

Pineapple Glaze

1 can (8 oz.) crushed
   pineapple, drained
1 teaspoon prepared mustard
⅛ to ¼ teaspoon thyme leaves
1 teaspoon brown sugar

Makes 1 cup
Serving size: 2 tablespoons

Combine ingredients in small bowl or 2-cup measure. Microwave at High 1 to 2 minutes, or until heated. Spread over pork tenderloin roast as directed.

Per Serving:
Calories:	17
Sodium:	0
Cholesterol:	0
Exchanges:	½ fruit

Fruit Glaze

½ cup low sugar apple or
   cherry spread

Makes ½ cup
Serving size: 1 tablespoon

Spread fruit over pork tenderloin roast as directed.

Per Serving:
Calories:	12
Sodium:	0
Cholesterol:	0
Exchanges:	free

Apple Glaze

½ cup unsweetened
   applesauce
¼ teaspoon nutmeg

Makes ½ cup
Serving size: 1 tablespoon

Mix applesauce and nutmeg. Spread on pork tenderloin roast as directed.

Per Serving:
Calories:	5
Sodium:	0
Cholesterol:	0
Exchanges:	free

Pork Tenderloin

2 lb. pork tenderloin roast

Serves 8

Cooking time: 12½ to 16½ minutes per lb.

Place tenderloin on roasting rack in 12 × 8-in. baking dish. Shield ends of roast with aluminum foil. Estimate total cooking time; divide in half. Microwave at High 3 minutes. Reduce power to 50% (Medium). Microwave remaining part of first half of time. Remove foil. Turn roast over. Spread one of the following fruit glazes over roast, if desired. Microwave at 50% (Medium) the remaining time, or until the internal temperature reaches 165°. Tent loosely with foil. Let stand 5 to 10 minutes, or until temperature is 170°.

Per Serving:
Calories:	256	Cholesterol:	75 mg.
Sodium:	69 mg.	Exchanges:	3 med. fat meat

Pork Stew

1 cup hot water
1 teaspoon instant chicken
    bouillon granules
¼ teaspoon bouquet sauce
2 tablespoons all-purpose
    flour
1 lb. lean boneless pork,
    cut into 1-in. cubes
1 large onion, thinly sliced
1 cup thinly sliced celery
1 can (16 oz.) whole tomatoes
8 oz. green beans, cut into
    1-in. lengths
2 medium yellow squash,
    thinly sliced
½ teaspoon crushed rosemary
¼ teaspoon salt, optional
    Dash pepper
⅛ teaspoon garlic powder
2 cups shredded lettuce

Serves 6

In 2-cup measure, blend hot water, bouillon, bouquet sauce and flour. Set aside.

Place remaining ingredients except lettuce in 3-qt. casserole. Stir in flour and water mixture. Cover. Microwave at High 10 minutes. Stir. Re-cover.

Reduce power to 50% (Medium). Microwave 35 to 40 minutes, or until meat and vegetables are tender. Stir in lettuce. Let stand, covered, 5 to 10 minutes.

NOTE: for low sodium diet substitute low-salt bouillon and bouquet sauce.

Per Serving:
  Calories: 240
  Sodium: 304 mg.
  Cholesterol: 49 mg.
  Exchanges: 1 vegetable, 1
              bread, 2 med.
              fat meat

Pork De-lite

1 pkg. (10 oz.) frozen
    asparagus cuts
½ cup chopped onion
¾ lb. butterflied pork chops,
    cut into ⅛-inch strips
1½ cups sliced fresh
    mushrooms

Sauce:

1 tablespoon cornstarch
1 tablespoon cold water
½ cup skim milk
⅓ cup cooking liquid from
    pork and vegetables
½ teaspoon low-sodium instant
    chicken bouillon granules
¼ teaspoon dried
    thyme leaves
¼ teaspoon lemon-pepper
    seasoning
    Dash ground sage

4 servings

Unwrap asparagus and place on plate. Microwave at High for 4 to 6 minutes, or until defrosted. Set aside.

Place onion in 2-quart casserole. Cover. Microwave at High for 2 minutes. Stir in pork, asparagus and mushrooms. Re-cover. Microwave at High for 4½ to 7½ minutes longer, or until pork is no longer pink, stirring after every 2 minutes. Drain pork and vegetables, reserving ⅓ cup liquid for sauce. Set aside.

For sauce, in 2-cup measure, blend cornstarch and water. Stir in milk, ⅓ cup cooking liquid, bouillon, thyme, lemon-pepper and sage. Microwave at High for 2½ to 4 minutes, or until sauce thickens, stirring 2 or 3 times. Stir sauce into pork and vegetables. Microwave at High for 1 minute, if necessary to heat through.

Per Serving:			
Calories:	377	Cholesterol:	74 mg.
Protein:	25 g.	Sodium:	75 mg.
Carbohydrates:	13 g.	Calcium:	85 mg.
Fat:	26 g.	Exchanges:	1 bread, 3 high-fat meat

Peppered Pork & Rice Casserole

1 cup uncooked brown rice
1 cup uncooked rotini pasta
2 tablespoons reduced-calorie margarine
1 clove garlic, minced
1 boneless pork loin chop, about 6 oz., cut into ½-inch cubes
½ cup chopped low-fat boiled ham
⅓ cup sliced green onions
1 small green pepper, cut into thin strips
1 medium tomato, seeded and chopped
2 cans (10½ oz. each) ready-to-serve low-sodium chicken broth
¼ to ½ teaspoon ground cumin
¼ teaspoon dried oregano leaves
¼ teaspoon salt*
⅛ teaspoon pepper

6 servings

In 3-quart casserole, combine rice, rotini, margarine and garlic. Microwave at High for 5 to 6 minutes, or until rice and rotini are lightly browned, stirring after every 2 minutes. Stir in remaining ingredients. Cover. Microwave at High for 5 minutes. Reduce power to 50% (Medium). Microwave for 40 to 50 minutes longer, or until liquid is absorbed and rice and rotini are tender. Let stand, covered, for 10 minutes.

*To reduce sodium omit salt.

Per Serving:	
Calories:	293
Protein:	13 g.
Carbohydrates:	34 g.
Fat:	12 g.
Cholesterol:	28 mg.
Sodium:	302 mg.
Calcium:	16 mg.
Exchanges:	2 bread, 2 med.-fat meat

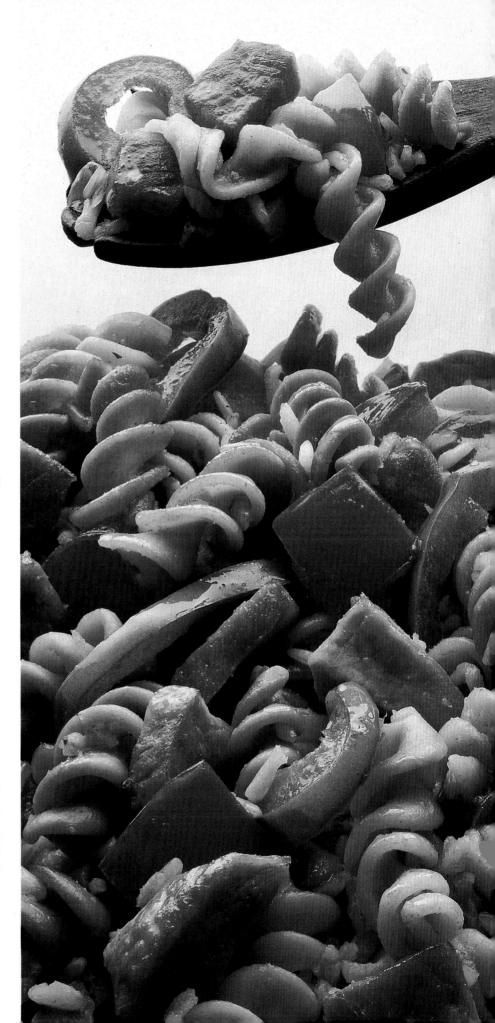

Coriander Pork Kabobs

Marinade:

¼ cup apple juice
1 tablespoon vegetable oil
1 clove garlic, minced
1 teaspoon ground coriander
½ teaspoon sugar
⅛ teaspoon cayenne
⅛ teaspoon pepper

¾ lb. pork tenderloin, cut into
    20 cubes, about 1 inch
8 whole water chestnuts
4 green onions, white portions
    cut into 8 pieces, about
    2 inches
1 medium carrot
1 medium zucchini, cut into 8
    chunks, about ½ inch thick
8 wooden skewers, 10-inch

4 servings

In medium mixing bowl, combine all marinade ingredients. Mix well. Add pork, water chestnuts and onions. Stir to coat. Chill for 1 hour.

Shave carrot into thin lengthwise strips using vegetable peeler. Wrap carrot strip around each water chestnut. For each kabob, assemble pork, onion, zucchini, pork, water chestnut/carrot, pork, zucchini, onion and pork on skewer. Repeat for remaining kabobs. Place kabobs on roasting rack. Cover with wax paper. Microwave at 50% (Medium) for 12 to 16 minutes, or until pork is no longer pink, turning kabobs over and rearranging twice.

Per Serving:
Calories:	317
Protein:	17 g.
Carbohydrates:	13 g.
Fat:	22 g.
Cholesterol:	58 mg.
Sodium:	356 mg.
Calcium:	45 mg.
Exchanges:	1 fruit, 2 high-fat meat, 2 fat

Cantonese Pork & Broccoli

⅓ cup cold water
2 tablespoons
    reduced-sodium
    soy sauce
1 tablespoon white wine
2 teaspoons cornstarch
1 clove garlic, minced
½ teaspoon grated
    orange peel
⅛ teaspoon pepper
¾ lb. fresh broccoli, separated
    into flowerets, stalk
    thinly sliced
¾ lb. pork tenderloin, trimmed
    and thinly sliced
1 can (8 oz.) sliced water
    chestnuts, drained
1⅓ cups hot cooked long grain
    white rice, page 230

4 servings

In 1½-quart casserole, blend water, soy sauce, wine, cornstarch, garlic, orange peel and pepper. Stir in broccoli. Cover. Microwave at High for 3 to 5 minutes, or until broccoli brightens in color, stirring once or twice. Add pork and water chestnuts. Mix well. Re-cover. Microwave at High for 5 to 9 minutes longer, or until pork is no longer pink, stirring twice. Let stand, covered, for 2 minutes. Serve over rice.

Per Serving:
Calories:	375
Protein:	21 g.
Carbohydrates:	30 g.
Fat:	18 g.
Cholesterol:	58 mg.
Sodium:	556 mg.
Calcium:	163 mg.
Exchanges:	2 bread, 3 med.-fat meat

Country Pork & Vegetable Stew ▶

1 can (15½ oz.) Great Northern
    beans
1 can (10½ oz.) ready-to-serve
    low-sodium tomato soup
1 can (10½ oz.) ready-to-serve
    low-sodium French
    onion soup
1 pkg. (10 oz.) frozen cut
    green beans
½ teaspoon ground sage
½ teaspoon dried
    marjoram leaves
¼ teaspoon garlic powder
¼ teaspoon salt*
2 bay leaves
1 acorn squash, about 1 lb.,
    peeled, seeded and cut into
    1-inch chunks
¾ lb. butterflied pork chops, cut
    into ¾-inch cubes

8 servings, 1 cup each

In 3-quart casserole, combine all ingredients, except pork. Mix well. Cover. Microwave at High for 25 to 30 minutes, or until squash is tender, stirring 2 or 3 times. Stir in pork. Re-cover. Reduce power to 50% (Medium). Microwave for 5 minutes longer, or until pork is no longer pink. Let stand, covered, for 10 minutes. Remove bay leaves.

*To reduce sodium omit salt.

Per Serving:
Calories:	192
Protein:	13 g.
Carbohydrates:	22 g.
Fat:	7 g.
Cholesterol:	27 mg.
Sodium:	163 mg.
Calcium:	33 mg.
Exchanges:	1 vegetable, 1 bread, 2 low-fat meat

Ribs

Spare ribs can be microwaved in 2 ways, depending on your tastes. Dry-roasted ribs are covered with wax paper to prevent spatters, and are chewy, finger food. Braised ribs are tightly covered and steamed in liquid so they almost slip off the bones.

Since ribs are bony, you will need ¾ to 1-lb. per person. The most important step in microwaving them is arranging, and rearranging them in the dish. Enough rib pieces to feed 3 to 4 people should be laid against the sides of the dish and overlapped slightly on the bottom. When rearranging, expose the least cooked portions and overlap the most cooked pieces.

Roasted Ribs

2½ to 3-lb. spare ribs, cut in 2 to 3-rib pieces
1 onion, thinly sliced
½ teaspoon basil
1 cup bottled barbecue sauce
2 teaspoons lemon juice

Serves 3 to 4

Braised Ribs

2½ to 3-lbs. spare ribs, cut in 2 to 3-rib pieces
1 onion, thinly sliced
½ teaspoon basil
1 lemon, thinly sliced
1 cup water
1 cup bottled barbecue sauce

Serves 3 to 4

Sweet-and-Sour Sauce

Prepare sauce before microwaving ribs by either the roasted or braised method. After draining liquid, substitute this for barbecue sauce.

¼ cup brown sugar
1 tablespoon cornstarch
½ cup pineapple juice
¼ cup vinegar
2 tablespoons soy sauce

In a 2-cup measure, combine brown sugar and cornstarch. Measure in remaining ingredients; stir well. Microwave at High 3 to 4 minutes, or until thick and translucent, stirring every minute.

	Roasted	Braised
Start at High	Finish at 50% (Medium)	Finish at 50% (Medium)
first 5 min.	25-35 min.	30-40 min.

How To Microwave Barbecued Ribs

Arrange ribs around sides and over bottom of 12×8-in. dish or 3-qt. casserole, overlapping slightly as needed. Spread with onion rings. Sprinkle with basil.

Roasted Ribs. Cover with wax paper, which prevents spatters without steaming ribs.

Braised Ribs. Add lemon slices and water. Cover tightly with lid or plastic wrap.

96

Pennsylvania Ribs and Kraut

2½ to 3-lbs. ribs, cut in
    2 to 3 rib pieces
2 tablespoons each bouquet
    sauce and water, combined
1 can (27-oz.) sauerkraut,
    drained
1 medium onion, chopped
1 medium apple, peeled and
    finely chopped
2 tablespoons brown sugar
1 teaspoon caraway seeds
    (optional)

Serves 3 to 4

Arrange ribs around sides and over bottom of a 3-qt. casserole, overlapping slightly as needed. Cover tightly. Microwave at High 5 minutes. Reduce power to 50% (Medium). Microwave 15 minutes.

Remove ribs. Brush with bouquet sauce mixture; set aside. Drain liquid from casserole.

Combine sauerkraut, onion, apple, brown sugar and caraway seed in casserole. Arrange ribs on top. Cover. Microwave 15 to 25 minutes, until ribs are fork tender and sauerkraut is heated through.

Microwave at High 5 minutes. Reduce power to 50% (Medium). Microwave for half the cooking time. Rearrange and turn ribs over, so least cooked pieces are exposed, and more cooked parts are overlapped. Re-cover.

Microwave remaining time or until fork tender. Drain liquid. Add sauce (and lemon juice for roasted ribs). Microwave uncovered 4 to 6 minutes.

Ham

Ham is available in many forms. Canned hams and boneless, rolled hams are fully cooked and ready to eat, although their flavor improves with heating. Bone-in hams may be labeled either "fully cooked" or "cook before eating". If the ham is not labeled, it is probably a "cook before eating" ham.

"Picnic hams" are cut from the shoulder, rather than the hind leg of pork, and contain more fat and tissue. They are available bone-in and boneless, fully cooked and "cook before eating" Many fully cooked picnic hams are not labeled, so it is best to check with the butcher. Either type of picnic shoulder should be microwaved tightly covered to tenderize it.

Canned & Boneless Rolled Ham

50% (Medium)

	Approx. Min./Lb.	Removal Temp.
Canned Ham	6-8	130°
Boneless, rolled ham	10-15	130°

How to Prepare Ham for Microwaving

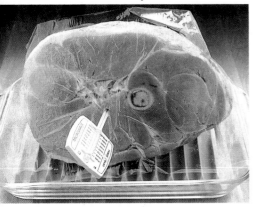

Bone-in Ham, fully cooked. Place on rack. Cover cut surface with plastic wrap. Shield, if used, must be at least 3-in. from top of oven. Insert thermometer into center of meatiest area, not touching fat or bone.

Bone-in Ham, "cook before eating". Place ham in cooking bag or tightly covered dish. Insert microwave thermometer, if used, into meatiest area, not touching fat or bone.

Picnic Ham. Place ham in cooking bag. If ham contains bones, check their position with a skewer before inserting microwave thermometer in meatiest area.

How to Microwave Bone-in Hams and Picnic Hams

Estimate the total cooking time and divide in half. Microwave at High 5 minutes. Reduce power to 50% (Medium). Microwave remaining part of first half of time.

Turn ham over. Insert probe, if used. Microwave second half of cooking time, or until internal temperature reaches removal time indicated on chart.

Let stand, loosely tented with foil, 10 minutes. Temperature will rise 5° to 10°.

Pasta & Ham Mornay

1¼ cups uncooked penne
   or mostaccioli pasta
½ cup sliced zucchini,
   ⅛ inch thick
⅓ cup frozen peas
2 tablespoons sliced
   green onion
1 tablespoon reduced-calorie
   margarine
2 teaspoons snipped
   fresh parsley
¼ teaspoon dried basil leaves
   Dash pepper
2 teaspoons all-purpose flour
½ cup evaporated
   skimmed milk
2 tablespoons shredded
   Swiss cheese
1 pkg. (4 oz.) low-fat boiled
   ham, cut into ¼-inch strips

4 servings

Prepare pasta as directed on package. Rinse with warm water. Drain. Set aside.

In 1½-quart casserole, combine zucchini, peas, onion, margarine, parsley, basil and pepper. Cover. Microwave at High for 2 to 3 minutes, or until vegetables are tender-crisp, stirring once. Stir in flour. Blend in milk. Microwave, uncovered, at High for 2½ to 3½ minutes longer, or until mixture thickens and bubbles, stirring once or twice. Stir in Swiss cheese, ham and pasta. Re-cover. Microwave at High for 1 to 3 minutes, or until heated through.

Per Serving:
Calories:	231
Protein:	16 g.
Carbohydrates:	39 g.
Fat:	12 g.
Cholesterol:	21 mg.
Sodium:	510 mg.
Calcium:	152 mg.
Exchanges:	2 bread, 2 med.-fat meat

Glazed Ham & Sweet Potatoes

1 can (23 oz.) sweet potatoes
(or yams) in syrup, drained
and cut in 1-in. cubes
1 to 1¼ lb. fully cooked,
boneless ham slices,
½-in. thick
¼ cup maple syrup
¼ cup brown sugar
¼ teaspoon dry mustard
Dash cloves

Serves 4

Arrange sweet potatoes around edges of 12×8-in. dish. Place ham slices in center, overlapping slightly to fit dish.

Combine remaining ingredients to make glaze; pour half over ham and sweet potatoes. Cover dish with wax paper. Microwave at High 4 minutes.

Pour remaining glaze over ham and sweet potatoes. Do not cover. Microwave at High 4 to 7 minutes or until ham is hot.

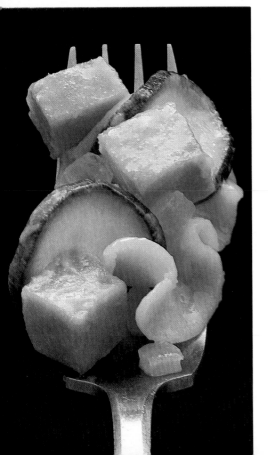

Ham & Zucchini in Cheese Sauce

4 servings rice or noodles
4 cups thinly sliced zucchini
¼ cup chopped onion
2 tablespoons water
2 tablespoons butter or
    margarine
2 tablespoons flour

½ teaspoon salt
⅛ teaspoon pepper
¾ cup milk
½ cup shredded Cheddar
    cheese
2 cups cubed cooked ham
¼ teaspoon paprika

Serves 4

Cook rice or noodles conventionally while microwaving sauce. Combine zucchini, onion and water in 2-qt. casserole. Cover. Microwave at High 4 to 7 minutes, or until zucchini is tender-crisp. Let stand covered while making sauce.

Melt butter in 4-cup measure at High 30 to 60 seconds. Stir in flour, salt and pepper until smooth. Blend in milk. Microwave at High 4 to 6 minutes, or until thickened, stirring every minute. Stir in cheese.

Drain zucchini. Add ham and cheese sauce to zucchini. Microwave at High 2 to 3½ minutes, or until thoroughly heated.

Stir mixture to redistribute sauce. Sprinkle paprika on top. Serve over rice or noodles.

Ham & Cheese Filled Cabbage Rolls

6 large cabbage leaves

Filling:

2 cups cooked cubed ham
1 cup shredded Cheddar
   cheese
1 egg
¼ cup seasoned bread crumbs
¼ teaspoon dry mustard

Topping:

3 tablespoons grated
   Parmesan cheese
2 tablespoons shredded
   Cheddar cheese
¼ teaspoon paprika

Note: To remove cabbage
leaves, microwave the whole
cabbage head at High 1 to 3
minutes,or until 6 outer leaves
can be separated easily. Refrigerate remaining cabbage for
future use.

Serves 6

How to Microwave Ham & Cheese Filled Cabbage Rolls

Cut out hard center rib from
each cabbage leaf. Place leaves
in 8×8-in. dish. Cover with
vented plastic wrap. Microwave
at High 1 to 2½ minutes, or until
leaves are pliable. Set aside.

Combine filling ingredients.
Place one-sixth of the mixture on
the base of each leaf. Fold in
sides of leaf. Roll up leaves to
enclose filling. Secure with a
pick if necessary. Place rolls,
seam side down, in 8×8-in. dish.
Cover with wax paper.

Microwave 4 to 6 minutes, or
until filling is set, rotating dish
after half the cooking time.
Combine topping ingredients.
Sprinkle over rolls. Microwave
uncovered 1½ to 2½ minutes, or
until cheese melts.

Bacon

There are several ways to microwave bacon. Choose the one that suits your needs and the type of bacon you prefer.

Bacon varies in thickness, number of slices per pound and the amount of salt and sugar used in curing. These factors affect cooking times and methods. Thick slices and home cures take more time. When microwaving several layers of bacon, reduce the time per slice.

Microwaved bacon doesn't curl or spatter; it shrinks less and needs less attention than conventionally fried. Clean-up is easy.

High Power
| 1 to 6 slices | ¾-1 min. per slice |
| Over 6 slices | ½-¾ min. per slice |

How To Microwave Bacon

Layer 3 paper towels. Place them directly on the oven floor or on a paper or microwave oven-proof plate.

Arrange 1 to 6 strips of bacon on towels and cover with another towel. Microwave and let stand 5 minutes. Paper may develop brown spots and stick slightly if bacon has a high sugar content.

Roasting Rack Method

Use a roasting rack or trivet in a baking dish when you wish to save drippings, or if you prefer the broiled type of bacon. Cover bacon with a paper towel before microwaving to absorb spatters.

Let bacon stand 5 minutes after microwaving. It should be removed from the oven while fat is still slightly translucent and bubbly. Bacon cooked on a roasting rack will not be as flat or crisp as bacon cooked on paper towels. Timings in chart are for medium-cooked bacon.

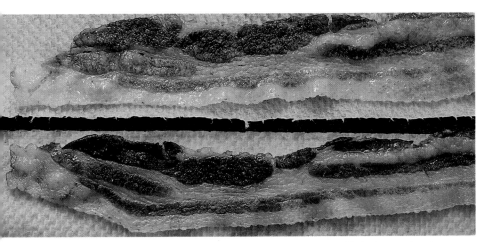

Remove bacon from oven while it still looks slightly underdone. After standing it will be evenly cooked and brown. Microwave bacon on paper towels if you prefer crisp-cooked bacon.

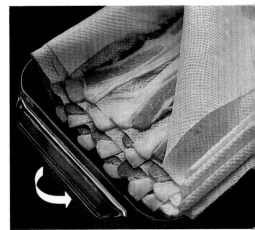

Use a paper towel lined baking dish for several layers of bacon. Cover each with towel. Rotate dish after ½ cooking time.

Sausages

Wieners and frankfurters vary in size. Times in the chart are for medium wieners (10 to 12 per lb.). When heating smaller wieners, check at the minimum time. Wieners and franks are fully cooked and take little time to heat.

Larger sausages, such as bratwurst, knockwurst and Polish sausage are also fully cooked. They take a little longer to heat and should be turned over after ½ the time.

Uncooked breakfast sausage links and patties vary greatly in fat content, which affects the amount of shrinkage. If you use the roasting rack method, you will want a browning agent, since plain microwaved sausage is gray when fully cooked.

Wieners in Buns

High Power

1 wiener	½-¾ min.
2 wieners	¾-1¼ min.
4 wieners	1¾-2¾ min.

How to Microwave Wieners

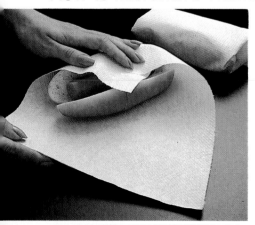

Place wiener in bun. Wrap in paper napkin or towel. Microwave at High according to chart.

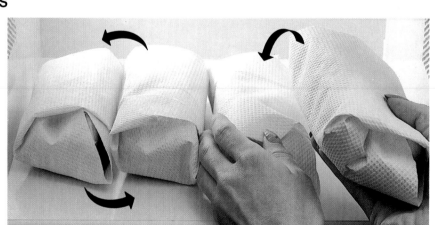

Rearrange once when heating 4 wieners by moving outside ones to center. When wieners are heated without buns, times are slightly shorter.

How to Microwave Sausage Patties or Links

Roasting rack method. Place rack in 12×8-in. baking dish. Arrange sausage on rack. Brush with equal parts bouquet sauce and water. Cover with wax paper. Microwave on first side. Turn over. Brush with sauce mixture. Cover. Microwave second side.

Browning dish method. Preheat browning dish as manufacturer directs. Place sausage in dish. Microwave first side. Turn sausage over. Microwave second side.

High Power

Patties, 2-oz., 3-in. diameter

Quantity	1st side Minutes	2nd side Minutes
Rack Method		
2	1 - 1½	2 - 2½
4	1½ - 2	2½ - 3
8	3 - 3½	4 - 4½
Browning Dish		
2	½	1
4	1½	1½ - 2
8	2	2½ - 3

Sausage Links

Quantity	1st side Minutes	2nd side Minutes
Rack Method		
2	1	1 - 1½
4	1	1 - 1½
8	1½ - 2	2
Browning Dish		
2	½	½ - 1
4	½ - 1	1
8	1 - 1½	1½

Brown & Serve Links

Quantity	1st side Minutes	2nd side Minutes
Rack Method		
2	½	½ - 1
4	½	1
8	1	1
Browning Dish		
2	¼	¼ - ½
4	½	½
8	½	½ - ¾

Wiener & Bean Pot Casserole

½ cup chopped onions
1 clove garlic, crushed
2 tablespoons butter or margarine
1 pkg. wieners (12 to 16-oz.) cut in quarters
1 can (16-oz.) baked beans
1 can (16-oz.) lima beans, drained

1 can (16-oz.) kidney beans, drained
½ cup brown sugar
½ cup catsup
1 tablespoon prepared mustard
½ teaspoon salt
¼ teaspoon pepper

Serves 4 to 6

Combine onions, garlic and butter in 3-qt. casserole. Microwave at High 1 to 2 minutes, until onions are soft and translucent. Add remaining ingredients. Push wieners to bottom of dish so they are buried under beans. Cover. Microwave 13 to 15 minutes, until heated through, stirring after ½ the time.

Shield wieners by pushing ▶ them underneath beans.

Poultry

Chicken is one of our best and most economical sources of protein. Most Americans eat it at least once a week. Chicken is an ideal food for microwaving; it's tender and juicy, responds to a variety of flavoring and cooks in fractions of the conventional time. The juices rendered are highly nutritious, and should be saved for sauces, soups or enriching vegetables.

Cornish hens and chicken pieces microwave so quickly they do not have time to crisp and brown. Use a browning agent or a crumb coating, or add flavor and eye appeal by cooking in a colorful sauce.

Defrosting Poultry

Type	Power Level	Time	Procedure
Chicken,			
Whole	30% (Low)	5 to 9 min./lb.	Unwrap and place breast-side down in baking dish. Cover with wax paper. Microwave for half of time. Turn breast-side up. Shield if needed. Microwave remaining time. Remove giblets. Let stand 5 to 10 minutes until cool but not icy.
Quarters, Legs, Thighs, Wings	50% (Med.)	4 to 6½ min./lb.	Unwrap and place in baking dish or on roasting rack. Microwave for half of time. Separate pieces. Arrange with thickest portions toward outside. Microwave remaining time. Let stand 10 to 15 minutes until cool but not icy.
Boneless Breasts	50% (Med.)	5½ to 8 min./lb.	Unwrap and place in baking dish or on roasting rack. Microwave for half of time. Separate pieces. Microwave remaining time until pliable but cold. Let stand 15 to 20 minutes.
Livers	50% (Med.)	4 to 7 min./lb.	Place package in microwave oven. Microwave for half of time. Unwrap and separate livers. Microwave remaining time. Let stand 5 minutes until livers can be pierced with fork.
Turkey,			
Whole, bone-in, no larger than 11 lbs.	50% (Med.)	3½ to 5½ min./lb.	Estimate total defrosting time and divide into 4 parts. Unwrap and place breast-side down in baking dish. Microwave for one-fourth of total time. Turn breast-side up. Microwave for one-fourth of time. Shield warm spots as needed. Let stand 15 minutes. Turn turkey on side. Microwave for one-fourth of time. Turn turkey on other side. Microwave remaining time. Remove giblets. Let stand in cool water 30 to 60 minutes until cool but not icy.
Whole, boneless, 5 to 6 lbs.	50% (Med.)	7½ to 9½ min./lb.	Unwrap and place on roasting rack. Microwave for half of time, turning over once. Let stand 15 minutes. Remove gravy packet. Turn turkey over. Microwave remaining time, turning over once. Let stand 20 minutes until cool but not icy.
Bone-in Breast	50% (Med.)	3½ to 5½ min./lb.	Unwrap and place skin-side down on roasting rack. Microwave for half of time. Remove gravy packet. Turn skin-side up. Shield if needed. Microwave remaining time. Rinse in cool water. Let stand 5 to 10 minutes until cool but not icy.
Boneless Breast, no larger than 5 lbs.	50% (Med.)	7½ to 9½ min./lb.	Unwrap and place on roasting rack. Microwave for half of time, turning over once. Let stand 15 minutes. Remove gravy packet. Shield if needed. Turn turkey over. Microwave remaining time, turning over once. Let stand 20 minutes until cool but not icy.
Legs, Thighs, Wings	50% (Med.)	5½ to 7½ min./lb.	Unwrap and place on roasting rack. Microwave for half of time. Turn over and rearrange. Microwave remaining time. Let stand 15 minutes until cool but not icy.
Tenderloins	50% (Med.)	4 to 6 min./lb.	Unwrap and place on roasting rack. Microwave for half of time. Shield thin portions. Microwave remaining time. Let stand 10 to 15 minutes until cool but not icy.
Cutlets	30% (Low)	7 to 11 min./lb.	Unwrap and place on roasting rack. Microwave for half of time. Separate and rearrange as soon as possible. Microwave remaining time, until pliable but still icy. Let stand to complete defrosting.
Ground	50% (Med.)	4 to 6 min./lb.	Unwrap and place in casserole. Microwave, removing defrosted portions to another dish. Let stand 10 minutes.
Cornish Hens	50% (Med.)	5 to 7 min./lb.	Unwrap and place breast-side down in baking dish. Cover with wax paper. Microwave for half of time. Turn breast-side up. Shield if needed. Rearrange hens. Microwave remaining time. Remove giblets. Let stand 5 minutes.
Duckling	50% (Med.)	4½ to 6 min./lb.	Unwrap and place breast-side down in baking dish. Cover with wax paper. Microwave for half of time. Turn breast-side up. Shield if needed. Microwave remaining time. Remove giblets. Let stand 5 to 10 minutes until cool but not icy.

Microwaving Poultry

Type	Power Level	Time	Procedure
Chicken, Whole	High	5 to 8 min./lb.	Place breast-side up on roasting rack. Cover with wax paper. Microwave until legs move freely and juices run clear, rotating rack twice. Let stand, covered, 10 minutes.
Quarters, Breasts, Legs, Thighs, Wings	High	4 to 8 min./lb.	Arrange on roasting rack with thickest portions toward outside. Cover with wax paper. Microwave until no longer pink and juices run clear, rearranging once or twice. Let stand, covered, 3 minutes.
Turkey, Whole, bone-in, no larger than 11 lbs.	High first 10 min., then 50% (Med.)	12 to 15 min./lb. total time	Estimate total cooking time and divide into 4 parts. Place turkey breast-side down in baking dish. Microwave at High for 10 minutes. Reduce power to 50% (Medium). Microwave remainder of first one-fourth of time. Turn breast-side up. Shield if needed. Baste. Microwave at 50% (Medium) for one-fourth of time. Drain. Turn turkey on side. Microwave at 50% (Medium) for one-fourth of time. Turn turkey on other side. Baste. Microwave remaining time until internal temperature of thickest portion of each thigh registers 180°F. Let stand, tented with foil, 20 to 30 minutes.
Whole, boneless, 5 to 6 lbs.	High first 10 min., then 70% (Med. High)	11 to 15 min./lb. total time	Place turkey in nylon cooking bag. Secure bag loosely with string. Place in baking dish. Microwave at High for 10 minutes. Reduce power to 70% (Medium High). Microwave remaining time until internal temperature registers 175°F in several places, turning over 2 or 3 times. Let stand, tented with foil, 15 to 20 minutes.
Bone-in Breast	High first 5 min., then 50% (Med.)	12½ to 16½ min./lb. total time	Estimate total cooking time and divide into 4 parts. Place turkey skin-side down on roasting rack. Microwave at High for 5 minutes. Reduce power to 50% (Medium). Microwave remainder of first one-fourth of time. Turn turkey on side. Microwave at 50% (Medium) for one-fourth of time. Turn turkey on other side. Baste. Microwave at 50% (Medium) for one-fourth of time. Turn turkey skin-side up. Baste. Microwave remaining time until internal temperature registers 170°F. Let stand, tented with foil, 10 to 20 minutes.
Boneless Breast, no larger than 5 lbs.	High first 5 min., then 50% (Med.)	16 to 18 min./lb. total time	Place turkey on roasting rack. Microwave at High for 5 minutes. Reduce power to 50% (Medium). Microwave remaining time until internal temperature registers 170°F, turning over after half the time. Let stand, tented with foil, 10 to 20 minutes.
Legs, Thighs, Wings	70% (Med. High)	13 to 17 min./lb.	Place turkey in baking dish with ¼ cup broth or wine. Cover. Microwave until juices run clear, turning over after half the time. Let stand, covered, 5 minutes.
Ground	High	4 to 7 min./lb.	Crumble turkey into casserole. Cover. Microwave until firm and cooked through, stirring twice.
Cornish Hens	High	5½ to 8 min./lb.	Place breast-side up on roasting rack. Cover with wax paper. Microwave until legs move freely and juices run clear, rearranging once or twice. Brush with glaze. Let stand, covered, 5 minutes.
Duckling	High first 10 min., then 50% (Med.)	6½ to 9½ min./lb. total time	Estimate total cooking time and divide in half. Place duckling breast-side down on roasting rack. Secure neck skin to back with wooden picks. Microwave at High for 10 minutes. Drain. Reduce power to 50% (Medium). Microwave remainder of first half of time. Drain. Turn duckling breast-side up. Brush with glaze. Microwave at 50% (Medium) for remaining time. Drain. Brush with glaze. Let stand, tented with foil, 5 minutes.

Sunday Chicken Bake

This easy, dressed-up chicken dinner is microwaved at 50% power because sour cream curdles at high temperatures. Skinning the chicken allows more flavor to be absorbed by the meat.

4 servings cooked rice,
    page 230
4 half chicken breasts, boned
    and skinned
1 can (10¾-oz.) cream of
    mushroom soup, undiluted
8 oz. fresh mushrooms, sliced
1 cup dairy sour cream
½ cup dry sherry
1 tablespoon chopped,
    candied ginger
2 tablespoons snipped fresh
    parsley

Serves 4

How to Microwave Sunday Chicken Bake

Microwave rice; set aside covered. Arrange chicken breasts in 8×8-in. dish.

Combine rest of ingredients in small bowl. Pour over chicken. Cover with vented plastic wrap.

Microwave at 50% power (Medium) for 15 minutes. Turn chicken over. Re-cover. Microwave 10 to 20 minutes, until chicken is fork tender.

Crispy Coated Chicken

1 2½ to 3½-lb. broiler-fryer, quartered or cut in pieces

Coating mixture:

1 cup corn flake crumbs
6 tablespoons grated
   Parmesan cheese
2 teaspoons parsley flakes
1 small clove garlic, crushed
½ teaspoon salt
   Dash pepper

Dipping mixture:

¼ cup butter
2 eggs, beaten

High Power

5½-8 minutes per pound

How to Microwave Crispy Coated Chicken

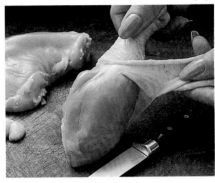

Skin chicken and remove excess fat.

Combine coating ingredients in a 1-qt. casserole.

Melt butter at High ¾ to 1 minute. Stir into beaten eggs.

Dip chicken in egg mixture, then turn in crumbs to coat well.

Arrange chicken over rice on serving platter. Spoon some of sauce onto chicken. Serve rest in gravy boat. Garnish with paprika and chopped olives.

Arrange in 12x8-in. dish with bony sides down and thick pieces to outside of dish. Cover with wax paper. Microwave ½ the time.

Rearrange chicken so that areas which are least cooked come to outside of dish. Discard wax paper. Microwave for second ½ of time.

Whole Chickens

A whole chicken turns a light golden brown during micro-waving. For richer color, you can brush the chicken with glaze half way through cooking, or use a browning sauce as suggested below. Because chicken skin is very fatty, dilute the bouquet sauce with butter and rub it into the skin. Brushed-on liquid beads up and streaks.

High Power, 3 min.

50% Power, 10-12 min./lb.

How to Microwave a Whole Chicken

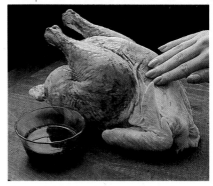

Dry chicken thoroughly. Rub a mixture of equal parts brown bouquet sauce and melted butter into skin.

Place chicken breast side down in baking dish. Micro-wave at High 3 minutes. Reduce power to 50%. Micro-wave for ½ of time.

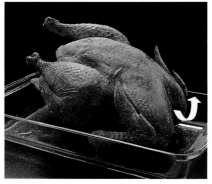

Turn chicken breast side up. Microwave second ½ of time, or until legs move easily and meat around bone is done.

Rice Stuffing

2 tablespoons butter or margarine	2 teaspoons parsley flakes
½ cup sliced brazil nuts or almonds	½ teaspoon salt
	⅛ teaspoon rosemary
½ cup finely chopped celery	⅛ teaspoon sage
¼ cup chopped onion	⅛ teaspoon thyme
1½ cups cooked rice	⅛ teaspoon pepper
¼ cup raisins	

Makes 4 servings

Combine butter, nuts, celery and onion in 1-qt. casserole. Cover. Microwave 2 to 4 minutes at High, or until celery is tender and onions are translucent. Set aside. In small bowl, mix together remaining ingredients; stir into nut mixture. Use to stuff 4 cornish hens or a 3 to 4-lb. chicken. To serve as a side dish, microwave covered 1 to 2 minutes on High, or until heated through.

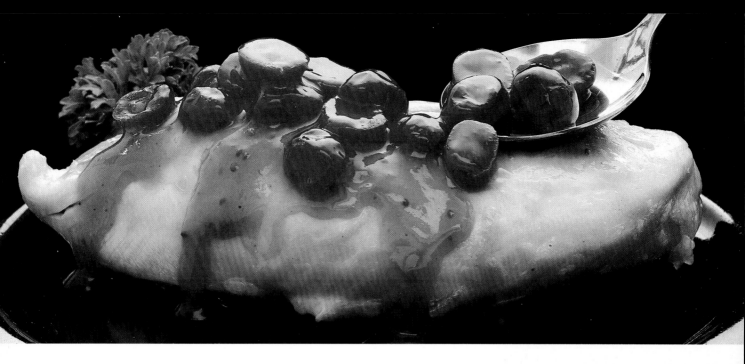

Cranberry Orange ▲ Glazed Chicken

⅔ cup freshly squeezed orange
  juice
⅔ cup fresh cranberries, halved
1 teaspoon sugar
2 teaspoons cornstarch
  Dash ground cloves
2 whole bone-in chicken
  breasts, halved, skin
  removed

Serves 4

In 2-cup measure combine all
ingredients except chicken.
Microwave at High 3 to 4
minutes, or until mixture
thickens, stirring 2 or 3 times
during cooking. Set aside.

Arrange chicken on roasting
rack with meatiest portions to
outside. Cover with wax paper.
Microwave at High 5 minutes.
Rearrange chicken. Microwave
at High 3 minutes. Cover with
one-third of glaze. Microwave at
High 2 to 4 minutes longer, or
until meat near bone is no
longer pink. Serve remaining
glaze over chicken.

Per Serving:
  Calories: 197
  Sodium: 90 mg.
  Cholesterol: 60 mg.
  Exchanges: 1 fruit, 3 low
            fat meat

Lemon Seasoned ▶ Chicken Breasts

1 tablespoon water
½ teaspoon bouquet sauce
1 tablespoon lemon juice
1 teaspoon lemon pepper
½ teaspoon salt, optional
2 whole bone-in chicken
  breasts, halved, skin
  removed
1 to 2 teaspoons parsley
  flakes, optional

Serves 4

In small dish combine all
ingredients except chicken and
parsley. Arrange chicken
breasts bone-side up on
microwave roasting rack, with
meatiest portions to outside of
dish. Brush with half of
seasoned mixture. Microwave at
High 5 minutes.

Turn pieces over and brush with
remaining mixture. Microwave
10 to 15 minutes, or until meat
near bone is no longer pink,
rotating once during cooking. If
desired, sprinkle with parsley
before serving.

Per Serving:
  Calories: 165
  Sodium: 132 mg.
  Cholesterol: 63 mg.
  Exchanges: 3 low fat meat

Curried Chicken

2½ to 3-lb. broiler-fryer chicken, cut into 8 pieces, skin removed
1½ cups buttermilk
2 to 3 teaspoons curry powder
⅛ teaspoon pepper
Dash ground cinnamon
Dash ground cloves
1 medium onion, thinly sliced
2 cloves garlic, cut in half
1 cup julienne carrots (1½ × ¼-inch strips)
1 medium potato, cut into ½-inch cubes
1 medium green pepper, cut into chunks
1 cup evaporated skimmed milk
2 tablespoons cornstarch

6 servings

In 3-quart casserole, arrange chicken. In small bowl, blend buttermilk, curry, pepper, cinnamon, cloves, onion and garlic. Pour over chicken, lifting pieces to coat. Cover. Marinate for 30 minutes. Add carrots, potato and green pepper to chicken. Cover. Microwave at High for 20 to 30 minutes, or until vegetables are tender and chicken near bone is no longer pink, turning chicken over and rearranging after half the time. Remove chicken. Remove meat from bones. Cut into bite-size pieces. Set aside. Add milk to vegetable mixture. Remove a small amount of liquid and blend in cornstarch. Stir into vegetable mixture. Microwave at High for 5 to 9 minutes, or until sauce thickens and bubbles. Add chicken to sauce.

Per Serving:
Calories:	186
Protein:	23 g.
Carbohydrates:	15 g.
Fat:	4 g.
Cholesterol:	60 mg.
Sodium:	390 mg.
Calcium:	213 mg.
Exchanges:	1 bread, 2½ low-fat meat

Oriental Chicken
with Peanut Sauce

1 boneless whole chicken
   breast (about 12 oz.) skin
   removed, cut into ½-inch
   strips
¼ cup sliced green onions
3 tablespoons reduced-sodium
   soy sauce
2 tablespoons lemon juice
1 teaspoon honey
1 clove garlic, minced
½ teaspoon peeled, grated
   gingerroot
¼ teaspoon ground coriander
⅛ teaspoon dried crushed red
   pepper
⅛ teaspoon sesame oil
3 tablespoons unsalted dry
   roasted peanuts
1 pkg. (3¾ oz.) cellophane
   noodles
8 oz. fresh spinach, trimmed
   and torn, about 6 cups
¼ cup shredded carrot

4 servings

Per Serving:
Calories:	146
Protein:	18 g.
Carbohydrates:	7 g.
Fat:	5 g.
Cholesterol:	34 mg.
Sodium:	237 mg.
Calcium:	94 mg.
Exchanges:	½ bread, 2 low-fat meat

How to Microwave Oriental Chicken with Peanut Sauce

Combine chicken and onions in 2-quart casserole. Cover. Set aside. In 2-cup measure, combine soy sauce, lemon juice, honey, garlic, gingerroot, coriander, red pepper and sesame oil. Set aside. Place peanuts in blender; chop until fine particles form. Set aside.

Prepare noodles as directed on package. Keep warm on platter. Microwave chicken and onions at High for 2 to 5 minutes, or until chicken is no longer pink, stirring once. Add spinach. Re-cover. Microwave at High for 2 to 2½ minutes longer, or until spinach wilts. Stir.

Drain cooking liquid into soy sauce mixture. Microwave at High for 2 minutes to blend flavors. Stir in peanuts. Top noodles with chicken and spinach mixture. Pour sauce over chicken and sprinkle with carrot.

Gingered Chicken & Chinese Cabbage

2 tablespoons sliced almonds
2 teaspoons reduced-calorie margarine
1 boneless whole chicken breast (about 12 oz.) skin removed, cut into ½-inch strips
2 cups coarsely sliced Chinese cabbage
¼ cup chopped carrot
1 can (8 oz.) bamboo shoots, rinsed and drained, cut into ¼-inch strips
⅓ cup sliced green onions, ½ inch thick

Sauce:

½ cup ready-to-serve low-sodium chicken broth
1 tablespoon reduced-sodium soy sauce
1 tablespoon sherry
2 teaspoons cornstarch
¼ teaspoon peeled, grated gingerroot
¼ teaspoon sugar
⅛ teaspoon chili powder
Dash cayenne

4 servings

In 1-quart casserole, combine almonds and margarine. Microwave at High for 4 to 5 minutes, or just until almonds begin to brown, stirring once. Set aside. In 2-quart casserole, combine chicken, cabbage and carrot. Cover. Microwave at High for 5 to 7 minutes, or until chicken is no longer pink, stirring twice. Stir in bamboo shoots and onions. Set aside. In 2-cup measure, blend all sauce ingredients. Microwave at High for 2 to 3 minutes, or until mixture bubbles, stirring twice. Stir into chicken. Microwave at High for 2 to 3 minutes longer, or until hot. Top with almonds.

Per Serving:
Calories:	137
Protein:	16 g.
Carbohydrates:	8 g.
Fat:	5 g.
Cholesterol:	34 mg.
Sodium:	204 mg.
Calcium:	56 mg.
Exchanges:	2 low-fat meat, 1 vegetable

Pasta, Chicken & Broccoli

1½ cups uncooked whole wheat elbow macaroni
2 tablespoons lemon juice
2 cups frozen broccoli cuts
⅓ cup chopped onion
1 clove garlic, minced
2 tablespoons water
1½ cups cut-up cooked chicken
¼ teaspoon Italian seasoning
⅛ teaspoon pepper
1 cup low-fat plain yogurt
2 tablespoons grated Parmesan cheese
2 tablespoons chopped walnuts

6 servings

Prepare macaroni as directed on package, adding 2 table-spoons lemon juice to cooking water. Drain. Set aside.

In 2-quart casserole, combine broccoli, onion, garlic and 2 tablespoons water. Cover. Microwave at High for 6 to 8 minutes, or until tender-crisp, stirring once. Stir in macaroni, chicken, Italian seasoning and pepper. Re-cover. Microwave at High for 3 to 6 minutes longer, or until heated through, stirring once. Blend in yogurt and Parmesan cheese. Sprinkle with walnuts before serving.

Per Serving:
Calories:	198
Protein:	18 g.
Carbohydrates:	20 g.
Fat:	5 g.
Cholesterol:	30 mg.
Sodium:	397 mg.
Calcium:	136 mg.
Exchanges:	1 bread, 2 low-fat meat

Coriander Chicken with Sweet & Sour Sauce

2 boneless whole chicken
    breasts (about 12 oz. each)
    skin removed, split in half

Herb Filling:
1 tablespoon finely chopped
    green onion
1 teaspoon dried parsley flakes
¼ teaspoon ground coriander
⅛ teaspoon garlic powder
⅛ teaspoon pepper

1 can (8 oz.) unsweetened
    pineapple chunks, drained
    (reserve juice)
¼ cup water
2 tablespoons low-sugar
    orange marmalade
1 tablespoon cornstarch
1 tablespoon no-salt ketchup
2 teaspoons reduced-sodium
    soy sauce
1½ teaspoons white wine vinegar
½ teaspoon low-sodium instant
    chicken bouillon granules
½ cup halved seedless green
    grapes

4 servings

Per Serving:
Calories:	203
Protein:	27 g.
Carbohydrates:	19 g.
Fat:	2 g.
Cholesterol:	68 mg.
Sodium:	173 mg.
Calcium:	—
Exchanges:	2½ low-fat meat, 1 bread

How to Microwave Coriander Chicken with Sweet & Sour Sauce

Pound each chicken breast half to ¼-inch thickness. Set aside. In small bowl, combine all filling ingredients. Mix well.

Spread about 1 teaspoonful filling over each chicken breast half. Fold in sides and roll up, enclosing filling.

Place breast seam-side down in 9-inch square baking dish. Add pineapple chunks to chicken. Set aside.

Combine remaining ingredients, except grapes, with pineapple juice in 2-cup measure. Mix well.

Microwave at High for 3 to 4 minutes, or until mixture thickens, stirring after every minute. Pour over chicken. Cover with wax paper.

Microwave at High for 6 to 10 minutes, or until chicken is no longer pink, rotating dish once. Sprinkle grapes over chicken during last 2 minutes.

Ham-stuffed Turkey Tenderloins ▲

2 turkey tenderloins
   (about 1¼ lbs.)

Stuffing:

1 tablespoon butter or
   margarine
2 tablespoons chopped onion
1 tablespoon finely chopped
   celery
1 tablespoon finely chopped
   red or green pepper
¼ lb. ground fully cooked ham
⅓ cup fresh bread crumbs
1 teaspoon dried parsley
   flakes

1 tablespoon milk
¼ teaspoon dried crushed
   sage leaves
   Dash salt
   Dash pepper

Basting Sauce:

1 tablespoon butter or
   margarine
1 teaspoon dried parsley
   flakes
⅛ teaspoon dried crushed
   sage leaves

4 to 6 servings

Cut lengthwise slit in each turkey tenderloin to within ½ inch of edge to form pocket for stuffing. Set aside. In 1-quart casserole, combine butter, onion, celery and red pepper. Cover. Microwave at High for 2 to 3 minutes, or until celery is tender-crisp. Stir in remaining stuffing ingredients. Fill each tenderloin with half of stuffing. Secure with string in 2 or 3 places. Arrange in 9-inch square baking dish with stuffing opening toward center of dish. Set aside. In custard cup, combine all basting sauce ingredients. Microwave at High for 45 seconds to 1 minute, or until butter melts. Brush on each tenderloin. Cover with wax paper. Microwave at 70% (Medium High) for 11 to 18 minutes, or until turkey is firm and no longer pink, rotating dish twice. Let stand, covered, for 3 minutes. Remove string.

Barbecued Turkey Thighs

2 turkey thighs (1 to 1½ lbs.
   each)
1 can (8 oz.) tomato sauce
1 tablespoon honey
2 teaspoons cider vinegar
2 teaspoons Worcestershire
   sauce
½ teaspoon prepared mustard
¼ teaspoon salt
⅛ teaspoon celery seed
⅛ teaspoon pepper
⅛ teaspoon instant minced
   garlic

4 servings

Arrange turkey thighs in 10-inch square casserole with thickest portions toward outside of casserole. Set aside. In small mixing bowl, combine remaining ingredients. Mix well. Pour over turkey. Cover. Marinate in refrigerator for at least 4 hours.

Place casserole with turkey and marinade in microwave oven. Microwave at High for 5 minutes. Reduce power to 70% (Medium High). Microwave for 30 to 40 minutes, or until turkey is tender and cooked through, turning turkey over and basting with sauce twice. Remove turkey from bones and serve in sauce.

Apple-Plum Spiced Turkey Breast

5¼ to 6¼-lb. bone-in turkey
    breast, defrosted

Marinade:

½ cup apple juice
⅓ cup plum jelly
⅓ cup Hoisen sauce
1 tablespoon soy sauce
¼ teaspoon fennel seed,
    crushed
¼ teaspoon ground cinnamon
⅛ teaspoon anise seed,
    crushed
⅛ teaspoon ground cloves

6 to 8 servings

Remove gravy packet from turkey breast and discard. Place turkey in large plastic food storage bag in baking dish. In 4-cup measure, combine all marinade ingredients. Microwave at High for 2½ to 3½ minutes, or until mixture boils, stirring after every minute. Cool slightly. Pour over turkey. Secure bag. Marinate in refrigerator overnight, turning bag occasionally.

Remove turkey breast from marinade, reserving marinade. Place turkey skin-side down on roasting rack. Estimate total cooking time at 12½ to 16½ minutes per pound and divide total cooking time into 4 parts. Microwave at High for first 5 minutes. Reduce power to 50% (Medium). Microwave the remainder of first one-fourth of time. Turn turkey on side. Brush with marinade. Microwave at 50% (Medium) for second one-fourth of time. Turn turkey on other side. Brush with marinade. Microwave at 50% (Medium) for third one-fourth of time. Turn turkey skin-side up. Brush with marinade. Microwave the remaining one-fourth of time, or until internal temperature registers 170°F in several places. Let stand, tented with foil, for 10 to 20 minutes before carving.

Hungarian Turkey Goulash

1 teaspoon vegetable oil
1 medium onion, cut in half
    lengthwise and thinly
    sliced
1 clove garlic, minced
1 tablespoon all-purpose flour
1 can (8 oz.) whole tomatoes
⅓ cup water
2 teaspoons paprika
1½ teaspoons instant beef
    bouillon granules
½ teaspoon salt
¼ teaspoon caraway seed,
    crushed
2 medium potatoes, thinly
    sliced, about 2 cups
1½ cups cubed turkey, ¾-inch
    cubes
⅓ cup dairy sour cream

4 servings

In 1½-quart casserole, combine oil, onion and garlic. Cover. Microwave at High for 4 to 6 minutes, or until onion is tender, stirring once. Stir in flour. Mix in tomatoes and water, stirring to break apart tomatoes. Stir in paprika, bouillon, salt, caraway, potatoes and turkey. Re-cover. Microwave at High for 15 to 20 minutes, or until potatoes are tender, stirring 3 times. Let stand, covered, for 5 minutes. Stir in sour cream.

Cutlets with Cheese ▲

⅓ cup mayonnaise
⅓ cup dairy sour cream
1 tablespoon Dijon mustard
½ teaspoon Worcestershire
    sauce
⅛ teaspoon cayenne
4 turkey cutlets (2 to 3 oz.
    each) ¼ inch thick
2 cups garlic and onion
    seasoned croutons,
    crushed
4 slices (½ oz. each) Cheddar
    cheese, cut into
    3 × 1½-inch strips

4 servings

In 9-inch square baking dish, combine mayonnaise, sour cream, mustard, Worcestershire sauce and cayenne. Mix well. Add turkey cutlets, turning to coat. Cover. Chill for 1 to 2 hours. Scrape excess sour cream mixture from cutlets. Dip each cutlet in crumbs, pressing lightly to coat both sides. Arrange cutlets on roasting rack. Microwave at 70% (Medium High) for 3 minutes. Rotate rack half turn. Top each cutlet with Cheddar cheese. Microwave at 70% (Medium High) for 5 to 6 minutes, or until cheese melts and turkey is firm and no longer pink, rotating rack after half the time.

Herb & Vegetable-stuffed Turkey Tenderloins

1 cup frozen cut green beans
2 tablespoons butter or
   margarine
¼ cup chopped carrot
¼ cup chopped celery
2 tablespoons finely chopped
   onion
½ cup herb seasoned stuffing
   mix
¼ teaspoon salt

Gravy:

1 tablespoon butter or
   margarine
2 tablespoons all-purpose flour
2 teaspoons dried parsley
   flakes
¼ teaspoon salt
⅛ teaspoon pepper
¼ teaspoon bouquet sauce
½ cup ready-to-serve chicken
   broth
¾ cup milk

2 turkey tenderloins
   (about 1 lb.)
   Paprika

4 servings

How to Microwave Herb & Vegetable-stuffed Turkey Tenderloins

Place beans on plate. Microwave at High for 1 to 2½ minutes, or until defrosted. Coarsely chop beans. In 1-quart casserole, combine beans, butter, carrot, celery and onion. Cover.

Microwave at High for 4 to 5 minutes, or until vegetables are tender, stirring after every 2 minutes. Stir in stuffing mix and salt. Re-cover. Set aside. Place butter in 4-cup measure. Microwave at High for 45 seconds to 1 minute, or until butter melts.

Stir in flour, parsley, salt, pepper and bouquet sauce. Blend in broth until smooth. Blend in milk. Microwave at High for 3 to 3½ minutes, or until mixture thickens, stirring after every minute.

Cut lengthwise slit in each tenderloin to within ½ inch of edge to form pocket. Fill each tenderloin with half of stuffing mixture.

Arrange in 9-inch square baking dish with stuffing opening toward center of dish. Pour gravy over turkey. Sprinkle with paprika. Cover with wax paper.

Microwave at 70% (Medium High) for 13 to 18 minutes, or until turkey is firm and no longer pink, rotating dish after every 3 minutes.

Turkey Cutlets
& Golden Pilaf

Golden Pilaf:

- 1 slice bacon, cut-up
- 2 tablespoons sliced green onion
- 1½ cups ready-to-serve chicken broth
- ½ cup chopped red apple
- ⅓ cup raisins
- ½ teaspoon dried parsley flakes
- ¼ teaspoon salt
- ¼ teaspoon turmeric
- ¼ teaspoon lemon pepper seasoning
- 1½ cups instant rice

- ½ cup cornflake crumbs
- 1 teaspoon dried parsley flakes
- ½ teaspoon lemon pepper seasoning
- 12 oz. turkey cutlets (2 to 3 oz. each) ¼ inch thick
- 2 tablespoons chopped walnuts

4 servings

In 2-quart casserole, combine bacon and onion. Cover. Microwave at High for 2 to 4 minutes, or until bacon is brown. Stir in remaining pilaf ingredients, except rice. Re-cover. Microwave at High for 5 to 8 minutes, or until mixture boils. Quickly stir in rice. Re-cover. Set aside.

On wax paper, combine cornflake crumbs, parsley and lemon pepper. Roll each cutlet in crumb mixture, pressing lightly to coat. Arrange cutlets on roasting rack. Cover with wax paper. Microwave at 70% (Medium High) for 5 to 11 minutes, or until turkey is firm and no longer pink, rotating rack once. Add walnuts to pilaf. Stir. Spoon pilaf onto serving platter. Serve cutlets with pilaf.

Turkey Tamale Pie

Topping:

½ cup dairy sour cream
⅛ teaspoon ground cumin
⅛ teaspoon ground coriander
   Dash salt

Crust:

1 cup all-purpose flour
⅓ cup yellow cornmeal
¾ teaspoon salt
¼ teaspoon chili powder
   Dash cayenne
6 tablespoons shortening
4 to 6 tablespoons cold water

Filling:

1 lb. ground turkey
⅓ cup chopped green pepper
1 clove garlic, minced
1 teaspoon chili powder
¼ teaspoon salt
⅛ teaspoon ground cumin
⅛ teaspoon ground coriander
⅛ teaspoon ground oregano
   Dash cayenne
2 cups shredded Cheddar
   cheese
¼ cup chili sauce

6 servings

In small mixing bowl, combine all topping ingredients. Chill topping while preparing crust and filling.

For crust, in small mixing bowl, combine flour, cornmeal, salt, chili powder and cayenne. Cut in shortening to form coarse crumbs. Sprinkle with water, 1 tablespoon at a time, mixing with fork until particles are moistened and cling together. Form dough into a ball. Roll out on lightly floured board at least 2 inches larger than inverted 9-inch pie plate. Ease into plate. Trim and flute edges. Prick thoroughly. Microwave at High for 6 to 9 minutes, or until crust appears dry and opaque, rotating plate after every 2 minutes. Set aside.

In 2-quart casserole, combine all filling ingredients, except cheese and chili sauce. Microwave at High for 4 to 6 minutes, or until turkey is firm and cooked through, stirring after every 2 minutes. Drain. Stir in cheese and chili sauce. Press mixture into prepared crust. Spread topping over filling to within 1 inch of edge. Microwave at 50% (Medium) for 8 to 14 minutes, or until heated through, rotating plate after every 3 minutes. Serve with chopped tomato and sliced green onion.

Greek Pasticchio ▲

1 lb. ground turkey
⅓ cup chopped onion
¾ teaspoon ground cinnamon
⅛ teaspoon ground nutmeg
⅔ cup ricotta cheese
½ teaspoon dried parsley flakes
¼ teaspoon salt
⅛ teaspoon pepper

Sauce:

2 tablespoons butter or margarine

2 tablespoons all-purpose flour
½ teaspoon salt
1¼ cups milk
¼ cup grated Parmesan cheese

1⅓ cups fine egg noodles, cooked
Snipped fresh parsley (optional)

4 to 6 servings

In 1½-quart casserole, combine turkey and onion. Microwave at High for 4 to 7 minutes, or until firm, stirring twice. Drain. Stir in cinnamon and nutmeg. Microwave at High for 1 minute. Place turkey mixture in medium bowl. Set aside. In small mixing bowl, blend ricotta cheese, parsley, salt and pepper. Set aside.

For sauce, place butter in small mixing bowl. Microwave at High for 45 seconds to 1 minute, or until butter melts. Stir in flour and salt. Blend in milk. Microwave at High for 4 to 6½ minutes, or until mixture thickens and bubbles, stirring 2 or 3 times with whisk. Blend in Parmesan cheese. In same 1½-quart casserole, layer half of noodles, half of turkey, half of ricotta cheese mixture and one-third of sauce. Repeat once, ending with remaining two-thirds of sauce. Microwave at High for 5 minutes. Rotate casserole half turn. Reduce power to 50% (Medium). Microwave for 6 to 12 minutes, or until heated through, rotating casserole twice. Let stand for 3 minutes. Garnish with snipped fresh parsley.

Burrito Bake ▶

¾ lb. ground turkey
6 oz. pork sausage
⅓ cup chopped onion
1 teaspoon ground cumin
½ teaspoon salt
¼ teaspoon garlic powder
¼ teaspoon dried crushed red pepper
¼ teaspoon pepper
1¼ cups taco or salsa sauce, divided
¼ cup chopped black olives
⅔ cup refried beans
4 flour tortillas, 10-inch
1 cup shredded Monterey Jack cheese
½ cup shredded Cheddar cheese

Toppings:

Sliced avocado
Shredded lettuce
Chopped tomato
Dairy sour cream

4 servings

In 2-quart casserole, combine turkey, sausage and onion. Microwave at High for 6 to 8 minutes or until meats are firm, stirring 2 or 3 times. Drain. Add cumin, salt, garlic powder, red pepper, pepper, ½ cup taco sauce and olives. Mix well. Stir in refried beans. Microwave at High for 3 minutes, stirring once. Set aside.

Prepare tortillas as directed on package for enchiladas. Spoon one-fourth of turkey mixture down center of each tortilla. Fold in one end of tortilla and then two sides. Roll to enclose filling. Place burritos seam-side down in 10-inch square casserole. Top with remaining ¾ cup taco sauce. Sprinkle with Monterey Jack and Cheddar cheeses. Microwave at 70% (Medium High) for 6 to 9 minutes, or until cheese melts and burritos are hot, rotating once or twice. Let stand, covered, for 3 minutes. Serve with toppings.

◀ Cornish Hen Friccasee

     2 tablespoons butter or
         margarine
    ½ cup chopped onion
    ½ cup thinly sliced celery
    ¼ cup thinly sliced carrot
     1 cup fresh mushroom halves
    ⅓ cup water
    ¼ cup rosé wine
     1 teaspoon instant chicken
         bouillon granules
    ½ teaspoon salt
    ¼ teaspoon dried basil leaves
    ⅛ teaspoon dried thyme leaves
    ⅛ teaspoon pepper
     2 Cornish hens (18 oz. each)
         split in half through
         breastbone
     2 tablespoons all-purpose flour
    ¼ cup half-and-half
    ¼ teaspoon bouquet sauce

                            2 servings

In 10-inch square casserole,
combine butter, onion, celery
and carrot. Cover. Microwave at
High for 6 to 8 minutes, or until
tender, stirring twice. Stir in
mushrooms, water, wine, bouillon,
salt, basil, thyme and pepper.
Arrange Cornish hens skin-side
up on vegetables. Re-cover.
Reduce power to 70% (Medium
High). Microwave for 16 to
24 minutes, or until Cornish
hens are no longer pink and
juices run clear, rearranging
hens twice. Drain cooking liquid
into 4-cup measure. Set aside.
Cover Cornish hens and vegetables. Set aside.

In small mixing bowl, blend flour
and half-and-half until smooth.
Blend in hot cooking liquid and
bouquet sauce. Microwave at
High for 3 to 4 minutes, or until
mixture thickens and bubbles,
stirring after every minute. Pour
sauce over Cornish hens and
vegetables.

Cheesy Crab-stuffed Cornish Hens

Stuffing:
- 2 slices bacon, cut-up
- 1 can (6 oz.) crab meat, rinsed, drained and cartilage removed
- ½ cup Cheddar cheese croutons
- ¼ cup finely shredded Cheddar cheese
- 1 tablespoon sliced green onion
- ⅛ teaspoon salt
- ⅛ teaspoon pepper
- 2 Cornish hens, (18 oz. each*)

Glaze:
- 1 tablespoon French dressing
- ½ teaspoon bouquet sauce.

2 servings

Place bacon in 1-quart casserole. Cover. Microwave at High for 2½ to 4 minutes, or until crisp, stirring once. Stir in remaining stuffing ingredients. Fill cavity of Cornish hens with stuffing. Secure legs together with string. In custard cup, blend all glaze ingredients. Brush glaze on Cornish hens. Arrange hens breast-side up on roasting rack. Microwave at High for 12 to 17 minutes, or until legs move freely and juices run clear, rearranging hens and brushing with glaze once or twice. Let stand, tented with foil, for 5 minutes.

*For Cornish hens weighing 24 oz. each, microwave at High for 17 to 20 minutes.

Crisp-roasted Duckling ▲

- 4 to 5-lb. duckling
- 1 small onion, cut into 8 pieces
- 2 slices lemon

2 to 3 servings

Place duckling breast-side down on roasting rack. Secure neck skin to back with wooden picks. Cover with wax paper. Estimate total cooking time at 6½ to 9½ minutes per pound. Microwave at High for 10 minutes. Drain. Fill cavity with onion and lemon. Return duckling breast-side down on roasting rack. Re-cover. Reduce power to 50% (Medium). Microwave the remainder of first half of total cooking time. Drain. Turn duckling breast-side up. Re-cover. Microwave at 50% (Medium) for second half of time, or until legs move freely and juices run clear. Meanwhile, preheat conventional oven to 400°F. Place duckling in conventional roasting pan. Bake until skin on duckling is crisp and brown, 15 to 20 minutes.

Fish & Seafood

Microwaving is an excellent way of preparing fish and seafood. Quick, moist cooking and minimal handling is best for these delicate foods which dry out, toughen or break apart easily.

Many microwave oven owners believe that microwaved fish tastes far less "fishy" than conventionally cooked. You may notice a slight fishy odor when defrosting and microwaving frozen fish, but it seems to disappear after cooking.

Be careful not to overcook fish and seafood. They are done as soon as they flake or lose their translucent appearance.

50% Power (Medium)
3-5 min. per lb.

30% Power (Low)
6½-8½ min. per lb.

How to Defrost Fish Fillets, Steaks & Small Whole Fish

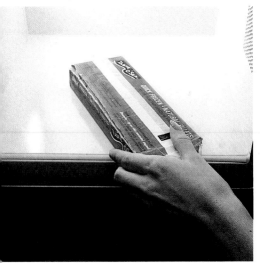

Open package. If pieces can be separated, place them in dish in which they will be cooked. Place dish or package in oven.

Defrost for ½ the time. Separate, rearrange or turn fish over so less defrosted parts are brought to top and outside of dish.

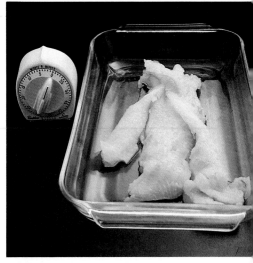

Defrost remaining time, or until fish is pliable on outside but icy in center or thick areas. Let stand 5 minutes. Rinse well.

How to Microwave Salmon or Halibut Steaks
50% Power (Medium), 10-13 min. per lb.

Arrange steaks in baking dish. Melt 2 tablespoons butter for each pound of fish. Add 1 teaspoon lemon juice. Brush on steaks.

Cover with vented plastic wrap. Microwave at 50% power (Medium) for ½ the cooking time.

Turn steaks over. Brush with lemon-butter; cover. Microwave remaining time until fish flakes easily.

Defrosting Fish & Shellfish

Type	Power Level	Time	Procedure
Fish,			
Whole, small	50% (Med.)	3½ to 6½ min./lb.	Unwrap and place in baking dish or on roasting rack. Microwave for half of time. Separate and rearrange. Shield heads and tails. Microwave remaining time until fish is pliable but icy in center. Let stand 5 to 10 minutes.
Fillets, block	50% (Med.)	6 to 10 min./lb.	Unwrap and place in baking dish or on roasting rack. Microwave for half of time. Separate fillets as soon as possible. Microwave remaining time until fish is pliable but still icy. Let stand 10 minutes.
Fillets, glazed	50% (Med.)	5 to 8 min./lb.	Unwrap and arrange on roasting rack. Microwave for half of time. Rearrange once. Microwave remaining time until fish is pliable but still icy. Let stand 10 minutes.
Steaks	50% (Med.)	4 to 7 min./lb.	Unwrap and place in baking dish or on roasting rack. Microwave for half of time. Separate and rearrange. Shield thin portions. Microwave remaining time until fish is pliable but icy in center. Let stand 5 to 10 minutes.
Lobster Tails,			
2, about 8 oz. each	30% (Low)	10 to 14 min. total	Unwrap and place in baking dish or on roasting rack. Arrange with thickest portions toward outside. Shield thin portions after half of time. Microwave until tails are pliable but still icy in centers. Rearrange once or twice. Let stand 10 to 15 minutes.
4, about 8 oz. each	30% (Low)	15 to 19 min. total	
Oysters,			
Shucked, 1 pint	50% (Med.)	6 to 9 min./pint	Place plastic package in microwave oven. Microwave for half of time. Remove from package and place in baking dish. Microwave remaining time until oysters are pliable but still icy, stirring once. Let stand 10 minutes.
Scallops,	50% (Med.)	4½ to 6 min./lb.	Unwrap and place in baking dish. Microwave for half of time. Separate scallops as soon as possible. Microwave remaining time until cold but not icy, stirring 2 or 3 times. Rinse with cold water. Let stand 5 minutes.
Shrimp,			
Shelled, deveined	50% (Med.)	4 to 8 min./lb.	Unwrap and place in baking dish. Microwave for half of time. Separate shrimp as soon as possible. Microwave remaining time until cold but not icy, stirring 2 or 3 times. Rinse with cold water. Let stand 5 minutes.

Microwaving Fish & Shellfish

Type	Power Level	Time	Procedure
Fish, Whole, small	70% (Med. High)	6 to 9 min./lb.	Arrange in baking dish with backbones toward outside. Brush with melted butter or lemon juice. Cover with wax paper. Microwave for half of time. Rearrange. Microwave remaining time until fish flakes easily near thickest portion of backbone. Let stand, covered, 3 minutes.
Fillets	High	3½ to 6 min./lb.	Arrange in baking dish or on roasting rack. Brush with melted butter or lemon juice. Cover with wax paper. Microwave for half of time. Rearrange or rotate dish. Microwave remaining time until fish flakes easily with fork. Let stand, covered, 3 minutes.
Steaks	70% (Med. High)	7 to 9 min./lb.	Arrange in baking dish or on roasting rack. Brush with melted butter or lemon juice. Cover with wax paper. Microwave for half of time. Rearrange. Microwave remaining time until fish flakes easily with fork. Let stand, covered, 3 minutes.
Clams 1 lb., 12 to 15	High	3 to 5½ min./lb.	Scrub outside of shells thoroughly. Discard any broken or open clams. Soak in salted spring water for at least 3 hours to clean. Discard any open or floating clams. Rinse and drain clams. Place ½ cup water in 2-quart casserole. Microwave at High for 2 to 3½ minutes until boiling. Add clams. Cover. Microwave until clams open, stirring once.
Lobster Tails, 2, about 8 oz. each	50% (Med.)	7 to 11 min. total	Remove membrane from underside. Arrange in baking dish shell-side down. Brush with melted butter. Cover with plastic wrap. Microwave until lobster is firm and opaque, rotating dish once or twice. Shield 1 inch of flesh after half of time. Let stand, covered, 3 minutes.
4, about 8 oz. each	50% (Med.)	11 to 15 min. total	
Mussels, 1 lb., about 20	High	1½ to 3 min./lb.	Remove beard and scrub outside of shells thoroughly. Discard any broken or open mussels. Soak in salted spring water for at least 3 hours to clean. Discard any open or floating mussels. Rinse and drain mussels. Place ½ cup water in 2-quart casserole. Microwave at High for 2 to 3½ minutes until boiling. Add mussels. Cover. Microwave until mussels open, stirring once.
Scallops	70% (Med. High)	5 to 8 min./lb.	Arrange in single layer in baking dish. Cover with vented plastic wrap. Microwave for half of time. Stir to rearrange. Re-cover. Microwave remaining time until scallops are opaque. Let stand, covered, 1 to 2 minutes.
Shrimp	70% (Med. High)	5 to 8 min./lb.	Arrange in single layer in baking dish. Cover with vented plastic wrap. Microwave for half of time. Stir to rearrange. Re-cover. Microwave remaining time until shrimp are opaque. Let stand, covered, 1 to 2 minutes.

◄ Trout with Walnut Stuffing

Stuffing:

- 2 tablespoons butter or margarine
- 2 tablespoons finely chopped celery
- 2 tablespoons sliced green onion
- 1 tablespoon snipped fresh parsley
- 1 cup herb seasoned croutons
- ¼ cup chopped walnuts
- 3 tablespoons ready-to-serve chicken broth or water
- ¼ teaspoon salt
- ¼ teaspoon lemon pepper seasoning
- ⅛ teaspoon dried marjoram leaves

- 2 whole trout (6 to 8 oz. each) heads removed

2 servings

In 1-quart casserole, combine butter, celery, onion and parsley. Cover. Microwave at High for 2 to 3 minutes, or until tender-crisp. Add remaining stuffing ingredients. Mix well. Fill each trout with half of stuffing. Arrange trout in 10-inch square casserole with backbones toward outside of casserole. Cover with wax paper. Microwave at 70% (Medium High) for 9 to 14 minutes, or until fish flakes easily with fork near backbone. Let stand, covered, for 2 to 3 minutes.

Poached Trout with Onions & Capers

- 1 bottle (8 oz.) clam juice
- 3 tablespoons fresh lemon juice
- 1 small onion, thinly sliced, separated into rings
- ½ teaspoon salt
- ¼ teaspoon pepper
- 2 whole trout (6 to 8 oz. each) heads removed
- ½ cup seasoned croutons, crushed
- 2 tablespoons butter or margarine
- 1 tablespoon capers, drained
- ⅛ teaspoon dried thyme leaves
- Dash garlic powder

2 servings

In 10-inch square casserole, combine clam juice, lemon juice, onion, salt and pepper. Cover. Microwave at High for 6 to 9 minutes, or just until mixture boils. Arrange trout in casserole with backbones toward outside of casserole. Re-cover. Reduce power to 70% (Medium High). Microwave for 6 to 9 minutes, or until fish flakes easily with fork near backbone, turning fish over after half the time. Place trout on serving platter. Top each trout with onion and croutons. Set aside. In 1-cup measure, combine butter, capers, thyme and garlic powder. Microwave at High for 1 to 1½ minutes, or until butter melts. Spoon evenly over trout.

Salmon with Red Wine Sauce

- 4 salmon steaks (7 to 9 oz. each) 1½ inches thick

Red Wine Sauce:

- 3 tablespoons butter or margarine
- 2 tablespoons red wine
- ½ teaspoon onion powder
- ½ teaspoon dried chervil leaves
- ¼ teaspoon celery salt
- ⅛ teaspoon paprika
- ⅛ teaspoon pepper

4 servings

Arrange salmon steaks in 9-inch square baking dish with thickest portions toward outside of dish. Set aside. In 1-cup measure, combine all Red Wine Sauce ingredients. Microwave at 70% (Medium High) for 1½ to 2½ minutes, or until butter melts. Brush half of sauce on salmon. Cover with wax paper. Microwave at 70% (Medium High) for 14 to 19 minutes, or until fish flakes easily with fork, rotating dish and brushing with sauce twice. Let stand, covered, for 3 minutes.

Orange Roughy with Vegetables

- 1 medium cucumber, peeled, seeded and cut into 2 × ¼-inch strips
- 1 medium tomato, seeded and chopped
- 1 cup sliced fresh mushrooms
- 1 teaspoon dried tarragon leaves
- 12 oz. orange roughy fillets, ½ inch thick, cut into 4 serving-size pieces
- 2 tablespoons butter or margarine
- 2 tablespoons all-purpose flour
- ¼ teaspoon salt
- ⅛ teaspoon pepper
- ½ cup half-and-half
- ¼ cup white wine
- 1 teaspoon snipped fresh parsley

4 servings

In 9-inch square baking dish, combine cucumber, tomato, mushrooms and tarragon. Cover. Microwave at High for 4 minutes, stirring once. Top with orange roughy pieces. Re-cover. Reduce power to 70% (Medium High). Microwave for 5 to 8 minutes, or until fish flakes easily with fork, turning pieces over after half the time. Drain. Reserve ¼ cup cooking liquid. Set aside. Arrange vegetables and orange roughy on serving platter. Cover. Set aside.

Place butter in 4-cup measure. Microwave at High for 45 seconds to 1 minute, or until butter melts. Stir in flour, salt and pepper. Blend in reserved cooking liquid, half-and-half and wine. Reduce power to 70% (Medium High). Microwave for 2 to 3 minutes, or until mixture thickens and bubbles, stirring after every minute. Pour sauce over orange roughy. Sprinkle with parsley.

Sole with ▶ Swiss Cheese Sauce

- 1 small zucchini, cut in half lengthwise, sliced ¼ inch thick
- ½ cup sliced celery, ¼ inch thick

Swiss Cheese Sauce:

- 2 tablespoons butter or margarine
- 1 tablespoon sliced green onion
- 2 teaspoons snipped fresh parsley
- ¼ teaspoon salt
- ⅛ teaspoon dried marjoram leaves
   Dash pepper
- 2 tablespoons all-purpose flour
- 1 cup milk
- 1 cup shredded Swiss cheese

- 1 lb. sole fillets, about ¾ inch thick, cut into serving-size pieces

4 to 6 servings

In 9-inch square baking dish, combine zucchini and celery. Cover with plastic wrap. Microwave at High for 3 to 4 minutes, or until tender-crisp, stirring once. Set aside.

For sauce, in 4-cup measure, combine butter, onion, parsley, salt, marjoram and pepper. Microwave at High for 1 to 1¼ minutes, or until butter melts. Stir in flour. Blend in milk. Microwave at High for 3 to 4½ minutes, or until mixture thickens and bubbles, stirring 3 times. Stir in cheese until melted.

Arrange sole pieces in 9-inch square baking dish with thickest portions toward outside of dish. Spoon zucchini and celery over sole. Pour cheese sauce over sole and vegetables. Microwave, uncovered, at High for 7 to 11 minutes, or until fish flakes easily with fork, rearranging pieces after half the time.

Grouper in Herb Butter

- 1 lb. grouper fillets, about 1 inch thick, cut into 4 serving-size pieces
- ¼ cup butter or margarine
- 1 teaspoon lemon juice
- ½ teaspoon dried parsley flakes
- ⅛ teaspoon Italian seasoning
   Dash garlic powder
   Dash fennel seed, crushed
- 1 to 2 tablespoons grated Parmesan cheese

4 servings

Arrange grouper pieces in 9-inch square baking dish with thickest portions toward outside of dish. Set aside. In 1-cup measure, combine butter, lemon juice, parsley, Italian seasoning, garlic powder and fennel. Microwave at High for 1 to 1½ minutes, or until butter melts. Pour over grouper pieces. Cover with wax paper. Microwave at High for 6 to 10 minutes, or until fish flakes easily with fork, rotating dish twice. Sprinkle with Parmesan cheese. Let stand, covered, for 2 to 3 minutes.

Shrimp Moutarde

Marinade:
¼ cup olive oil
2 tablespoons red wine vinegar
2 teaspoons Dijon mustard
1 teaspoon dried parsley flakes
1 teaspoon freeze-dried chives
½ teaspoon sugar
Dash pepper

1 lb. extra-large shrimp, shelled and deveined

3 to 4 servings

In small mixing bowl, blend all marinade ingredients. In large plastic food storage bag, combine marinade and shrimp. Secure bag. Marinate in refrigerator for 3 hours. Pour shrimp and marinade into 2-quart casserole. Cover. Microwave at 70% (Medium High) for 6 to 9 minutes, or until shrimp are opaque, stirring after every 2 minutes. Let stand, covered, for 2 to 3 minutes.

Saucy Shrimp & Vegetables

¼ cup butter or margarine
2 cups thinly sliced bok choy
1 medium yellow summer squash, cut into 2 × ¼-inch strips
1 cup sliced fresh mushrooms
1 can (16 oz.) whole tomatoes, drained and cut-up
1 tablespoon white wine
¾ teaspoon bouquet garni seasoning
½ teaspoon salt
¼ teaspoon garlic powder
¼ teaspoon pepper
1 tablespoon all-purpose flour
¾ lb. medium shrimp, shelled, deveined and butterflied
¼ cup whipping cream

4 servings

In 2-quart casserole, combine butter, bok choy, squash, mushrooms and tomatoes. Cover. Microwave at High for 5½ to 6½ minutes, or until vegetables are tender-crisp, stirring after every 2 minutes. Remove vegetables with slotted spoon. Set aside. Reserve cooking liquid in casserole. Add wine, bouquet garni, salt, garlic powder and pepper. Stir in flour. Add shrimp. Re-cover. Reduce power to 50% (Medium). Microwave for 6 to 8 minutes, or until shrimp are opaque, stirring after every 2 minutes. Stir in vegetable mixture. Blend in cream. Microwave, uncovered, at 50% (Medium) for 4 to 5 minutes, or until heated through, stirring after half the time. Serve over hot cooked noodles or rice.

Cajun Shrimp ▶

Crumb Topping:
1 tablespoon butter or margarine
¼ cup unseasoned dry bread crumbs
⅛ teaspoon pepper
Dash cayenne

½ cup chopped green pepper
¼ cup sliced green onions
1 clove garlic, minced
¼ teaspoon dry mustard
¼ teaspoon chili powder
⅛ teaspoon dried thyme leaves
1 can (8 oz.) tomato sauce
½ lb. medium shrimp, shelled and deveined
¼ lb. bay scallops
¼ teaspoon salt
¼ teaspoon sugar

4 servings

For topping, place butter in custard cup. Microwave at High for 30 seconds to 1 minute, or until butter melts. Stir in remaining topping ingredients. Set aside.

In 1-quart casserole, combine green pepper, onions, garlic, dry mustard, chili powder and thyme. Cover. Microwave at High for 2 to 4 minutes, or until onion is tender, stirring once. Stir in tomato sauce, shrimp, scallops, salt and sugar. Spoon into 4 individual soufflé dishes or casseroles. Microwave at 70% (Medium High) for 8 to 13 minutes, or until shrimp and scallops are opaque, rearranging dishes twice. Add crumb topping during last minute of cooking time.

◄ Shrimp Pasta Sauce

3 tablespoons olive oil
⅔ cup chopped fresh
    mushrooms
½ cup cubed zucchini, ½-inch
    cubes
¼ cup finely chopped onion
2 tablespoons snipped fresh
    parsley
1 clove garlic, minced
½ teaspoon dried basil leaves
¼ teaspoon dried thyme leaves
1 can (16 oz.) whole tomatoes
1 can (6 oz.) tomato paste
¼ teaspoon salt
¼ teaspoon sugar
¼ teaspoon pepper
½ lb. extra-small shrimp,
    shelled and deveined

4 to 6 servings

In 2-quart casserole, combine
olive oil, mushrooms, zucchini,
onion, parsley, garlic, basil and
thyme. Cover. Microwave at
High for 3 to 6 minutes, or until
vegetables are tender, stirring
once. Add remaining ingredients, except shrimp, stirring to
break apart tomatoes. Cover
with wax paper. Reduce power
to 70% (Medium High). Microwave for 10 to 15 minutes, or
until flavors are blended, stirring
once. Stir in shrimp. Re-cover.
Microwave at 70% (Medium
High) for 3 to 4 minutes, or until
shrimp are opaque, stirring
once. Let stand, covered, for
3 minutes. Serve over hot
cooked pasta.

Oysters Deluxe

2 slices bacon
2 tablespoons butter or
    margarine
½ cup chopped red pepper
¼ cup finely chopped onion
¼ teaspoon dried marjoram
    leaves
2 tablespoons all-purpose
    flour
⅔ cup half-and-half
1½ teaspoons lemon juice
¾ teaspoon salt
¼ teaspoon dry mustard
4 to 5 drops hot pepper
    sauce
1 pint fresh oysters, drained

4 servings

Place bacon on paper towel-
lined plate. Cover with another
paper towel. Microwave at High
for 2 to 2½ minutes, or until
crisp and brown. Cool slightly.
Crumble. Set aside.

In 1-quart casserole, combine
butter, red pepper, onion and
marjoram. Cover. Microwave at
High for 3 to 5 minutes, or until
vegetables are tender, stirring
once. Stir in flour. Blend in
half-and-half. Stir in lemon juice,
salt, dry mustard and hot
pepper sauce. Reduce power
to 70% (Medium High). Microwave for 3 to 5 minutes, or until
mixture thickens and bubbles,
stirring twice. Mixture will be
very thick. Stir in oysters.
Reduce power to 50% (Medium).
Microwave for 6 to 10 minutes,
or until oysters are firm and
edges begin to curl, stirring
twice. Serve over toast points.
Sprinkle with bacon.

Oyster Casserole

2 tablespoons butter or
    margarine
½ cup chopped onion
½ cup chopped celery
½ cup chopped green pepper
¼ cup snipped fresh parsley
½ teaspoon salt
⅛ teaspoon pepper
⅛ teaspoon cayenne
1 cup oyster crackers, crushed
1 can (8 oz.) whole tomatoes,
    drained and cut-up
¼ cup ketchup
1 tablespoon all-purpose flour
2 eggs, slightly beaten
1 pint fresh oysters, drained
    and chopped (reserve
    ¼ cup oyster liquor)

Topping:
2 tablespoons butter or
    margarine
⅛ teaspoon cayenne
1 cup oyster crackers

4 to 6 servings

In 2-quart casserole, combine
butter, onion, celery, green
pepper, parsley, salt, pepper
and cayenne. Cover. Microwave
at High for 5 to 6 minutes, or
until vegetables are tender,
stirring after every 2 minutes.
Add cracker crumbs, tomatoes,
ketchup, flour and eggs. Mix
well. Stir in oysters and
reserved liquor. Set aside.

For topping, place butter in
small mixing bowl. Microwave at
High for 45 seconds to 1 minute,
or until butter melts. Stir in
cayenne and crackers. Toss to
coat. Arrange topping around
outside edge of casserole.
Microwave at 50% (Medium) for
18 to 28 minutes, or until heated
through, rotating casserole after
every 5 minutes. Let stand,
covered, for 5 minutes.

◄ Scallops with Wine & Cheese Sauce

1 lb. bay scallops
⅓ cup white wine
3 tablespoons butter or margarine
½ teaspoon dry mustard
¼ teaspoon garlic powder, divided
2 cups shredded Colby cheese
1 tablespoon all-purpose flour
¼ cup seeded chopped tomato
1 tablespoon snipped fresh parsley
1 tablespoon sliced green onion
1 teaspoon olive oil
4 English muffins, split and toasted

4 servings

Place scallops in 9-inch square baking dish. Cover with plastic wrap. Microwave at 50% (Medium) for 6 to 9 minutes, or until scallops are opaque, stirring 2 or 3 times. Set aside. In 2-quart casserole, combine wine, butter, dry mustard and ⅛ teaspoon garlic powder. Microwave at High for 2½ to 3½ minutes, or until mixture boils. In large plastic food storage bag, combine cheese and flour. Shake to coat. Stir into wine and butter mixture. Reduce power to 50% (Medium). Microwave for 1½ to 2 minutes, or until mixture can be stirred smooth, stirring after every minute. Drain scallops. Stir scallops into cheese sauce. Microwave at 50% (Medium) for 1 to 2 minutes, or until heated through. In small mixing bowl, combine tomato, parsley, onion, olive oil and remaining ⅛ teaspoon garlic powder. Mix well. Spoon scallops and cheese sauce over English muffins. Top with tomato mixture.

Creamy Scallops in Patty Shells ▲

8 frozen patty shells
2 tablespoons butter or margarine
2 tablespoons finely chopped celery
1 tablespoon finely chopped green onion
2 tablespoons all-purpose flour

1¼ cups milk
1 cup sliced fresh mushrooms
½ teaspoon salt
½ teaspoon Worcestershire sauce
¼ teaspoon dried tarragon leaves
Dash cayenne
½ lb. bay scallops

4 servings

Bake patty shells according to package directions. Set aside. In 1½-quart casserole, combine butter, celery and onion. Cover. Microwave at High for 3 to 4 minutes, or until tender, stirring once. Stir in flour. Blend in milk. Stir in mushrooms, salt, Worcestershire sauce, tarragon and cayenne. Microwave, uncovered, at High for 5 to 7 minutes, or until mixture thickens and bubbles, stirring after every 2 minutes. Stir in scallops. Reduce power to 70% (Medium High). Microwave for 4 to 6 minutes, or until scallops are firm and opaque, stirring once. Spoon into prepared patty shells.

Tuna & Potato Chip ▲ Casserole

3 cups crushed potato chips
1 can (10¾ oz.) condensed cream of mushroom soup
1 can (6½ oz.) tuna, drained
1 can (4 oz.) mushroom stems and pieces, drained
1 jar (2 oz.) pimiento-stuffed green olives, sliced
½ cup shredded Cheddar cheese
½ cup milk
2 tablespoons frozen chopped onion or 1½ teaspoons dried onion flakes

Serves 4

Place one-third of crushed chips in 1½-qt. casserole. In medium bowl combine remaining ingredients except chips. Spread half of tuna mixture over chips. Top with another one-third of chips and remaining tuna. Sprinkle remaining chips over top. Microwave at High 4 to 6 minutes, or until heated, rotating dish ¼ turn after half the cooking time.

Tuna Potato Casserole

1 pkg. (9 oz.) frozen French-style green beans
1 pkg. (5½ oz.) au gratin potato mix
2½ cups hot water
1 can (6½ oz.) tuna, drained
¾ cup milk
1 envelope (single-serving size) instant onion soup mix
2 tablespoons butter or margarine
1 can (3 oz.) French fried onion rings

Serves 4 to 6

Place green beans in 2-qt. casserole; cover. Microwave at High 3 to 4 minutes, or until beans can be broken apart easily. Mix in remaining ingredients except onion rings; cover. Microwave at High 18 to 25 minutes, or until potatoes are tender and sauce thickened, stirring 3 or 4 times during cooking. Sprinkle with onion rings during last 2 minutes of cooking. Let stand 5 minutes.

Shrimp Fried Rice

1 pkg. (6¼ oz.) fried rice mix
2 tablespoons butter or margarine
2 cups hot water
1 pkg. (10 oz.) frozen large cooked shrimp
1 pkg. (6 oz.) frozen pea pods
2 eggs
1½ teaspoons soy sauce
1 can (8 oz.) sliced water chestnuts, drained

Serves 4

Place rice and butter in 2-qt. casserole. Microwave at High 2 to 3 minutes, or until rice begins to brown, stirring after half the time. Stir in hot water and seasoning mix from rice package; cover. Microwave at High 5 to 7 minutes, or until boiling. Stir. Reduce power to 50% (Medium). Microwave 10 to 20 minutes, or until rice is tender. Let stand, covered, 10 to 15 minutes, or until no visible moisture remains in bottom of dish.

Place shrimp in single layer in 8 × 8-in. baking dish. Microwave at 50% (Medium) 2 to 4 minutes, or until no longer icy, stirring after half the time. Rinse under cool water. Set aside.

Place pea pods in 1-qt. casserole. Increase power to High. Microwave 2 to 4 minutes, or until defrosted. Set aside.

Beat eggs and soy sauce in medium bowl. Increase power to High. Microwave 1½ to 2 minutes, or until eggs are almost set, stirring after half the cooking time. Break up eggs into small pieces.

Stir eggs, water chestnuts, shrimp and pea pods into rice. Microwave at High 1 to 2 minutes, or until heated.

Shrimp & Rice Medley ▲

1 pkg. (10 oz.) frozen large
  cooked shrimp
2 tablespoons butter or
  margarine
⅓ cup seasoned bread crumbs
1 pkg. (10 oz.) frozen rice with
  peas and mushrooms

1 pkg. (10 oz.) frozen long
  grain white and wild rice
1 can (10¾ oz.) condensed
  cream of shrimp soup
2 tablespoons white wine

Serves 4

Place shrimp in single layer in 8 × 8-in. baking dish. Microwave at 50% (Medium) 2 to 4 minutes, or until no longer icy, stirring to break apart after half the time. Rinse under cool water. Set aside.

Place butter in small bowl or custard cup. Increase power to High. Microwave 30 to 60 seconds, or until melted. Stir in bread crumbs. Set aside.

Cut a large "X" in one side of each rice pouch. Place pouches side by side, cut side down, in 12 × 8-in. baking dish. Microwave at High 6 to 8 minutes, or until heated. Empty rice into dish. Stir. Add shrimp, soup and wine. Cover with wax paper. Microwave at High 8 to 9 minutes, or until heated, stirring every 3 minutes. Sprinkle bread crumb mixture over top.

Deli Seafood Casserole

2 tablespoons butter or
  margarine
¼ cup plus 2 tablespoons
  seasoned bread crumbs
1 qt. delicatessen-style
  macaroni tuna salad
2 cans (4¼ oz. each) shrimp,
  drained and rinsed
1 cup frozen peas
¼ cup milk

Serves 4 to 6

Place butter in small dish. Microwave at High 30 to 60 seconds, or until melted. Stir in bread crumbs. Set aside.

Combine remaining ingredients in 2-qt. casserole; cover. Microwave at High 6 to 8 minutes, or until heated, stirring after half the time. Sprinkle with crumbs. Microwave at High 1 to 2 minutes, or until heated.

Meatless Main Dishes

Tomato Cheese Pie

½ cup unbleached all-purpose
   flour
½ cup whole wheat flour
1 tablespoon yellow cornmeal
¼ teaspoon salt*
⅓ cup vegetable shortening
3 to 4 tablespoons ice water

Filling:

1 cup part-skim ricotta cheese
½ cup shredded Cheddar
   cheese
½ cup low-fat cottage cheese
2 eggs, beaten
1 tablespoon all-purpose flour
½ teaspoon dried oregano
   leaves
¼ teaspoon garlic powder

Topping:

1 medium tomato, thinly sliced
1 tablespoon grated Parmesan
   cheese
1 tablespoon snipped fresh
   parsley
¼ teaspoon dried oregano
   leaves

6 servings

In medium mixing bowl, combine all-purpose flour, whole wheat flour, cornmeal and salt. Cut in shortening to form coarse crumbs. Sprinkle with water, 1 tablespoon at a time, mixing with fork until particles are moistened and cling together. Form dough into a ball. Roll out on lightly floured board at least 2 inches larger than inverted 9-inch pie plate. Ease into plate. Trim and flute edge. Prick thoroughly. Microwave at High for 6 to 8 minutes, or until crust appears dry and opaque, rotating plate after every 2 minutes. Set aside.

For filling, in medium mixing bowl, combine all ingredients. Mix well. Spread evenly into prepared crust. Place pie plate on saucer in oven. Microwave at 50% (Medium) for 11 to 19 minutes, or until center is soft-set, rotating plate one-half turn after every 3 minutes. Top with tomato slices. In small bowl, blend all remaining topping ingredients. Sprinkle over tomato slices. Let stand for 10 minutes before serving.

*To reduce sodium omit salt.

Per Serving:			
Calories:	315	Cholesterol:	115 mg.
Protein:	14 g.	Sodium:	308 mg.
Carbohydrates:	20 g.	Calcium:	220 mg.
Fat:	26 g.	Exchanges:	1 vegetable, 1 bread, 2 high-fat meat

Tofu Vegetable Sauté ▲

1 cup uncooked couscous
1 pkg. (10 oz.) frozen
   asparagus cuts
1 lb. tofu, rinsed and cut into
   ¾-inch cubes
2 cups sliced fresh mushrooms
1 can (8 oz.) bamboo shoots,
   rinsed and drained
½ cup thinly sliced green
   onions
¼ cup reduced-sodium soy
   sauce

1 tablespoon cornstarch
1 tablespoon white wine
1 clove garlic, minced
2 teaspoons vegetable oil
1 teaspoon sugar
¼ teaspoon peeled, minced
   gingerroot
¼ teaspoon sesame oil
⅛ teaspoon cayenne

4 servings

Prepare couscous as directed on package. Set aside. Unwrap
asparagus. Place on plate. Microwave at High for 4 to 5 minutes,
or until defrosted. Stir to break apart. In 3-quart casserole,
combine asparagus, tofu, mushrooms, bamboo shoots and onions.
Set aside.

In small mixing bowl, blend remaining ingredients, except
couscous. Pour over tofu and vegetable mixture. Stir to coat.
Cover. Microwave at High for 12 to 13 minutes, or until sauce
thickens and is translucent, stirring after every 4 minutes. Serve
over couscous.

Per Serving:
		Cholesterol:	—
Calories:	295	Cholesterol:	—
Protein:	17 g.	Sodium:	523 mg.
Carbohydrates:	41 g.	Calcium:	178 mg.
Fat:	9 g.	Exchanges:	2 bread, 2 med.-fat meat

Spinach Pie

Filling:
 2 pkgs. (10 oz. each) frozen
    chopped spinach
¾ cup part-skim ricotta cheese
½ cup evaporated skimmed
    milk
¼ cup chopped
    water chestnuts
 1 egg
 1 egg yolk
 2 teaspoons cider vinegar
¾ teaspoon dried basil leaves
¼ teaspoon ground nutmeg

Crust:
 2 cups cooked brown rice,
    page 230
 1 egg white
 3 tablespoons grated
    Parmesan cheese

4 servings

Unwrap spinach. Place on
plate. Microwave at High for 6
to 8 minutes, or until defrosted,
rotating plate once. Drain. Press
to remove excess moisture. In
medium mixing bowl, combine
spinach and remaining filling
ingredients. Mix well. Set aside.

In small mixing bowl, combine
all crust ingredients. Mix well.
Press firmly against bottom
and sides of 9-inch pie plate.
Microwave at High for 4 to 7
minutes, or until center is set,
rotating plate once.

Spread filling evenly into rice
crust. Microwave at High for
5 minutes. Reduce power to
50% (Medium). Microwave for
15 to 25 minutes longer, or until
center is firm to touch, rotating
plate once or twice. Let stand
for 3 minutes.

Per Serving:
Calories:	285
Protein:	18 g.
Carbohydrates:	39 g.
Fat:	8 g.
Cholesterol:	87 mg.
Sodium:	320 mg.
Calcium:	509 mg.
Exchanges:	2 vegetable, 2 bread, 1½ fat

Vegetable Curry

1 medium onion, cut into
    ½-inch pieces
1 medium green pepper, cut
    into thin strips
1 small red baking apple,
    cored and chopped
½ cup thinly sliced carrot
1 clove garlic, minced
2 tablespoons reduced-calorie
    margarine
1 can (16 oz.) pinto beans,
    rinsed and drained
1 medium tomato, seeded
    and chopped
¼ cup raisins
1 tablespoon olive oil
1½ teaspoons curry powder
½ teaspoon salt*
¼ teaspoon dried dill weed
¼ teaspoon pepper
2 cups cooked brown rice,
    page 230
1 tablespoon unsalted
    sunflower nuts

4 servings

In 2-quart casserole, combine
onion, green pepper, apple,
carrot, garlic and margarine.
Cover. Microwave at High for 6
to 10 minutes, or until onion and
carrot are tender, stirring after
every 2 minutes. Add remaining
ingredients, except rice and
sunflower nuts. Mix well.
Re-cover. Microwave at High for
6 to 7 minutes longer, or until
heated through and flavors are
blended. Serve over brown rice.
Sprinkle with sunflower nuts.

*To reduce sodium omit salt.

Per Serving:	
Calories:	342
Protein:	9 g.
Carbohydrates:	45 g.
Fat:	14 g.
Cholesterol:	—
Sodium:	442 mg.
Calcium:	29 mg.
Exchanges:	1 fruit, 1 vegetable, 2 bread, 3 fat

How to Microwave Middle Eastern Cabbage

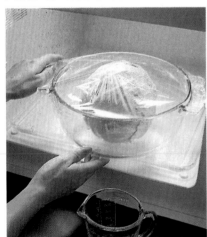

Combine cabbage and water in 2-quart casserole. Cover with plastic wrap. Microwave at High for 6 to 9 minutes, or until outer leaves are pliable, rotating dish once. Drain. Cool slightly.

Place cooled cabbage on 2 crisscrossed sheets of plastic wrap. Gently pull back pliable outer leaves. Cut out inside of cabbage, leaving outer leaves attached to stem. Chop enough cabbage to equal 1 cup.

Combine chopped cabbage, tomato and onions in 2-quart casserole. Cover. Microwave at High for 2 to 3 minutes, or until cabbage is tender-crisp. Stir in remaining ingredients, except lemon wedges. Mix well.

◄ Middle Eastern Cabbage

1 medium head cabbage,
    about 2 lbs.
½ cup water
1 medium tomato, seeded and
    chopped
3 tablespoons sliced green
    onions
2 cups cooked brown rice,
    page 230
¼ cup wheat germ
¼ cup chopped almonds
1 egg
1 tablespoon lemon juice
½ teaspoon ground cinnamon
½ teaspoon salt*
⅛ teaspoon pepper
⅛ teaspoon ground allspice
⅛ teaspoon ground ginger
4 lemon wedges

4 servings

*To reduce sodium omit salt.

Per Serving:
Calories: 221
Protein: 9 g.
Carbohydrates: 32 g.
Fat: 8 g.
Cholesterol: 69 mg.
Sodium: 284 mg.
Calcium: 69 mg.
Exchanges: 2 bread, 1 med.-fat
                   meat

One-Dish Garbanzo Bake

2¼ cups water
¾ cup bulgur or cracked
    wheat
1 small green pepper, cut into
    1-inch chunks
1 small onion, thinly sliced
    and separated into rings
1 parsnip, cut into ½-inch
    cubes, about ¾ cup,
    discard woody core
1 tablespoon olive oil
1 can (15 oz.) garbanzo
    beans, rinsed and drained
1 can (8 oz.) no-salt tomato
    sauce
½ cup thinly sliced yellow
    squash
⅓ cup water
¼ teaspoon dried rosemary
    leaves
¼ teaspoon salt*
⅛ teaspoon pepper

4 servings

Place 2¼ cups water in 4-cup
measure. Microwave at High for
4 to 6 minutes, or until water
boils. Place bulgur in small
mixing bowl. Add boiling water.
Cover and let stand for 30
minutes to soften. Drain and
press to remove excess
moisture. Set aside.

In 2-quart casserole, combine
green pepper, onion, parsnip
and olive oil. Cover. Microwave
at High for 4 to 5 minutes, or
until tender-crisp, stirring once.
Stir in remaining ingredients,
except bulgur. Re-cover. Microwave at High for 9 to 14
minutes longer, or until vegetables are tender, stirring twice.
Let stand, covered, for 5
minutes. Serve over bulgur.

*To reduce sodium omit salt.

Per Serving:
Calories: 230
Protein: 9 g.
Carbohydrates: 37 g.
Fat: 6 g.
Cholesterol: —
Sodium: 579 mg.
Calcium: 24 mg.
Exchanges: 2 bread, 1 med.-fat
                   meat

Lift cabbage leaves and plastic
wrap and place in deep bowl or
2-quart measure. Spoon stuffing
into cabbage shell. Gently pull
leaves toward center to enclose
stuffing. Secure plastic wrap
tightly around cabbage.

Microwave at High for 7 to 10
minutes, or until internal
temperature in center registers
140°F. Let stand, covered, for 5
minutes. Cut cabbage into
wedges. Squeeze lemon juice
over each serving.

Cuban Black Beans

2 cups chopped onions
1 medium green pepper,
　chopped
2 cloves garlic, minced
2 tablespoons olive oil
5 cups hot water
1 lb. dried black beans,
　rinsed and drained
3 tablespoons red wine
　vinegar
1½ teaspoons dried oregano
　leaves
½ teaspoon dried basil leaves
½ teaspoon dried marjoram
　leaves
½ teaspoon salt*
⅛ teaspoon dried crushed red
　pepper
2 bay leaves
3 cups hot cooked rice,
　page 230

Topping:
⅓ cup chopped onion
　Red wine vinegar

6 servings, about 1 cup each

In deep 3-quart casserole,
combine onions, green pepper,
garlic and olive oil. Stir. Cover.
Microwave at High for 5 to 7
minutes, or until tender-crisp,
stirring once. Add remaining
ingredients, except rice and
topping. Stir. Re-cover. Microwave at High for 10 minutes.
Reduce power to 50% (Medium).
Microwave for 1½ hours, or until
beans are tender, stirring once
or twice. Microwave, uncovered,
at High for 10 to 30 minutes
longer, or until thick. Remove
bay leaves. Serve over rice.
Top each serving with onion
and vinegar.

*To reduce sodium omit salt.

Per Serving:
Calories:	352
Protein:	15 g.
Carbohydrates:	63 g.
Fat:	6 g.
Cholesterol:	—
Sodium:	549 mg.
Calcium:	68 mg.
Exchanges:	4 bread, 1 low-fat meat

Simmered Beans & Artichokes ▲

3 cups water
1 cup bulgur or cracked wheat
1 pkg. (9 oz.) frozen artichoke
　hearts
½ cup coarsely chopped onion
½ cup coarsely chopped green
　pepper
1 clove garlic, minced
1 tablespoon olive oil
1 can (16 oz.) Great Northern
　beans, rinsed and drained
1 can (14½ oz.) no-salt stewed
　tomatoes

½ cup white wine
1 tablespoon packed brown
　sugar
¼ teaspoon salt*
¼ teaspoon dried oregano
　leaves
⅛ teaspoon dried marjoram
　leaves
1 medium white potato, cut in
　half lengthwise and sliced
　¼ inch thick

6 servings

Place water in 4-cup measure. Microwave at High for 5½ to 7½
minutes, or until water boils. Place bulgur in medium mixing bowl.
Add boiling water. Cover and let stand for 30 minutes to soften.
Drain and press out excess moisture. Set aside.

In 2-quart casserole, combine artichoke hearts, onion, green
pepper, garlic and olive oil. Cover. Microwave at High for 6 to 9
minutes, or until onion is tender-crisp, stirring once. Stir in
remaining ingredients, except bulgur and potato. Re-cover.
Microwave at High for 5 to 8 minutes, or until bubbly around
edges. Stir in potato. Re-cover. Microwave at High for 15 to 25
minutes longer, or until potato is tender, stirring twice. Serve
over bulgur.

*To reduce sodium omit salt.

Per Serving:
Calories:	281	Cholesterol:	—
Protein:	9 g.	Sodium:	122 mg.
Carbohydrates:	53 g.	Calcium:	35 mg.
Fat:	3 g.	Exchanges:	2 vegetable, 3 bread, ½ fat

Whole Wheat ► Mac-N-Cheese

1 cup uncooked whole wheat
   elbow macaroni
¼ cup chopped carrot
1 tablespoon finely chopped
   onion
1 tablespoon reduced-calorie
   margarine
2 tablespoons all-purpose flour
⅛ teaspoon dried tarragon
   leaves
   Dash pepper
1 cup buttermilk
½ cup frozen peas
1 cup shredded pasteurized
   process American cheese

4 servings

Prepare macaroni as directed on package. Rinse with warm water. Drain. Set aside.

In 1½-quart casserole, combine carrot, onion and margarine. Cover. Microwave at High for 2 to 3 minutes, or until carrot is tender-crisp. Stir in flour, tarragon and pepper. Blend in buttermilk. Stir in peas. Reduce power to 70% (Medium High). Microwave, uncovered, for 6 to 8½ minutes, or until sauce thickens and bubbles, stirring 2 or 3 times. Add macaroni and American cheese. Mix well. Microwave at 70% (Medium High) for 2 to 3 minutes longer, or until hot, stirring once.

Per Serving:
Calories:	280
Protein:	14 g.
Carbohydrates:	29 g.
Fat:	14 g.
Cholesterol:	32 mg.
Sodium:	259 mg.
Calcium:	289 mg.
Exchanges:	2 bread, 2 med.-fat meat

Wild Rice & Barley Dinner

4½ cups hot water, divided
½ cup uncooked medium
   pearl barley
½ cup uncooked wild rice,
   rinsed and drained
½ cup sliced fresh mushrooms
½ cup sliced carrot, ¼ inch
   thick
¼ cup sliced green onions
2 tablespoons snipped fresh
   parsley
1 clove garlic, minced
½ teaspoon bouquet garni
   seasoning

½ teaspoon low-sodium instant
   chicken bouillon granules
½ teaspoon salt*
⅛ teaspoon pepper
½ lb. fresh broccoli, cut into
   flowerets, stalk sliced
   ¼ inch thick, about
   2½ cups
1 cup frozen whole kernel
   corn
½ cup evaporated skimmed
   milk

6 servings

In 3-quart casserole, combine 1½ cups water and barley. Cover. Microwave at High for 5 minutes. Reduce power to 50% (Medium). Microwave for 10 minutes. Rinse and drain. Return to same casserole. Stir in remaining 3 cups water, wild rice, mushrooms, carrot, green onions, parsley, garlic, bouquet garni, bouillon, salt and pepper. Re-cover. Microwave at High for 3 minutes. Reduce power to 50% (Medium). Microwave for 45 to 55 minutes longer, or until wild rice kernels begin to open, stirring after every 15 minutes. Add remaining ingredients. Re-cover. Microwave at High for 8 to 11 minutes longer, or until broccoli is tender-crisp, stirring twice.

*To reduce sodium omit salt.

Per Serving:
Calories:	184	Cholesterol:	1 mg.
Protein:	8 g.	Sodium:	207 mg.
Carbohydrates:	39 g.	Calcium:	149 mg.
Fat:	1 g.	Exchanges:	2 vegetable, 2 bread

Vegetable & Brown Rice Bake

½ cup low-fat cottage cheese
⅓ cup part-skim ricotta cheese
¼ cup buttermilk
 1 teaspoon dried basil leaves
¼ teaspoon dried marjoram
     leaves
 2 cups cooked brown rice,
     page 230, divided
 1 medium zucchini, thinly
     sliced, divided
 1 large tomato, seeded and
     chopped, divided
 2 teaspoons grated Parmesan
     cheese
½ cup hot Tomato Sauce,
     page 187

4 servings

In food processor or blender bowl, combine cottage cheese, ricotta cheese, buttermilk, basil and marjoram. Process until smooth. In 1-quart casserole, layer one-half the rice. Press lightly. Top with one-half the zucchini, one-half the tomato and one-half the cottage cheese mixture. Repeat layers. Sprinkle with Parmesan cheese. Cover. Microwave at 70% (Medium High) for 11 to 18 minutes, or until internal temperature in center registers 140°F, rotating dish once or twice. Let stand, covered, for 1 minute. Top each serving with 2 tablespoons Tomato Sauce.

Per Serving:			
Calories:	201	Cholesterol:	9 mg.
Protein:	10 g.	Sodium:	182 mg.
Carbohydrates:	32 g.	Calcium:	118 mg.
Fat:	4 g.	Exchanges:	2 bread, 1 med.-fat meat

154

Riviera Eggplant Bake

1 medium onion, chopped
⅛ teaspoon garlic powder
½ cup chopped green pepper
1 tablespoon olive oil
1 can (6 oz.) tomato paste
½ cup tomato juice
2 teaspoons sugar
¼ teaspoon oregano
¼ teaspoon basil
⅛ teaspoon pepper
1 bay leaf
1 medium eggplant
8 oz. shredded mozzarella
    cheese, divided
1 tablespoon grated Parmesan
    cheese

Serves 4

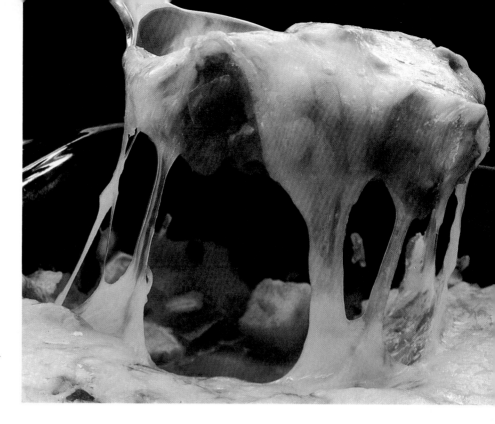

How to Microwave Riviera Eggplant Bake

Combine onion, garlic, green pepper and olive oil in 2-qt. casserole. Microwave at High 2½ to 3 minutes or until tender.

Stir in tomato paste, tomato juice, sugar and seasonings. Microwave at High 3 to 6 minutes, or until bubbly, stirring once during cooking. Set aside.

Cut eggplant into ½-in. cubes while microwaving sauce. Arrange cubes in 8×8-in. dish.

Cover with wax paper; microwave at High 6 to 8 minutes, or until tender and translucent.

Sprinkle half the mozzarella over eggplant. Spoon on sauce. Top with remaining mozzarella and Parmesan cheese.

Microwave at High 4 to 5 minutes, or until cheese melts, rotating dish ½ turn after half the cooking time.

Eggs & Cheese

Eggs illustrate one difference between conventional and microwave cooking. When you poach or shirr an egg conventionally, it cooks first in the outer, or white portion. This is also true of boiled eggs, which must always be cooked conventionally.

The oposite is true in microwaving. Since an egg yolk contains more fat than the white, it attracts more energy. If you microwave an egg until the white is set, the yolk will toughen. Standing time is necessary to cook the white completely without hardening the yolk. When yolks and whites are mixed together, microwaving is even, but standing time is still used to cook eggs delicately.

Most cheeses melt rapidly in the microwave oven because of their relatively high fat contents. But all cheeses do not soften at the same rate. In general, a soft, moist cheese melts easily, while aged, drier cheeses are slower to melt.

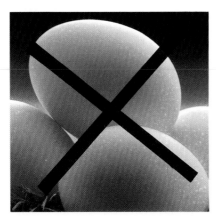

Never microwave an egg in its shell. Steam builds up inside and egg will burst.

Browning Dish Bacon and Eggs

Preheat browning dish 2 minutes at High. Cut 2 strips of bacon in half. Place them against sides of dish; microwave 2 minutes. Break 2 eggs into dish, baste with bacon fat. Remove and drain bacon on paper towel. Cover dish; microwave 15 to 30 seconds. Let eggs stand 2 to 3 minutes, until set.

Scrambled Eggs

Microwave-scrambled eggs are fluffier and have more volume than conventionally-scrambled. You can microwave and serve or eat them from the same dish. Butter suggested in these directions is for flavor only; it isn't needed to prevent sticking, so if you're calorie conscious, you can omit it and also substitute water for milk.

Tastes differ in scrambled eggs; you may prefer them more or less firm. Remove them from the oven while they still look underdone. Overcooking makes them rubbery. If, after standing, they are not done to your satisfaction, microwave them a few seconds longer.

High Power

Eggs	Butter	Milk	Time
1	1 tbsp.	1 tbsp.	35-45 sec.
2	1 tbsp.	2 tbsp.	1¼-1¾ min.
4	1 tbsp.	2 tbsp.	2-3 min.
6	2 tbsp.	¼ cup	3¼-4¼ min.
10	3 tbsp.	½ cup	5¼-6½ min.

How to Microwave Scrambled Eggs

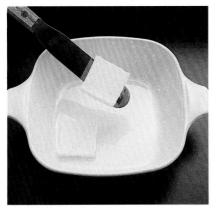

Place butter in serving dish or casserole. Microwave 30 seconds at High until butter melts.

Add eggs and milk. Scramble with a fork. Microwave at High for about half the cooking time.

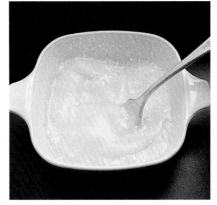

Open the oven door. Eggs are beginning to set around the edges, where they receive most energy.

Break up set parts and push them to center of dish. Cook remaining time, stirring once or twice more.

Remove eggs from oven while they are still soft and moist. Let them stand 1 to 4 minutes.

Eggs continue to cook and will be set after standing. Stir eggs before serving.

Sunday Brunch Eggs

Dice 1 slice bacon per egg. Microwave at High 30 seconds per slice. Chop 1 tablespoon each mushroom and green onion. Add to bacon.

Microwave 30 seconds more per slice. Drain off fat. Add eggs and milk; scramble. Microwave and stir as directed above. Increase time if necessary.

Serve for a special breakfast. Try different flavor combinations, such as chopped ham, green pepper and tomato for Western style eggs.

Poached Eggs

Eggs are easy to poach in the microwave oven if you observe these simple rules: Bring water and vinegar to a full boil before adding the egg. Reduce the power level so egg will poach gently. Standing time is important. It allows the white to set without overcooking the yolk. After standing, slip the egg into a slotted spoon to drain. If the bottom is not set to your satisfaction, turn egg over into custard cup and microwave a few seconds more.

50% Power (Medium)

1 egg	45 sec. to 1 min. 20 sec.
2 eggs	1 min. 5 sec. to 1 min. 35 sec.
4 eggs	2 min. 15 sec. to 3 min. 15 sec.

How to Microwave Poached Eggs

Measure 2 tablespoons water and ¼ teaspoon vinegar into 6-oz. custard cup. (One per egg.) Cover with plastic wrap. Bring to a boil at High power, 30 to 40 seconds per cup.

Break large eggs into cups. Cover. Microwave at 50% power until most of the white is opaque but not set. When poaching more than 1 egg, rotate dishes every 45 seconds.

Let stand 2 to 3 minutes. Shaking cups gently once or twice during standing helps set white. Do not remove cover until standing time is completed.

Eggs Florentine. Serve poached eggs on a bed of spinach, garnished with crumbled crisp bacon.

Puffy Omelet

4 large eggs
¼ cup milk
½ teaspoon salt
¼ teaspoon baking powder
⅛ teaspoon pepper
1 tablespoon butter or margarine

Serves 2 to 4

Filling:
One or more of the following:
Shredded cheese; crumbled crisp bacon; sliced cooked mushrooms; chopped ham; chopped green pepper; chopped green onion; sautéed onion slices; chopped tomato; diced, cooked potato; shredded chipped beef; chopped cooked shrimp.

How to Microwave a Puffy Omelet

Separate eggs, placing whites in 1-qt. mixing bowl and yolks in smaller bowl.

Beat whites until stiff but not dry. Blend together yolks, milk, salt, baking powder and pepper.

Fold yolk mixture into beaten egg whites gently, using rubber spatula.

Melt butter in 9-in. pie plate at High 30 to 45 seconds. Pour in eggs. Microwave at 50% power 3 to 5 minutes until partially set.

Lift edges with spatula so uncooked portion spreads evenly. Microwave 2½ to 4½ minutes, until center is almost set.

Sprinkle desired filling over ½ of omelet. Loosen omelet with spatula and fold in half. Gently slide onto serving plate.

Egg Foo Yung

1 cup water
1 tablespoon cornstarch
1 tablespoon soy sauce
2 teaspoons instant chicken
    bouillon granules
1 teaspoon sugar
    Dash ginger
3 green onions chopped
½ medium green pepper,
    chopped
1 tablespoon butter or
    margarine
6 eggs, well beaten
1 can (16 oz.) bean sprouts,
    drained
½ teaspoon salt

Serves 4

Variation:
Add 1 can (4½ oz.) tiny shrimp, drained, with the bean sprouts. Microwave at 50% (Medium) 2½ to 3½ minutes longer.

How to Microwave Egg Foo Yung

Combine water, cornstarch, soy sauce, chicken bouillon, sugar and ginger in 1-qt. measure. Microwave at High 3½ to 5 minutes, or until thickened, stirring twice. Let stand while preparing eggs.

Place onion, green pepper and butter in 2-qt. casserole. Microwave at High 3½ to 5 minutes, or until green pepper is tender-crisp, stirring after half the time. Add beaten eggs, bean sprouts and salt to green pepper and onion.

Microwave 3 minutes. Stir to break up; push cooked portions to center. Reduce power to 50% (Medium). Microwave 7 to 11 minutes, or until set, rotating dish ¼ turn twice during cooking. Pour sauce over eggs before serving.

Dutch Omelet

1 small onion, chopped
½ lb. ground pork sausage
2 cups shredded potatoes
¾ teaspoon salt, divided

6 eggs
¼ cup milk
⅛ teaspoon pepper
    Dash cayenne pepper

Serves 4

How to Microwave Dutch Omelet

Place onion and sausage in 2-qt. casserole. Microwave at High 3½ to 5 minutes, or until sausage loses its pink color, stirring once or twice.

Remove sausage and onion to paper towels. Discard all but 1 tablespoon fat from casserole.

Add potatoes to casserole. Cover. Microwave 4 to 6 minutes, or until tender. Sprinkle ¼ teaspoon salt over potatoes and stir to coat.

Combine eggs, ½ teaspoon salt, milk, pepper and cayenne. Pour over potatoes. Sprinkle sausage mixture on top. Microwave uncovered 3 minutes.

Lift edges with spatula so uncooked portion spreads evenly, taking care not to disrupt potatoes. Reduce power to 50% (Medium).

Microwave 8 to 14 minutes, or until eggs are almost set, rotating dish twice during cooking. Let stand loosely tented with foil 2 minutes before serving.

◄ Double Cheese Quiche

2 tablespoons dry bread
    crumbs
½ cup shredded Swiss
    cheese
½ cup shredded Cheddar
    cheese.
2 tablespoons finely chopped
    onion
2 tablespoons finely chopped
    green pepper
¼ cup buttermilk baking mix
¾ teaspoon salt
⅛ teaspoon pepper
5 eggs
1⅓ cups half and half

Serves 6

Butter bottom of 8- or 9-in.
quiche dish. Coat with crumbs.
Sprinkle Swiss and Cheddar
cheese in dish. In 2-qt.
casserole combine onion and
green pepper. Microwave at
High 2 to 4 minutes, or until
tender, stirring 2 or 3 times. Stir
in baking mix, salt and pepper
until vegetables are coated.
Beat in eggs and half and half.

Reduce power to 50%
(Medium). Microwave 5 to 8
minutes, or until very hot but not
set, stirring with wire whip every
2 minutes. Stir; pour into dish.
Microwave at 50% (Medium) 8
to 12 minutes, or until knife
inserted halfway between center
and edge comes out clean and
quiche is almost set, rotating
dish ¼ turn every 3 to 4
minutes. Let stand 10 minutes
before cutting.

Advance preparation: Cover
and refrigerate microwaved
quiche no longer than 8 hours
or overnight. Microwave at 50%
(Medium) 10 to 15 minutes, or
until heated.

162

Egg & Sausage Bake ▲

1 pkg. (12 oz.) seasoned bulk
   pork sausage
¼ cup chopped green pepper
¼ cup chopped onion
8 eggs
½ cup milk
¼ teaspoon salt
⅛ teaspoon pepper
1 cup shredded Cheddar
   cheese
1 cup shredded Swiss cheese

Serves 4

Crumble sausage into 2-qt.
casserole. Add green pepper
and onion. Microwave at High 3
to 6 minutes, or until meat is no
longer pink, stirring to break
apart after half the time. Break
sausage into small pieces; drain
well. Spread in 8 × 8-in. baking
dish. Set aside.

Beat eggs, milk, salt and
pepper in 2-qt. casserole. Reduce power to 50% (Medium).
Microwave 5 to 9 minutes, or
until eggs are set but still very
moist, stirring every 2 minutes.
Stir in cheeses; pour over
sausage. Cover with wax paper.

Place on inverted saucer in
oven. Microwave at 50%
(Medium) 10 to 12 minutes, or
until center is set, but slightly
moist on top, rotating ¼ turn
every 3 minutes. Let stand,
covered, 5 minutes.

Party Quiche

Crust:
⅓ cup shortening
1 tablespoon butter or
   margarine
1¼ cups all-purpose flour
½ teaspoon salt
2 to 3 tablespoons cold water
   with 2 drops yellow food
   coloring
1 egg, separated
½ teaspoon water

Filling:
10 slices bacon, chopped
4 eggs
1 can (13 oz.) evaporated
   milk
½ teaspoon salt
⅛ teaspoon cayenne
1 cup shredded Swiss
   cheese
⅓ cup chopped green onion

Serves 8

Cut shortening and butter into flour and salt until particles resemble
small peas. Sprinkle with water mixture, 1 tablespoon at a time,
stirring with fork until dough forms a ball. Roll out to 12-in. square
on floured surface. Gently place in 10-in. square casserole. Crimp
edges so dough covers ¾ to 1 inch up sides of casserole. Prick
with fork. Microwave at High 3 to 6 minutes, or until crust is dry.

Combine egg yolk and ½ teaspoon water. Brush crust with yolk
mixture. Microwave at High 30 to 60 seconds, or until yolk is set.
Set crust aside.

In 2-qt. casserole microwave bacon at High 6 to 9 minutes, or until
crisp, stirring 2 or 3 times. Remove bacon to paper towel with
slotted spoon. Discard fat.

In the same casserole combine reserved egg white and the 4
eggs, evaporated milk, salt and cayenne. Blend thoroughly.
Reduce power to 50% (Medium). Microwave 4 to 6 minutes, or
until very hot but not set, stirring with wire whip every 1 to 2
minutes during cooking time.

Layer cheese, bacon and green onion in crust. Pour in egg
mixture. Cover with wax paper. Place in oven on inverted pie plate
or dinner plate. Reduce power to 30% (Medium-Low). Microwave
20 to 28 minutes, or until just set, rotating 3 or 4 times during
cooking time. Let stand 10 minutes.

Advance preparation: Prepare the day before or early in the day;
refrigerate. To serve, cut into 16 pieces and place on platter.
Cover with wax paper. Microwave at 50% (Medium) 3 to 6
minutes, or until heated, rearranging pieces once.

Broccoli Quiche

1 pie shell (9-in.), baked, cooled
1 pkg. (10 oz.) broccoli cuts
3 eggs, slightly beaten
⅓ cup milk
1 can (3 oz.) French fried onion
   rings, divided
1 cup shredded Cheddar
   cheese, divided
½ teaspoon salt
⅛ teaspoon pepper

Serves 4 to 6

Defrost broccoli in package at High 3½ to 4 minutes. Drain.

In medium mixing bowl beat eggs and milk; stir in broccoli, ½ can onion rings, ½ cup cheese, salt and pepper. Pour into pie shell. Microwave at 50% (Medium) 8 to 15 minutes, or until almost set, rotating ¼ turn every 4 minutes.

Sprinkle remaining onion rings and cheese over top. Microwave at 50% (Medium) 1½ to 2½ minutes, or until cheese melts. Let stand 5 minutes.

Sweet Potato Puff

¼ cup butter or margarine
¼ cup flour
½ teaspoon salt
⅛ teaspoon cinnamon
   Dash nutmeg
1 cup milk
¼ cup brown sugar

1 cup mashed, cooked sweet
   potatoes or yams (can be
   canned or precooked)
4 eggs, separated
1 teaspoon cream of tartar
2 tablespoons chopped
   pecans, optional

Serves 2 to 4

In 2-qt. casserole microwave butter at High 30 to 45 seconds, or until melted. Blend in flour and seasonings. Slowly stir in milk.

Microwave at High 3 to 3½ minutes, or until thickened, stirring every minute. Add brown sugar, sweet potatoes or yams and slightly beaten egg yolks.

In large mixing bowl beat egg whites with cream of tartar until stiff peaks form. Gently fold egg whites into thickened sauce.

Microwave at 50% (Medium) 15 to 19 minutes, or until top edges appear dry and center seems set, rotating ¼ turn about every 3 minutes. Sprinkle with pecans, if desired.

Spanish Scrambled Eggs

½ cup chopped green pepper
1 tablespoon butter or
　margarine
6 beaten eggs
2 tablespoons milk
½ teaspoon salt

¼ teaspoon pepper
¼ teaspoon oregano leaves
½ cup finely chopped, peeled,
　seeded tomato
½ cup shredded mozzarella or
　¼ cup grated Parmesan

Serves 2 to 3

In 1-qt. casserole, combine green pepper and butter. Microwave covered at High 1½ to 2½ minutes, or until butter is melted and green pepper is hot.

In small bowl, blend eggs, milk, salt, pepper and oregano. Mix into green pepper. Microwave 3½ to 5 minutes, or until eggs are soft and moist, stirring and pushing cooked portions to center after 2 minutes, 1 minute, then every 30 seconds.

Stir in tomatoes. Cover. Let stand covered 1 minute. If desired, sprinkle on, or stir in cheese and allow to stand covered 1 to 2 more minutes.

Denver Sandwiches

3 tablespoons chopped
　green pepper
2 tablespoons chopped onion
2 teaspoons butter or margarine
3 eggs
½ cup fully cooked
　chopped ham
1 tablespoon milk
⅛ teaspoon dry mustard
⅛ teaspoon salt
⅛ teaspoon pepper
　Bread or toast

Serves 4

Combine green pepper, onion and butter in small mixing bowl. Microwave at High 1 to 2½ minutes, or until vegetables are tender.

Stir in eggs, chopped ham, milk and seasonings. Pour into two small saucers. Microwave at High 2 to 5 minutes, or until eggs are almost set, pushing cooked portions toward center of dish and rotating saucers once or twice during cooking.

Serve open face or as sandwiches with bread or toast.

Crab Meat Baked Eggs

1 can (6½ oz.) crab meat,
    rinsed and drained
3 slices (¾ oz. each) low fat
    American cheese
4 large eggs
    Dash paprika

Serves 4

NOTE: for low sodium diet use
well drained frozen crab and
low sodium cheese product.

Per Serving:
Calories:	196
Sodium:	592 mg.
Cholesterol:	298 mg.
Exchanges:	3 low fat meat, ½ fat

How to Microwave Crab Meat Baked Eggs

Flake crab. Reserve one-fourth. Divide remainder into 4 custard cups; form a well in each. Quarter 2 cheese slices. Arrange 2 quarters in each cup.

Break an egg into each cheese-filled depression. Top with remaining crab and strips of last cheese slice. Sprinkle with paprika. Cover each with plastic wrap.

Microwave at 50% (Medium) 4½ to 5½ minutes for soft-cooked eggs, or 5½ to 6½ minutes for hard-cooked.

Let stand, covered, 2 to 3 minutes until yolk is just soft or hard set.

Overnight Cheese Stratas

4 slices white bread
　　Butter or margarine
2 tablespoons finely chopped
　　onion
2 cups shredded Swiss cheese
1 can (5⅓ oz.) evaporated milk
½ cup milk
3 eggs
1 teaspoon salt
½ teaspoon dry mustard
2 teaspoons parsley flakes

Serves 4

Variation:
Microwave ½ lb. ground pork
sausage at High 2½ to 4
minutes, or until meat loses its
pink color. Crumble and drain.
Add with onion and cheese.

How to Microwave Overnight Cheese Stratas

Assemble the night before and microwave the next day. Butter one side of each slice of bread. Place slices buttered side down, in four individual casseroles. Top with onion and cheese.

Combine remaining ingredients except parsley flakes. Pour one-fourth of mixture over each slice of bread. Top each casserole with ½ teaspoon parsley flakes. Cover; refrigerate overnight.

Microwave uncovered at 50% (Medium) 18 to 26 minutes, or until set, rearranging dishes twice during cooking. Let stand 3 minutes.

American-Swiss Fondue ▶

1 clove garlic, halved
8 oz. grated cheddar cheese
8 oz. grated Swiss cheese
3 tablespoons flour
  Dash nutmeg
1 cup dry white wine
  Cubes of crusty French bread

Serves 4

Rub a 2-qt. casserole with cut garlic. Discard. Shake cheese, flour and nutmeg together in small bag. Measure wine into casserole. Microwave at 50% power (Medium) 3 to 4 minutes, until wine is hot but not boiling.

Stir in cheese mixture. Microwave 6 to 8 minutes, until smooth, stirring vigorously every 2 minutes with a fork or wire whip. Serve hot with bread cubes for dipping.

Macaroni & Cheese ▶

1 pkg. (7-oz.) elbow
  macaroni
3 tablespoons butter or
  margarine
3 tablespoons flour
1 teaspoon salt
½ teaspoon dry mustard
¼ teaspoon pepper
1½ cups milk
2 cups grated cheese

Serves 6

Photo directions opposite.

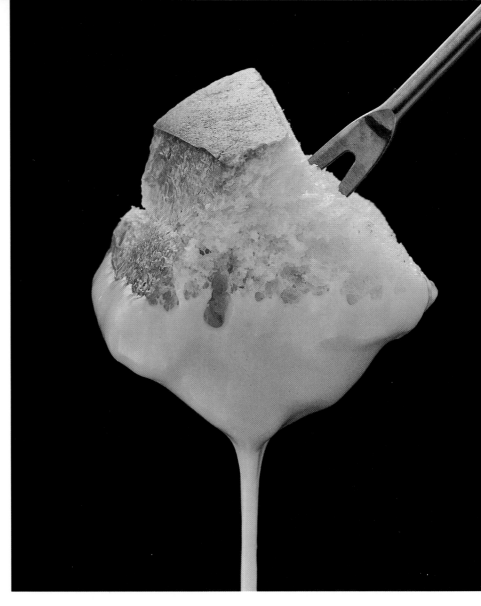

Grilled Cheese Sandwiches

This sandwich can be made outside the oven; heat from the browning dish is sufficient to brown the bread and melt the cheese.

For each sandwich:
2 slices bread   2 slices processed cheese
   Butter or margarine   (American, Swiss, cheddar)

Variations:

Spread ¼ teaspoon prepared mustard between cheese slices. Substitute 1 slice ham for 1 slice cheese.

How to Microwave Grilled Cheese Sandwiches

Preheat browning dish 4 to 5 minutes or browning grill 6½ to 7½ minutes at High power.

Place cheese between bread slices. Butter outside of sandwich on both sides. Place 1 or 2 sandwiches in preheated dish.

Flatten slightly with spatula. Let stand 15 to 20 seconds. Turn over; let stand 20 to 25 seconds. If necessary, microwave 15 to 25 seconds to finish melting cheese.

How to Microwave Macaroni & Cheese

Cook macaroni conventionally. Drain; set aside. Melt butter in 2-qt. casserole at High power, 40 to 55 seconds. Stir in flour and seasonings until smooth.

Microwave 30 to 45 seconds until heated. Blend in milk smoothly. Microwave 4½ to 5½ minutes until thickened, stirring every minute.

Stir in cheese until melted, microwaving 15 to 20 seconds, if needed. Mix in macaroni well. Microwave 5 to 6 minutes to heat through, stirring once.

169

Soups

Minestrone

½ cup thinly sliced celery
½ cup thinly sliced carrot
2 cloves garlic, minced
¾ cup (1 large) potato, cut
    into ½-in. cubes
1 can (16 oz.) tomatoes,
    undrained
1 cup thinly sliced zucchini
½ lb. green beans, cut into
    1-in. pieces
½ cup broken spaghetti
3 cups hot water
2 teaspoons instant beef
    bouillon granules
1 teaspoon basil leaves
1 tablespoon parsley flakes

Serves 6

In 3-qt. casserole, combine all ingredients. Cover. Microwave at High 25 to 35 minutes or until vegetables are tender, stirring once or twice.

NOTE: for low sodium diet substitute low-salt bouillon.

Per Serving:
Calories:	35
Sodium:	315 mg.
Cholesterol:	0
Exchanges:	1½ vegetable

◄ Chicken Noodle Soup

2½ to 3 lbs. chicken pieces
6 cups hot water, divided
2 large stalks celery, thinly sliced
2 medium carrots, thinly sliced
½ teaspoon dried basil
¼ teaspoon rosemary
¼ teaspoon pepper
1 teaspoon salt, optional
½ cup thin egg noodles

Serves 8

In 5-qt. casserole combine chicken, 4 cups water, celery, carrots, basil, rosemary, pepper and salt; cover. Microwave at High 30 to 40 minutes, or until chicken falls easily from bone, stirring twice during cooking.

Remove chicken from bones. Discard bone and skin. Dice meat and return to casserole. Add 2 cups hot water and noodles. Cover. Microwave at High 8 to 10 minutes, or until water boils. Microwave at High 7 to 10 minutes, or until noodles are tender.

Per Serving:
Calories: 111
Sodium: 274 mg.
Cholesterol: 6 mg.
Exchanges: 1 vegetable, 1½ low fat meat

Easy Cream of ▲ Asparagus Soup

½ cup water
½ cup uncooked instant rice
¼ cup chopped onion
¼ cup chopped celery
1 pkg. (10 oz.) frozen asparagus cuts, defrosted
2 tablespoons flour
Dash pepper
Dash nutmeg
½ teaspoon salt, optional
1 teaspoon instant chicken bouillon granules
1½ cups skim milk
¼ teaspoon paprika

Serves 4

Microwave water in small bowl at High 1½ to 2½ minutes, or until boiling. Add rice. Let stand, covered, 5 minutes, or until water is absorbed. In 2-qt. casserole combine onion, celery and asparagus. Cover. Microwave at High 4 to 6 minutes, or until tender, stirring twice.

Mash asparagus mixture with fork. Stir in flour, seasonings, rice and milk. Cover. Microwave at High 7 to 8 minutes, or until thickened. Sprinkle with paprika.

NOTE: .for low sodium diet substitute low-salt bouillon.

Per Serving:
Calories: 110
Sodium: 554 mg.
Cholesterol: 0
Exchanges: ½ milk, 1 vegetable, ½ bread

Egg Drop Soup ▶

4 cups hot water
2 teaspoons instant chicken
    bouillon granules
2 teaspoons soy sauce
1 green onion, chopped
2 eggs, slightly beaten

Serves 4

In 2-qt. casserole combine
water, bouillon, soy sauce and
onion. Microwave at High 7½ to
12 minutes, or until boiling. Pour
eggs in a thin circular stream
over boiling broth; let threads
coagulate. Serve immediately.

NOTE: for low sodium diet
substitute low-salt bouillon.

Per Serving:
  Calories: 39
  Sodium: 678 mg.
  Cholesterol: 126 mg.
  Exchanges: ½ med. fat meat

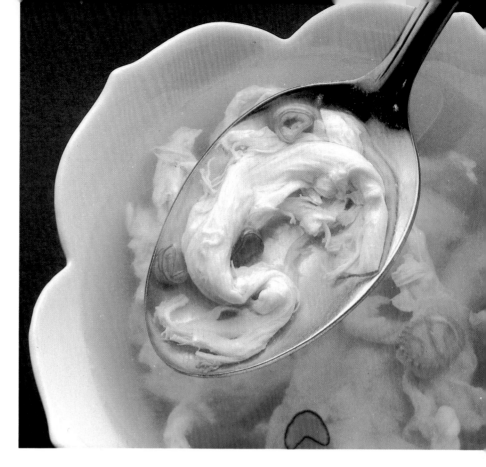

Cabbage Soup ▶

2 slices bacon, chopped
6 cups chopped cabbage
1 medium onion, sliced and
    separated into rings
¼ teaspoon dill weed
¼ teaspoon caraway seed
⅛ teaspoon pepper
1½ teaspoons salt, optional
4 cups hot water, divided

Serves 6

Place bacon in 3-qt. casserole;
cover. Microwave at High 3 to
5 minutes, or until bacon
begins to crisp. Stir in
cabbage, onion, seasonings
and 2 cups water; cover.
Microwave at High 10 minutes.
Add remaining water; cover.
Microwave at High 8 to 12
minutes, or until cabbage and
onions are tender.

NOTE: for low sodium diet
omit bacon.

Per Serving:
  Calories: 48
  Sodium: 547 mg.
  Cholesterol: 12 mg.
  Exchanges: 1 vegetable, ½ fat

French Onion Soup

2 tablespoons margarine or
    butter
1 large onion, sliced and
    separated into rings
3 cups hot water
3 teaspoons instant beef
    bouillon granules
½ teaspoon Worcestershire
    sauce
    Dash pepper
2 slices thin bread, toasted
4 oz. shredded mozzarella
    cheese
4 teaspoons Parmesan cheese

Serves 4

Per Serving:
Calories: 135
Sodium: 158 mg.
Cholesterol: 15 mg.
Exchanges: ½ bread, ½ high
fat meat, 1 fat

How to Microwave French Onion Soup

Combine margarine and onion in 2-qt. casserole. Cover.
Microwave at High 8 to 11 minutes, or until onions are translucent
and tender, stirring once or twice. Add water, bouillon,
Worcestershire sauce and pepper. Re-cover.

Microwave at High 6 to 8
minutes, or until boiling. Reduce
power to 50% (Medium).
Microwave 5 minutes.

Divide soup into 4 individual casseroles or bowls. Top each with
½ slice toasted bread and 2 tablespoons mozzarella. Sprinkle with
Parmesan. Place bowls in oven.

Microwave at High 2 to 3
minutes, or until cheese melts;
rearrange bowls after half
the time.

Cream of Broccoli ▲ & Cauliflower Soup

1 pkg. (10 oz.) frozen chopped broccoli
1 pkg. (10 oz.) frozen cauliflower
1 cup shredded potato
1 cup water
2 tablespoons chopped onion
2 teaspoons low-sodium instant chicken bouillon granules
¼ teaspoon pepper
⅛ teaspoon ground nutmeg
3 cups skim milk

9 servings, ¾ cup each

In 2-quart casserole, combine all ingredients, except milk. Cover. Microwave at High for 15 to 21 minutes, or until vegetables are tender, stirring 2 or 3 times. Let stand, covered, for 5 minutes. Process half the vegetables in food processor or blender bowl until pureed. Repeat with remaining vegetables. Return to casserole. Blend in milk. Microwave, uncovered, at High for 7 to 13 minutes, or until heated through, stirring once or twice.

Per Serving:
Calories: 59
Protein: 4.6 g.
Carbohydrates: 10 g.
Fat: —
Cholesterol 1.3 mg.
Sodium: 56.3 mg.
Calcium: 122.6 mg.
Exchanges: 2 vegetable

Tomato Rice Soup

1 can (14½ oz.) no-salt stewed tomatoes
1 can (12 oz.) no-salt tomato juice
1 cup hot water
1 cup cooked brown rice, page 230
¼ cup thinly sliced carrot
1 tablespoon frozen orange juice concentrate
1 teaspoon low-sodium instant chicken bouillon granules
⅛ teaspoon pepper
Dash ground cloves
Dash ground nutmeg
1 cup frozen peas

10 servings, ½ cup each

In 2-quart casserole, combine all ingredients, except peas. Stir. Cover. Microwave at High for 10 minutes. Add peas. Re-cover. Microwave at High for 5 to 10 minutes longer, or until carrot is tender. Let stand, covered, for 5 minutes.

Per Serving:
Calories: 55
Protein: 1.9 g.
Carbohydrates: 12 g.
Fat: .3 g.
Cholesterol
Sodium: 30.6 mg.
Calcium: 4.1 mg.
Exchanges: 1 bread

Creamy Pumpkin Soup

1 cup hot water
¾ cup canned pumpkin
3 tablespoons thinly sliced green onions
2 teaspoons frozen orange juice concentrate
1½ teaspoons low-sodium instant chicken bouillon granules
¼ teaspoon ground cinnamon
⅛ teaspoon ground ginger
½ cup skim milk

4 servings, ½ cup each

In 1-quart casserole, combine all ingredients, except milk. Mix well. Cover. Microwave at High for 3½ to 5½ minutes, or until bubbly and onions are just tender-crisp, stirring once. Stir in milk. Microwave at High for 30 seconds to 1 minute longer, or until hot. Stir before serving.

Per Serving:
Calories: 36
Protein: 2 g.
Carbohydrates: 7 g.
Fat: —
Cholesterol —
Sodium: 20 mg.
Calcium: 52.75 mg.
Exchanges: ½ bread

◄ Oriental Soup

1 cup (½-inch cubes) turnips
½ cup julienne carrots
   (2 × ⅛-inch strips)
1 clove garlic, minced
2 cups shredded lettuce
1 cup bean sprouts
1 pkg. (6 oz.) frozen pea pods
3 cups hot water
2 tablespoons reduced-sodium
   soy sauce
1 tablespoon low-sodium
   instant chicken bouillon
   granules
¼ teaspoon sesame oil
⅛ teaspoon white pepper
⅛ teaspoon ground ginger

5 servings, 1 cup each

In 2-quart casserole, combine turnips, carrots and garlic. Cover. Microwave at High for 6 to 7 minutes, or until tender. Add remaining ingredients. Re-cover. Microwave at High for 10 to 15 minutes longer, or until hot and lettuce is wilted, stirring after half the time to break apart pea pods.

Per Serving:
Calories:	68
Protein:	2 g.
Carbohydrates:	9 g.
Fat:	23 g.
Cholesterol:	25 mg.
Sodium:	264 mg.
Calcium:	—
Exchanges:	2 vegetable, ½ fat

Split Pea & Ham Soup ▲

1 lb. dried green split peas,
   sorted, rinsed and drained
6 cups hot water
1 cup (¼-inch cubes) potato
½ cup thinly sliced carrot
⅓ cup chopped low-fat boiled
   ham (about 2 oz.)
2 teaspoons low-sodium
   instant chicken bouillon
   granules
1 teaspoon dried thyme leaves
1 bay leaf
24 whole peppercorns

10 servings, ¾ cup each

In 5-quart casserole, combine all ingredients. Stir. Cover. Microwave at High for 10 minutes. Reduce power to 50% (Medium). Microwave for 30 minutes. Stir and re-cover. Microwave at 50% (Medium) for 30 to 45 minutes longer, or until peas are tender. Let stand, covered, for 10 to 15 minutes. Remove bay leaf and peppercorns before serving.

Per Serving:
Calories:	83
Protein:	5 g.
Carbohydrates:	13 g.
Fat:	1.5 g.
Cholesterol:	3 mg.
Sodium:	93 mg.
Calcium:	25 mg.
Exchanges:	1 bread

Spinach & Crab Soup

- 1 pkg. (10 oz.) frozen chopped spinach
- 3 tablespoons butter or margarine
- ¼ cup chopped onion
- ¼ cup chopped celery
- 3 tablespoons all-purpose flour
- 2 cups half-and-half
- 1 can (14½ oz.) ready-to-serve chicken broth
- 1 pkg. (6 oz.) frozen crab meat, defrosted, drained and cartilage removed
- ½ teaspoon salt
- ⅛ teaspoon ground mace
- 2 tablespoons dry sherry (optional)

4 to 6 servings

Unwrap spinach and place on plate. Microwave at High for 4 to 5 minutes, or until defrosted. Let stand for 5 minutes.

Drain thoroughly, pressing to remove excess moisture. Set aside.

In 2-quart casserole, combine butter, onion and celery. Cover. Microwave at High for 3 to 4 minutes, or until vegetables are tender, stirring once. Stir in flour. Blend in remaining ingredients, except sherry. Re-cover. Reduce power to 50% (Medium). Microwave for 20 to 26 minutes, or until hot, stirring 3 times. Stir in sherry.

Spinach & Seafood Soup:
Follow recipe above, substituting cut-up seafood sticks for crab meat.

177

Sandwiches

With a microwave oven, a hot sandwich can be ready in about 1 minute. Overheating toughens bread, but a piece of foil on the bottom of the oven will shield the bread from below while the filling protects it from above. Place a paper napkin or towel between bread and foil to absorb excess steam. Toasting the bread before microwaving keeps it from becoming soggy. For other popular sandwiches, see hamburgers, page 72; wieners, page 104 and grilled cheese, page 169.

Open-Face Bacon, Tomato & Cheese Sandwich

For each sandwich:
2 to 3 slices bacon, halved
1 slice bread
2 to 3 slices tomato
1 slice cheese

Microwave the bacon, following directions on page 102. While bacon is standing, toast bread; place on paper napkin. Lay thin tomato slices on toast, add bacon and top with cheese. Place sandwich and napkin on foil in oven.

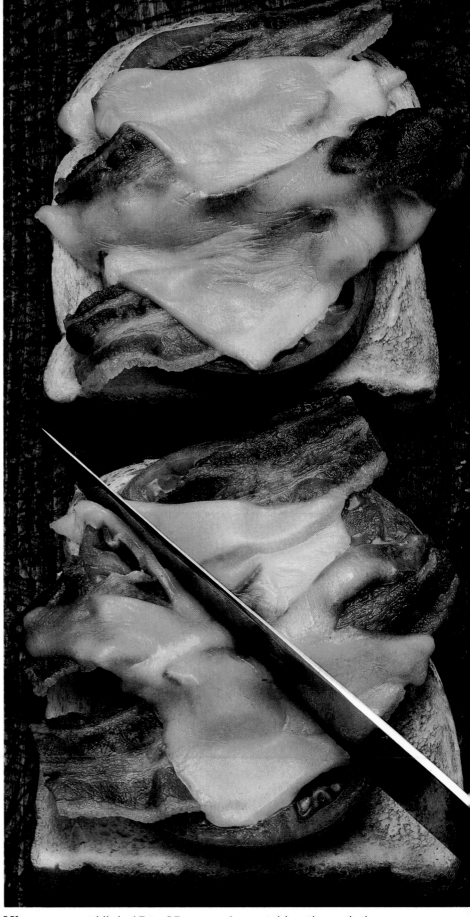

Microwave at High 15 to 35 seconds, watching through the oven door, until cheese melts. Serve whole as a sandwich or cut in fingers to serve as an appetizer.

Smoked Cheese & ▶ Turkey Salad Sandwiches

4 slices bacon
¼ cup chopped onion
¼ cup chopped green pepper
¼ cup chopped celery
1 tablespoon butter or margarine
2 cups cubed cooked turkey, ½-inch cubes
½ cup cubed smoked Cheddar cheese, ¼-inch cubes
⅓ cup mayonnaise
1 teaspoon prepared mustard
1 teaspoon Worcestershire sauce
4 Kaiser rolls, 4-inch, unsplit

4 servings

Place bacon on paper towel-lined plate. Cover with paper towel. Microwave at High for 3½ to 6 minutes, or until crisp. Crumble. Set aside. In 2-quart casserole, combine onion, green pepper, celery and butter. Micro-wave at High for 2 to 4 minutes, or until vegetables are tender-crisp. Stir in turkey, bacon and cheese. In small mixing bowl, blend mayonnaise, mustard and Worcestershire sauce. Add to turkey mixture. Mix well.

Cut thin slice from top of each roll. Scoop out center of each roll to within ¼ inch of edge. Fill each roll with turkey mixture. Arrange rolls on paper towel-lined platter. Cover with wax paper. Microwave at 50% (Medium) for 3 to 4 minutes, or just until cheese begins to melt, rotating platter after every minute.

Patty Melts

1 lb. ground turkey
1 tablespoon finely chopped onion
1 tablespoon milk
1 teaspoon Worcestershire sauce
¼ teaspoon salt
¼ teaspoon pepper
⅛ teaspoon garlic powder
4 slices (¾ oz. each) pasteurized process American cheese
4 English muffins, split and toasted

4 servings

In medium mixing bowl, combine ground turkey, onion, milk, Wor-cestershire sauce, salt, pepper and garlic powder. Mix well. Shape into 4 patties, about ½ inch thick. Arrange patties on roasting rack. Microwave at High for 4 minutes. Turn patties over and rearrange. Microwave at High for 3 to 6 minutes, or until cooked through. Top with cheese slices. Reduce power to 50% (Medium). Microwave for 2 to 4 minutes, or until cheese melts. Serve in toasted English muffins with ketchup or mustard.

Vegetable-Tuna ▲ Open-Face Sandwiches

2 slices bacon
1 can (3¼ oz.) tuna, drained
2 tablespoons mayonnaise or salad dressing
1 tablespoon chopped onion
2 slices whole wheat bread, toasted
4 to 6 thin slices avocado
¼ cup alfalfa sprouts
2 slices tomato
2 slices Colby cheese

Serves 2

Place bacon on paper towel-lined plate. Microwave at High 1½ to 2 minutes, or until brown. Crumble. In small bowl mix bacon, tuna, mayonnaise and onion. Spread half evenly on each toast slice. Top with two or three slices avocado, the sprouts, one slice tomato and cheese. Place on paper towel-lined plate. Reduce power to 50% (Medium). Microwave 1½ to 3½ minutes, or until heated and cheese melts.

Crab Meat Croissants

1 tablespoon butter or margarine
1 tablespoon chopped green onion
1 tablespoon plus 1½ teaspoons all-purpose flour
¼ teaspoon salt
⅛ teaspoon pepper
1 cup half and half
1 teaspoon white wine
1 can (6½ oz.) crab meat, rinsed, drained and cartilage removed
2 large croissants or 4 crescent rolls

Serves 2

Place butter and onion in 2-cup measure. Microwave at High 30 to 45 seconds, or until butter melts and onion is tender, stirring after half the time. Stir in flour, salt and pepper. Blend in half and half. Microwave at High 3 to 4 minutes, or until thickened, stirring every minute. Stir in wine and crab meat. Slice croissants in half lengthwise. Spread half of filling on bottom of each. Replace top of croissant.

Florentine Croissants

½ lb. fresh spinach, shredded
1 tablespoon butter or margarine
1 tablespoon plus 1½ teaspoons all-purpose flour
¼ teaspoon salt
⅛ teaspoon pepper
1 cup half and half
1 teaspoon white wine
2 large croissants or 4 crescent rolls
¼ lb. thinly sliced ham, cut into thin strips

Serves 2

Place spinach in 1½-qt. casserole; cover. Microwave at High 2½ to 3½ minutes, or until tender, stirring once. Drain well. Melt butter in 2-cup measure at High 30 to 45 seconds. Stir in flour, salt and pepper. Blend in half and half. Microwave at High 3 to 4 minutes, or until thickened, stirring with a wire whip after every minute. Stir in wine. Slice croissants in half lengthwise. Spread half of spinach on bottom of each. Top each with half the ham, one-fourth the sauce and top of croissant. Add remaining sauce.

Hot Deli Melt ▲

1 loaf (8 oz.) French bread,
   cut in half lengthwise
2 tablespoons Poppy Seed
   Dressing, right, or
   mayonnaise
¼ lb. thinly sliced cooked beef,
   turkey or ham

½ cup alfalfa sprouts
1 medium tomato, thinly sliced
½ cup sliced mushrooms
6 to 8 thin slices onion
6 to 8 thin slices green pepper
4 slices (¾ oz. each) Cheddar,
   Colby or Swiss cheese

Serves 2

Spread bread with Poppy Seed Dressing. Layer meat, sprouts,
tomato, mushrooms, onion, green pepper and cheese. Replace
top. Place sandwich on paper towel-lined plate. Microwave at 50%
(Medium) 4 to 6½ minutes, or until cheese melts. Cut in half.

Poppy Seed Dressing

¼ cup mayonnaise or salad
   dressing
¼ teaspoon prepared mustard
⅛ teaspoon poppy seed
   Dash garlic powder

Makes ¼ cup

In a small bowl mix all
ingredients. Use for Hot Deli
Melt or other sandwiches.

◄ Mexican Pizza Sandwich

2 medium tomatoes, chopped
¼ cup chopped onion
1 tablespoon chopped green
   chili peppers
¼ teaspoon garlic powder
¼ teaspoon ground cumin
¼ teaspoon oregano leaves
¼ teaspoon basil leaves
   Dash salt
   Dash cayenne pepper
2 slices firm bread, toasted
2 tablespoons shredded
   mozzarella cheese

Serves 2

In 1-qt. casserole combine
tomatoes, onion and chili
peppers. Microwave at High 5
to 6 minutes, or until tomatoes
are tender, stirring after half the
time. Drain. Stir in seasonings.

Arrange toasted bread in
bottom of 8 × 8-in. baking dish
or on serving dish. Place half of
tomato mixture on each slice.
Top each with 1 tablespoon
cheese. Microwave at High 1 to
2 minutes, or until cheese melts.
Rotate sandwiches once
during cooking.

Per Serving:	
Calories:	134
Sodium:	150 mg.
Cholesterol:	9 mg.
Exchanges:	1 vegetable, 1 bread, ½ med. fat meat

Zucchini Pocket Sandwich▲

1 cup shredded zucchini
½ cup sliced fresh mushrooms
1 cup chopped tomato
½ teaspoon basil leaves
¼ teaspoon garlic powder
2 tablespoons Parmesan
  cheese
4 small loaves pocket bread

Serves 4

In medium mixing bowl combine zucchini and mushrooms. Microwave at High 2 to 3 minutes, or until mushrooms are tender. Drain excess liquid.

Stir in tomato, seasonings and cheese. Split open one end of pocket bread. Place one-fourth of the filling in each.

Per Serving:
Calories: 114
Sodium: 140 mg.
Cholesterol: 8 mg.
Exchanges: 1 vegetable, 1
    bread

Vegie Melt Sandwich

1 tablespoon low calorie
  mayonnaise
½ teaspoon prepared mustard
2 slices firm bread, toasted
2 thin slices red onion
2 thin slices tomato
½ cup alfalfa sprouts
1 slice low fat American
  cheese, cut into 8 strips

Serves 2

In small bowl combine mayonnaise and mustard. Spread half of mixture on each slice of toast. Top each with 1 slice onion and tomato, then ¼ cup alfalfa sprouts. Arrange 4 strips cheese over each sandwich. Place on paper towel lined plate. Microwave at 50% (Medium) 1½ to 2½ minutes, or until cheese melts, rotating once during cooking.

Per Serving:
Calories: 118
Sodium: 280 mg.
Cholesterol: 3 mg.
Exchanges: 1 bread, ¼ low fat
    meat, ½ fat

Cheesy Shrimp Sandwich

1 oz. Neufchâtel cheese
2 tablespoons chopped onion
2 tablespoons chopped celery
1 can (4¼ oz.) cooked shrimp,
  drained and rinsed
  Dash celery seed
  Dash salt, optional
  Dash pepper
4 slices firm bread, toasted
16 thin slices cucumber

Serves 4

Place cheese, onion and celery in small mixing bowl or 1-qt. casserole. Microwave at 50% (Medium) 45 to 60 seconds, or until cheese softens. Add shrimp, celery seed, salt and pepper.

Place 4 cucumber slices on each slice of toast. Top each with one-fourth of shrimp mixture.

Per Serving:
Calories: 100
Sodium: 80 mg.
Cholesterol: 27 mg.
Exchanges: ½ bread, 1 low fat
    meat

Sauces

Tomato & Green Pepper Sauce

4 medium tomatoes, peeled and chopped
1 medium green pepper, cut into thin strips
1 small onion, chopped
½ teaspoon basil leaves
½ teaspoon salt, optional
¼ teaspoon oregano leaves
¼ teaspoon thyme leaves
¼ teaspoon marjoram leaves
⅛ teaspoon garlic powder
⅛ teaspoon black pepper
2 tablespoons water
1 tablespoon cornstarch

Serves 6
Serving size: ½ cup

In 1½-qt. casserole combine all ingredients except water and cornstarch. In small bowl blend cornstarch into water. Add to vegetable mixture. Cover. Microwave at High 5 minutes. Stir. Microwave at High 4 to 10 minutes, or until pepper is tender and sauce is slightly thickened, stirring once or twice. Serve with fish, meat or poultry.

Per Serving:
Calories: 31
Sodium: 169 mg.
Cholesterol: 0
Exchanges: 1 vegetable

Orange-Pineapple Sauce

Pictured opposite

1 can (8 oz.) crushed pineapple, packed in own juice
¼ cup low sugar orange marmalade
½ teaspoon parsley flakes

Serves 9
Serving size: 2 tablespoons

Combine all ingredients in 2-cup measure. Microwave at High 1½ to 3 minutes, or until marmalade melts. Serve over chicken or pork.

Per Serving:
Calories: 16
Sodium: 0
Cholesterol: 0
Exchanges: ½ fruit

Mushroom Sauce

8 oz. sliced fresh mushrooms
2 medium green onions, chopped
1 teaspoon instant beef bouillon granules
¼ teaspoon pepper
1¼ cups water
2 teaspoons cornstarch

Serves 5
Serving size: ¼ cup

In 1½-qt. casserole combine all ingredients except water and cornstarch. In small bowl blend cornstarch into water. Add to vegetable mixture. Cover. Microwave at High 3 to 6 minutes, or until mushrooms are tender and sauce is transparent, stirring once or twice. Serve with meat or fish.

NOTE: for low sodium diet substitute low-salt bouillon.

Per Serving:
Calories: 18
Sodium: 188 mg.
Cholesterol: 0
Exchanges: ½ vegetable

Sweet & Sour Sauce

½ cup unsweetened pineapple juice
5 tablespoons catsup
2 teaspoons vinegar
½ cup water
1 teaspoon instant minced onion

Serves 11
Serving size: 2 tablespoons

Combine all ingredients in 2-cup measure. Microwave at High 3 to 6 minutes, or until sauce is bubbly and onion is tender. Serve with beef, pork, chicken or vegetables.

NOTE: for low sodium diet substitute low-salt catsup.

Variation:
Barbecue Sauce: add 8 to 10 drops liquid hickory smoke flavoring.

Per Serving:
Calories: 11
Sodium: 82 mg.
Cholesterol: 0
Exchanges: free

Mint Sauce

⅔ cup water
1 teaspoon red wine vinegar
1½ teaspoons malt vinegar
2 teaspoons dry mint leaves
1 teaspoon sugar

Serves 8
Serving size: 1 tablespoon

Combine all ingredients in 2-cup measure. Microwave at High 1½ to 2½ minutes, or until boiling. Reduce power to 50% (Medium). Microwave 5 minutes, or until flavors blend. Use immediately or cover and refrigerate. Serve with lamb, pork, or vegetables.

Per Serving:
Calories: 0
Sodium: 0
Cholesterol: 0
Exchanges: free

Béchamel Sauce

2 tablespoons butter or
    margarine
2 teaspoons minced onion
2 tablespoons all-purpose flour
¼ teaspoon salt
    Dash white pepper
1 cup half and half
1 small bay leaf

Makes about 1 cup

Place butter and onion in 2-cup measure. Microwave at High 1 to 1½ minutes, or until tender. Stir in flour, salt and white pepper. Blend in half and half. Add bay leaf. Reduce power to 50% (Medium). Microwave 5 to 6½ minutes, or until thickened, stirring after each minute with wire whip. Discard bay leaf. Serve with poultry, pasta or vegetables.

Easy Béarnaise Sauce

3 egg yolks
1 teaspoon white vinegar
1 teaspoon white wine
½ teaspoon dried tarragon
    leaves

⅛ teaspoon salt
    Dash white pepper
½ cup butter or margarine
1 tablespoon minced onion

Makes ¾ cup

Combine egg yolks, vinegar, wine, tarragon, salt and white pepper in blender or food processor. Blend about 5 seconds, or until smooth. Place butter and onion in 2-cup measure. Microwave at High 45 seconds to 1¼ minutes, or until butter is melted and bubbly. Continue to blend egg yolks at low speed, adding hot butter and onion in slow and steady stream until sauce thickens. Serve immediately with fish or beef.

Easy Sauce

In the microwave oven, energy penetrates sauces from all directions, so they cook faster and require little stirring to achieve a smooth consistency. For easy clean-up, measure, mix and microwave in a measuring cup.

Sweet & Sour Cream Sauce ▶

2 tablespoons butter or
    margarine
2 tablespoons all-purpose
    flour
1 tablespoon sugar
¼ teaspoon caraway seed,
    optional
⅛ teaspoon salt
    Dash pepper
½ cup whipping cream
¼ cup milk
3 tablespoons vinegar

Makes 1 cup

In 1-qt. measure microwave
butter at High 30 to 60
seconds, or until melted. Stir in
flour, sugar, caraway, salt and
pepper until smooth. Blend in
cream and milk.

Microwave at High 2 to 4
minutes, or until thickened,
stirring every minute. Mix in
vinegar. Serve with cooked
cabbage, page 194.

White Sauce

2 tablespoons butter or
    margarine
2 tablespoons all-purpose
    flour
1 teaspoon chopped chives
¼ teaspoon salt
⅛ teaspoon pepper
1 cup milk

Makes 1 cup

Melt butter in 1-qt. measure at
High 30 to 60 seconds. Stir in
flour and seasonings until
smooth. Blend in milk. Microwave at High 2½ to 6 minutes,
or until mixture thickens; stir after
2 minutes, then every minute.

Variation:
Cheese Sauce: Add 1 cup
shredded Cheddar or American
cheese, 1 tablespoon sherry,
and ¼ teaspoon dry mustard to
hot white sauce. Stir until
cheese melts. Microwave at
High 30 seconds. Stir before
serving. Serve with broccoli,
cauliflower or Brussels sprouts.

Tomato Sauce

2 tablespoons chopped onion
2 tablespoons chopped green
    pepper
2 tablespoons butter or
    margarine
1 can (6 oz.) tomato paste
1 teaspoon sugar
¼ teaspoon whole oregano
⅛ teaspoon basil
⅛ teaspoon garlic powder
⅛ teaspoon salt
    Dash pepper
1 cup tomato juice

Makes 1¼ cups

In 1-qt. measure or casserole
combine onion, green pepper
and butter. Microwave at High
1 to 2 minutes, or until tender.

Stir in tomato paste, sugar and
seasonings until smooth. Blend
in tomato juice. Microwave at
High 3 to 4 minutes, or until hot
and bubbly, stirring after half
the cooking time. Serve over
noodles, poultry or cabbage.

Hollandaise Sauce

2 egg yolks
2 tablespoons lemon juice
    Dash cayenne pepper
½ cup butter or margarine

Makes ⅔ cup

In small bowl combine egg
yolks, lemon juice and cayenne.

In small bowl, microwave butter
at High 45 to 60 seconds, or
until melted. With whisk or fork,
stir egg yolk mixture into butter.

Reduce power to 50%
(Medium). Microwave 1 to
1½ minutes, or until thickened,
stirring every 30 seconds.
Stir before serving.

Variation:
Mousseline Sauce: Cool sauce
to room temperature. Fold in ¼
cup whipped cream. Serve with
broccoli, cauliflower or spinach.

Gravy

Microwaved gravies and sauces need far less stirring than constantly stirred conventional recipes. A wire whip or table fork is the best tool. If you do not have enough meat drippings for gravy, add butter to make ⅓ cup. Do all the measuring in the same cup.

Gravy

1½ cups broth or water
  1 teaspoon beef or chicken bouillon granules, optional
  ⅓ cup flour
  ⅓ cup drippings
    Salt and pepper

Makes 1½ cups

How to Microwave Gravy

Measure broth and bouillon into 4-cup measure. Stir in flour with wire whip until smooth.

Blend meat drippings into broth-flour mixture.

Microwave at High 4 to 6 minutes until thick, stirring twice. Season to taste before serving.

Sauce & Gravy Mixes

Sauce and gravy mixes are combined with either water or milk. Sauces can be microwaved at High because they are stirred after every minute with a wire whip. This prevents boil over and smooths the sauce.

How to Microwave Sauce & Gravy Mixes

Measure liquid as directed on package. Blend sauce mix and liquid in 2- or 4-cup measure.

Microwave at High as directed in chart, until sauce thickens or is hot and bubbly. Stir with wire whip after every minute.

Sauce & Gravy Mix Chart

Item	Preparation	Microwave Instructions
Water-Based Sauce & Gravy Mixes ¾ to 1¾ oz.	Follow photo directions, above.	If sauce contains ⅔ to 1 cup water, microwave at **High 1 to 3 minutes.** If sauce contains 1¼ cups water, microwave **3 to 5 minutes.**
Milk-Based Sauce & Gravy Mixes ¾ to 1¾ oz.	Follow photo directions, above. If butter is used, microwave in 1-qt. casserole at **High 1 to 2 minutes,** or until melted. Add sauce mix and milk as directed.	If sauce contains 1 cup milk, microwave at **High 2½ to 5 minutes.** If 1¼ cups milk is added, microwave **4 to 6 minutes;** microwave 2¼ cups milk **6 to 9 minutes.**
Exceptions: Spaghetti Sauce Mix 1½ to 2½ oz.	Use 1-qt. casserole. Measure liquid as directed on package. Add sauce mix and remaining ingredients as directed on package.	Microwave at **High 10 to 15 minutes,** or until hot and bubbly, stirring after every minute.
Béarnaise Sauce Mix ⅞ oz.	Melt ¼ cup butter in 4-cup measure at **High 1 to 1½ minutes.** Blend in liquid and sauce mix as directed.	Microwave at **High 3 to 4 minutes,** or until thickened, stirring after every minute.

Vegetables

Vegetable Basics

Vegetables retain flavor and nutrients when microwaved. Minerals and vitamins dissolve in water; the less you use, the more nutrients you save. Some vegetables microwave without added moisture. Others need only a little water or butter to provide steam. Learn these vegetable characteristics:

Piece Size. Large pieces take longer to cook than small ones. Keep pieces uniform in size and thickness for even microwaving.

Quantity. Microwaving time increases with the amount of food cooked. Small or medium amounts use energy most efficiently.

Tender Ends. Asparagus buds and broccoli flowerets are more tender than the stalks and need less energy to cook. Arrange them to the center of the dish.

Tight Skins. Prick or cut vegetables cooked in their skins to allow excess steam to escape.

Microwaving Vegetables

Most microwave techniques apply to vegetables. Doneness depends on personal taste. They can be crisp, just tender, or soft. Test after standing and add more time if needed.

Standing time allows vegetables to become tender without losing their texture. If large vegetables are microwaved until the center is tender, the outer portions become mushy.

Cover dish tightly and use a minimum of water. Wrap whole, skinless vegetables in plastic.

Turn over and rearrange large, whole vegetables. If they are stacked in the dish, rearrange from top to bottom and side to center, so all will receive equal energy.

Salt vegetables after cooking, or dissolve salt in cooking water before adding vegetables.

Arrange whole or halved vegetables in a ring, leaving the center open. Rotate both vegetables and dish part way through microwaving for even cooking.

Stir small, loose vegetables from outside to center once or twice to distribute heat.

Vegetable Chart

Type	Amount	Microwave Time at High	Procedure
Artichokes, fresh	2 med. 4 med.	5½ to 8½ min. 9½ to 15 min.	Trim stems. Cut 1 inch from tops. Trim sharp ends from each leaf. Rinse and shake off excess water. Brush with lemon juice to prevent browning. Wrap each with plastic wrap. Rearrange once. Let stand 3 minutes.
Hearts, frozen	9-oz. pkg.	6 to 8 min.	1-qt. casserole with 2 tablespoons water. Cover. Stir once. Let stand 3 minutes.
Asparagus, fresh	1 lb.	7 to 10 min.	Trim tough ends. 10-in. square casserole. Place tips to center. Add ¼ cup water. Cover. Rearrange once. Let stand 3 minutes.
frozen	10-oz. pkg.	7 to 9 min.	1-qt. casserole with 2 tablespoons water. Cover. Rearrange once. Let stand 3 minutes.
Beans, Green or Wax, fresh	1 lb.	12½ to 17½ min.	Trim ends. Cut into 1½-in. pieces. 1½-qt. casserole with ½ cup water. Cover. Stir once. Let stand 5 minutes.
Green, Wax or Lima, frozen	9-oz. pkg.	5 to 8 min.	1-qt. casserole with 2 tablespoons water. Cover. Stir once. Let stand 3 minutes.
Broccoli, Spears, fresh	1 lb.	8 to 12 min.	Trim tough stalk. Cut into spears. 10-in. square casserole. Place flowerettes to center. Add ¼ cup water. Cover. Rearrange once. Let stand 3 minutes.
frozen	10-oz. pkg.	7 to 10 min.	1-qt. casserole with 2 tablespoons water. Cover. Stir once. Let stand 3 minutes.
Brussels Sprouts, fresh	1 lb.	4 to 8 min.	Cut "X" in bottom of each sprout. 1½-qt. casserole with ¼ cup water. Cover. Stir once. Let stand 3 minutes.
frozen	1 lb.	6 to 8 min.	1-qt. casserole with 2 tablespoons water. Cover. Stir once. Let stand 3 minutes.
Cabbage, Shredded, fresh	¾ lb. (4 cups)	6 to 9 min.	1-qt. casserole with ¼ cup water. Cover. Stir once. Let stand 3 minutes.
Wedges, fresh	1 med. head (about 1½ lbs.)	12 to 19 min.	Cut into 4 wedges. 10-in. square casserole with ¼ cup water. Cover. Rotate dish once. Let stand 3 minutes.
Carrots, Sliced, fresh	2 cups sliced (⅛ in. thick)	4 to 8 min.	1-qt. casserole with 2 tablespoons water. Cover. Stir once. Let stand 3 minutes.
frozen	2 cups	6 to 8 min.	1-qt. casserole with 2 tablespoons water. Cover. Stir once. Let stand 3 minutes.
Baby, frozen	2 cups	5 to 7 min.	1-qt. casserole with 2 tablespoons water. Cover. Stir once. Let stand 3 minutes.
Cauliflower, Whole, fresh	1 med. (about 2 lbs.)	7½ to 14 min.	Remove leaf and stem. Rinse. Place core-side-up on platter. Cover with plastic wrap. Turn over after ½ time. Let stand 5 minutes.

Type	Amount	Microwave Time at High	Procedure
Cauliflower, Continued Flowerets, fresh	1 med. (about 2 lbs.) (5 cups)	7 to 10 min.	1½-qt. casserole with ¼ cup water. Cover. Stir once. Let stand 5 minutes.
frozen	10-oz. pkg.	5 to 8 min.	1-qt. casserole with 2 tablespoons water. Cover. Stir once. Let stand 3 minutes.
Corn, on Cob, fresh	2 med. ears 4 med. ears	5 to 10 min. 8 to 16 min.	Remove husk. 10-in. square casserole with 2 tablespoons water. Cover. Rearrange once. Let stand 5 minutes.
frozen	2 small ears 4 small ears	3 to 7 min. 5 to 10 min.	9-in. square baking dish with 2 tablespoons water. Cover. Rearrange once. Let stand 5 minutes.
Whole Kernel, frozen	10-oz. pkg.	5 to 7 min.	1-qt. casserole with 2 tablespoons water. Cover. Stir once. Let stand 3 minutes.
Peas, Black-eyed, frozen	10-oz. pkg.	8 to 9 min.	1-qt. casserole with ¼ cup water. Cover. Stir once. Let stand 3 minutes.
Green, fresh	2 cups (about 2 lbs.)	4 to 6 min.	Shell peas. 1-qt. casserole with ¼ cup water. Cover. Stir once. Let stand 3 minutes.
frozen	10-oz. pkg.	6 to 8 min.	1-qt. casserole with 2 tablespoons water. Cover. Stir once. Let stand 2 minutes.
Potatoes, Baking	2 med. 4 med.	6½ to 8 min. 10 to 14 min.	Pierce. Arrange in circle on paper towel in oven. Rearrange once. Let stand, wrapped in foil, 5 to 10 minutes.
New	1 lb. (2-in. dia.)	8 to 10 min.	Peel. Cut large potatoes. 1½-qt. casserole with ¼ cup water. Cover. Stir once. Let stand 5 minutes.
Spinach, fresh	1 lb.	6 to 9 min.	Wash. 2-qt. casserole with ¼ cup water. Cover. Stir once. Let stand 3 minutes.
frozen	10-oz. pkg.	5 to 8 min.	1-qt. casserole with 2 tablespoons water. Cover. Stir once. Let stand 3 minutes.
Squash, Acorn, fresh	1 whole 2 whole	8½ to 11 min. 13 to 16 min.	Cut in halves. Remove seeds. 9 or 10-in. baking dish with ¼ cup water. Cover with plastic wrap. Rearrange once. Let stand 5 minutes.
Mashed, frozen	10-oz. pkg.	6 to 8 min.	1-qt. casserole with no water. Cover. Stir once. Let stand 3 minutes.
Zucchini, Sliced, fresh	2 cups	3½ to 5½ min.	1-qt. casserole with 2 tablespoons water. Cover. Stir twice. Let stand 3 minutes.
Sweet Potatoes	2 small 4 small	5 to 9 min. 8 to 13 min.	Pierce. Arrange in circle on paper towel in oven. Rearrange once. Let stand, wrapped in foil, 5 to 10 minutes.

◄ Harvard Beets

2 teaspoons cornstarch
¼ teaspoon salt, optional
Dash pepper
Dash ground cloves
2 tablespoons cider vinegar
1 can (16 oz.) sliced beets, drained, ⅓ cup liquid reserved
1 tablespoon orange juice

Serves 4

In 1-qt. casserole combine cornstarch, salt, pepper and cloves. Blend in vinegar, beet liquid and orange juice.

Microwave at High 1¾ to 2½ minutes, or until clear and thickened, stirring every minute. Add beets. Microwave at High 1 to 4 minutes, or until beets are thoroughly heated.

Per Serving:
Calories: 40
Sodium: 172 mg.
Cholesterol: 0
Exchanges: 1½ vegetable

Broccoli & Cauliflower ▲ With Mustard Sauce

2 cups fresh broccoli flowerets
2 cups fresh cauliflowerets
⅓ to ½ cup skim milk
1 tablespoon all-purpose flour
2 teaspoons prepared mustard
¼ teaspoon salt, optional
Dash onion powder

Serves 4

Combine broccoli and cauliflower in baking dish. Cover. Microwave at High 8 to 11 minutes, or until tender, stirring once. Drain; set aside.

In medium bowl blend remaining ingredients with wire whip. Microwave at High 2 to 3 minutes, or until thickened, stirring every minute. Pour over vegetables. Toss to coat.

Per Serving:
Calories: 50
Sodium: 166 mg.
Cholesterol: 0
Exchanges: 2 vegetable

Italian Broccoli ▶ With Tomatoes

4 cups fresh broccoli flowerets
½ cup water
½ teaspoon oregano leaves
¼ teaspoon salt, optional
⅛ teaspoon pepper
2 medium tomatoes, cut
    into wedges
½ cup shredded mozzarella
    cheese

Serves 4

Place broccoli and water in 2-qt. casserole; cover. Microwave at High 5 to 8 minutes, or until tender-crisp. Drain. Stir in seasonings and tomatoes. Microwave, uncovered, at High 2 to 4 minutes, or until tomatoes are hot. Sprinkle with mozzarella. Microwave 1 minute, or until cheese melts.

Per Serving:
  Calories: 100
  Sodium: 160 mg.
  Cholesterol: 9 mg.
  Exchanges: 2½ vegetable, ½
                high fat meat

Lemon Brussels Sprouts ▶

. 1 pkg. (10 oz.) frozen
    Brussels sprouts
1 tablespoon water
½ teaspoon lemon juice
⅛ teaspoon grated lemon peel
⅛ teaspoon salt, optional
    Dash pepper

Serves 4

In 1-qt. casserole combine Brussels sprouts, water, lemon juice and lemon peel; cover. Microwave at High 3 minutes. Stir to break apart; re-cover. Microwave at High 2 to 3 minutes, or until Brussels sprouts are tender. Drain; sprinkle with seasonings.

Per Serving:
  Calories: 25
  Sodium: 63 mg.
  Cholesterol: 0
  Exchanges: 1 vegetable

Mushrooms Sautéed ▲ in Sherry

¼ cup chopped green onion
¼ cup sherry
½ teaspoon salt
⅛ teaspoon pepper
16 oz. fresh mushrooms, rinsed
    and drained, halved
2 tablespoons butter or
    margarine, optional

Serves 4 to 6

In 2-qt. casserole combine onion, sherry, salt and pepper. Add mushrooms; stir to coat. Dot with butter. Cover dish with wax paper. Microwave at High 3 to 7 minutes, or until desired doneness, stirring after half the cooking time.

Serve with steak or hamburgers.

Mushrooms in Garlic Butter

¼ cup butter or margarine
2 cloves garlic, minced
12 oz. fresh mushrooms, sliced
¼ teaspoon salt
    Dash pepper

Serves 4

Place butter and garlic in 2-qt. casserole. Microwave at High 2½ to 3½ minutes, or until butter melts and garlic browns; stir after half the time.

Add mushrooms, salt and pepper; stir to coat. Cover dish with wax paper. Microwave at High 3 to 5 minutes, or until desired doneness, stirring after half the cooking time.

Serve with steak or hamburgers.

Pickled Mushrooms

12 oz. fresh mushrooms, sliced
1 medium onion, thinly sliced
1 green pepper, cut into strips
1 clove garlic, minced
½ cup wine vinegar
3 tablespoons olive oil
¼ cup chopped stuffed
    green olives
1 teaspoon parsley flakes
½ teaspoon salt
¼ teaspoon black pepper
⅛ teaspoon whole thyme
1 bay leaf

Serves 6

Combine all ingredients in 2-qt. casserole; cover. Microwave at High 5 to 7 minutes, or until vegetables are tender-crisp, stirring after half the time. Refrigerate 6 to 8 hours. Drain.

Corn on the Cob ▶

10 to 12 ears corn in husk

Herb Butter, below

Serves 10 to 12

Arrange 1 to 4 unhusked ears of corn on oven floor with space between. No preparation is needed. Microwave following times in chart. Let stand 5 minutes. Husk corn after standing. Using paper napkin, hold corn with tip pointing down. Pull back leaves carefully to avoid steam. Grasp silk in other hand and pull sharply.

Amt.	Microwave Time	Procedure
1	3 to 5 min.	Turn over;
2	4 to 9 min.	rearrange after half the time.
3	9 to 12 min.	Turn over;
4	10 to 17 min.	rearrange every 4 minutes.

Herb Butter for Corn

1 cup butter or margarine
1 teaspoon dried chives
½ teaspoon sugar
½ teaspoon salt
¼ teaspoon pepper
2 tablespoons grated Parmesan cheese

Makes about 1 cup

In 1-qt. casserole combine butter, chives, sugar, salt and pepper. Microwave at High 2 to 3 minutes, or until butter melts, stirring after half the time. Stir in Parmesan cheese. Serve with corn on the cob.

Sweet & Sour Beans ▲

1 lb. fresh green beans, cut
   into 1-in. pieces
⅓ cup water
2 tablespoons brown sugar
2 teaspoons cornstarch
3 tablespoons lemon juice
1 tablespoon butter or
   margarine

Topping:
¼ cup dry bread crumbs
¼ cup slivered almonds
1 tablespoon butter or
   margarine, softened
Dash nutmeg

Serves 6

In 1½ to 2-qt. casserole combine beans and water; cover.
Microwave at High 9 to 11 minutes, or until tender-crisp, stirring
after half the cooking time. Let stand 5 minutes. Drain, reserving ¼
cup liquid. Set beans aside.

In small bowl or 2-cup measure, combine brown sugar and
cornstarch. Add lemon juice and reserved bean liquid. Microwave
at High 1½ to 2 minutes, or until thickened, stirring after half the
cooking time. Stir in butter.

Add thickened sauce mixture to beans. Combine topping
ingredients. Sprinkle over beans. Microwave, uncovered, at High 1
to 1½ minutes.

Variations:

Substitute 2 pkgs. (9 oz. each) frozen cut green beans for fresh.

Substitute 2 cans (15½ oz. each) cut green beans for fresh. Drain,
reserving ¼ cup bean liquid. Microwave beans and reserved liquid
at High 3 to 4 minutes, or until thoroughly heated. Drain, reserving
¼ cup liquid. Continue as directed above.

Herbed Green Beans ▲

1 pkg. (9 oz.) frozen French
   style green beans
⅓ cup chopped green pepper
¼ cup chopped onion
1 tablespoon olive oil
1 tomato, peeled and chopped
½ teaspoon salt
¼ teaspoon sugar
¼ teaspoon basil leaves
⅛ teaspoon crushed rosemary
Dash black pepper

Serves 4

Prepare beans as directed,
page 194. Set aside.

In small bowl or 1-qt. casserole,
combine green pepper, onion
and oil. Microwave at High 1 to
2 minutes, or until tender.

Drain beans. Add green pepper
mixture and remaining ingredients; cover. Microwave at High
1 to 2 minutes, or until heated.

Herb-steamed Cauliflower

½ cup ready-to-serve
    low-sodium chicken broth
½ teaspoon dried thyme leaves
¼ teaspoon dried marjoram
    leaves
1 bay leaf
1 medium head cauliflower,
    about 1½ lbs., trimmed

4 servings

In 3-quart casserole, combine
chicken broth, thyme, marjoram
and bay leaf. Place cauliflower
in casserole upside down. Cover.
Microwave at High for 13 to 20
minutes, or until base is tender,
turning cauliflower over after half
the time. Let stand, covered, for
5 minutes. Remove bay leaf.

Per Serving:
Calories:	26
Protein:	2 g.
Carbohydrates:	5 g.
Fat:	—
Cholesterol:	—
Sodium:	14 mg.
Calcium:	—
Exchanges:	1 vegetable

Cauliflower & Mushrooms with Yogurt Sauce

2 cups frozen cauliflowerets
2 tablespoons chopped onion
2 tablespoons water
1 tablespoon snipped fresh
    parsley
¼ teaspoon dried marjoram
    leaves

1 cup sliced fresh mushrooms

Yogurt Sauce:
⅓ cup low-fat plain yogurt
⅛ teaspoon salt*
    Dash pepper

4 servings

In 1-quart casserole, combine cauliflowerets, onion, water, parsley
and marjoram. Cover. Microwave at High for 4 minutes. Stir in
mushrooms. Re-cover. Microwave at High for 2 to 4 minutes
longer, or until vegetables are tender-crisp. Drain. Let stand,
covered, while preparing sauce.

In 1-cup measure, blend all sauce ingredients. Microwave at 50%
(Medium) for 30 seconds to 1 minute, or until heated through. Pour
over vegetables.

*To reduce sodium omit salt.

Per Serving:
Calories:	31	Cholesterol:	1 mg.
Protein:	3 g.	Sodium:	76 mg.
Carbohydrates:	5 g.	Calcium:	52 mg.
Fat:	1 g.	Exchanges:	1 vegetable

Nutty Cauliflower ▶ & Carrots

2 cups frozen cauliflowerets
1 cup cooked wild rice,
    page 230
⅓ cup chopped carrot
1 tablespoon slivered almonds
1 tablespoon reduced-calorie
    margarine
¼ teaspoon dried thyme leaves

4 servings

In 2-quart casserole, combine
all ingredients. Mix well. Cover.
Microwave at High for 8 to 9
minutes, or until carrot is tender-
crisp, stirring after half the time.

Per Serving:
Calories:	88
Protein:	3 g.
Carbohydrates:	14 g.
Fat:	5 g.
Cholesterol:	—
Sodium:	36 mg.
Calcium:	—
Exchanges:	1 bread, 1 fat

Glazed Baby Carrots ▲

12 oz. fresh baby carrots,
    scrubbed
2 tablespoons water

Glaze:

1½ tablespoons butter or
    margarine
1½ tablespoons brown sugar
¼ teaspoon cinnamon
⅛ teaspoon ground cloves
⅛ teaspoon salt
2 tablespoons chopped
    pecans, optional

Serves 4

Prepare carrots as directed,
page 194. Set aside.

In small bowl or 1-cup measure
microwave butter at High 30 to
45 seconds, or until melted. Stir
in brown sugar, cinnamon, cloves
and salt. Drain carrots. Pour
glaze over and stir to coat.
Microwave at High 20 seconds
to melt brown sugar, if needed.
Stir. If desired, garnish with
chopped pecans.

Variation:

Substitute 16 oz. frozen whole
baby carrots for the fresh.

Celery Carrots

6 medium carrots,
    sliced ¼ in. thick
2 stalks celery, thinly sliced
2 tablespoons water
½ teaspoon salt
1 can (16 oz.) stewed
    tomatoes, drained, ¼ cup
    liquid reserved
2 tablespoons all-purpose
    flour
4 slices bacon, microwaved
    and crumbled
½ teaspoon sugar
    Dash pepper

Serves 4 to 6

Combine carrots, celery, water
and salt in 1½ to 2-qt.
casserole. Cover. Microwave at
High 7 to 9 minutes, or until fork
tender, stirring after half the
cooking time. Do not drain.

In small dish blend ¼ cup
reserved tomato liquid and flour
until smooth. Add to casserole.

Stir in remaining ingredients.
Cover; microwave at High 3 to 4
minutes, or until thickened,
stirring once during cooking.

Carrots With Onion, ▲ Sour Cream & Dill

6 medium carrots, peeled
    and cut into julienne strips
2 tablespoons water
½ teaspoon salt, divided
¼ cup chopped green onion
¼ cup dairy sour cream
1 tablespoon packed brown
    sugar
¼ teaspoon dill weed

Serves 4 to 6

In 1½ to 2-qt. casserole
combine carrots, water and ¼
teaspoon salt. Cover.
Microwave at High 7 to 8
minutes, or until fork tender,
stirring after half the time. Drain
and reserve 1 tablespoon liquid.

Stir remaining ingredients and
reserved liquid into carrots.
Cover. Microwave at High 1 to 2
minutes, or until green onion is
tender-crisp.

Cheesy Asparagus ►

2 lbs. fresh asparagus, cut
   into 1 to 1½-in. pieces
¼ cup water
3 tablespoons butter or
   margarine, divided
¼ cup fine dry bread crumbs
¼ cup cashews
2 tablespoons all-purpose flour
¼ teaspoon salt
¼ teaspoon dry mustard
⅛ teaspoon pepper
1 cup milk
1 cup shredded Cheddar cheese

Serves 6 to 8

Variation:
Substitute 2 pkgs. (8 oz. each)
frozen cut asparagus spears
for fresh. Reduce water to 2
tablespoons.

How to Microwave Cheesy Asparagus

Combine asparagus and water
in 1½-qt. casserole; cover.
Microwave at High 8 to 12
minutes, or until tender, stirring
once. Drain; set aside.

Melt 1 tablespoon butter in
small bowl at High 30 to 60
seconds. Mix in bread crumbs
and cashews. Set aside.

Melt remaining butter in 1-qt.
measure at High 30 to 60
seconds. Stir in flour and
seasonings. Blend in milk.

Microwave at High 3 to 5
minutes, or until thickened and
bubbly, stirring after 2 minutes
and then every minute.

Remove half of asparagus from
casserole. Spread remaining
asparagus evenly in dish; pour
on half of sauce. Sprinkle half of
cheese over sauce.

Repeat layers. Top with crumb
mixture. Microwave at High 1 to
2 minutes, or until hot and
bubbly, rotating dish ½ turn
after half the time.

203

◄ Cabbage & Noodles

4 cups shredded cabbage
1 small onion, thinly sliced
  and separated into rings
3 tablespoons butter or
  margarine
½ teaspoon poppy seeds
½ teaspoon salt
  Dash pepper
2 cups cooked medium-sized
  egg noodles

Serves 4 to 6

In 2-qt. casserole combine all
ingredients except egg noodles.
Cover. Microwave at High 5 to 6
minutes, or until cabbage is
tender, stirring after half the
cooking time. Stir in noodles.

Cabbage-Bacon Sauté

6 slices bacon
3 cups shredded green
  cabbage
1 cup shredded red cabbage
1 tablespoon sugar
½ teaspoon salt
  Dash pepper
2 tablespoons vinegar

Serves 4

Arrange bacon on rack in
12 × 8-in. dish. Cover with paper
towel. Microwave at High 6
minutes. Let stand 3 to 5 minutes. Crumble bacon. Remove
rack from dish and discard all
but 3 tablespoons fat.

Add crumbled bacon, cab-
bage, sugar, seasonings and
vinegar to dish. Cover with
plastic wrap. Microwave at High
5 minutes, or until cabbage is
tender, stirring after half the
cooking time.

Bok Choy Sauté

3 large stalks bok choy
2 tablespoons butter or
  margarine
2 tablespoons soy sauce
¼ teaspoon garlic powder
1 teaspoon sugar
1 small carrot, cut into
  matchsticks
8 oz. fresh mushrooms,
  sliced

Serves 4 to 6

Slice bok choy stalks into ⅛-in.
slices and leaves into ½-in.
strips. In 2-qt. casserole melt
butter at High 1 to 1½ minutes.

Add soy sauce, garlic powder
and sugar. Stir in carrots, mushrooms and bok choy. Cover.

Microwave at High 4½ to 5½
minutes, or until tender-crisp,
stirring after half the time.

Creamy Sauerkraut

1 tablespoon butter or
  margarine
1 tablespoon all-purpose flour
¼ teaspoon salt
  Dash pepper
½ cup half and half
½ cup milk
1 can (16 oz.) sauerkraut,
  rinsed and drained
1 teaspoon caraway seeds
½ teaspoon sugar

Serves 4

In 1 to 1½-qt. casserole melt
butter at High 30 to 60
seconds. Stir in flour, salt and
pepper. Blend in half and half
and milk. Microwave at High 4
to 6 minutes, or until bubbly
and slightly thickened, stirring
every minute.

Stir in sauerkraut, caraway
seeds and sugar. Microwave at
High 1 to 2 minutes, or until
heated through.

Peas With Lettuce ▲

2 cups fresh shelled or 1 pkg.
   (10 oz.) frozen green peas
⅓ cup thinly sliced celery
2 tablespoons water
3 cups shredded head lettuce
1 tablespoon butter or
   margarine, melted
1 tablespoon all-purpose flour
½ teaspoon sugar
¼ teaspoon salt
   Dash pepper
¼ cup whipping cream

Serves 4

In 1½-qt. casserole combine
peas, celery and water; cover.
Microwave at High 5 to 7½
minutes, or until tender. Stir in
lettuce; re-cover. Microwave at
High 1 to 2 minutes, stirring
after every minute. Set aside.

In small dish combine butter,
flour, sugar, salt and pepper.
Blend in cream. Microwave at
High 1 to 2 minutes, or until
thickened, stirring every minute

Drain vegetables. Add sauce to
vegetables; toss to coat.

Black-eyed Peas & Rice ▶

1 pkg. (10 oz.) frozen
   black-eyed peas
2 slices bacon, microwaved
   crisply, crumbled
1 cup water
½ cup chopped green onion
1 clove garlic, pressed or
   minced
1 tablespoon butter or
   margarine
1 can (16 oz.) stewed
   tomatoes
½ cup long grain rice
⅓ cup water
½ teaspoon salt
¼ teaspoon paprika
   Dash cayenne pepper
   Dash black pepper

Serves 4

Prepare black-eyed peas
following directions, page 195.

Stir in remaining ingredients;
cover. Microwave at High 5
minutes. Reduce power to 50%
(Medium). Microwave 20 to 25
minutes, or until rice is tender
and liquid is absorbed, stirring
twice during cooking.

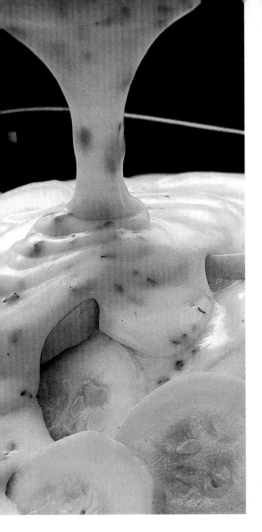

Squash in Cream Sauce ▲

1 lb. yellow summer squash,
    cut into ¼-in. slices
2 tablespoons water
1 tablespoon butter or
    margarine
1 tablespoon all-purpose flour
½ teaspoon chervil
½ teaspoon salt
    Dash pepper
¼ teaspoon sugar
½ cup half and half

Serves 4 to 6

In 1½-qt. casserole combine
squash and water. Cover.
Microwave at High 5 to 7
minutes, or until fork tender; stir
once. Drain and set aside.

In small bowl melt butter at
High 15 to 30 seconds. Stir in
flour, seasonings and sugar.
Blend in half and half. Microwave at High 1½ to 2½ minutes, or until thickened, stirring
twice. Pour sauce over squash
and toss to coat.

Stuffed Zucchini ▲

2 medium zucchini
1 small onion, chopped
1 cup coarsely chopped
    fresh mushrooms
½ cup chopped celery
1 medium tomato, chopped
1 tablespoon butter or
    margarine

¾ cup soda cracker crumbs
1 egg
½ cup grated Cheddar cheese
2 tablespoons grated
    Parmesan cheese
½ teaspoon salt
⅛ teaspoon pepper
½ teaspoon paprika

Serves 4

Halve zucchini lengthwise. Scoop out pulp, leaving ¼-in. shell;
chop pulp coarsely. Combine with onion, mushrooms, celery,
tomatoes and butter in 1½ to 2-qt. casserole. Cover. Microwave at
High 4 to 6 minutes, or until tender, stirring once during cooking
time. Drain.

Stir in cracker crumbs, egg, Cheddar cheese, Parmesan cheese,
salt and pepper. Mound one-fourth of filling in each zucchini shell.
Sprinkle with paprika.

Arrange stuffed zucchini on microwave roasting rack. Cover with
plastic wrap. Microwave at High 5 to 7 minutes, or until filling is set
and zucchini is fork tender, rotating dish ½ turn and rearranging
zucchini after half the cooking time.

Stuffed Tomatoes ▶

4 medium ripe tomatoes
4 slices bacon, cut into ½-in.
  wide strips
2 tablespoons finely
  chopped onion
2 tablespoons finely
  chopped celery
1 cup cooked, drained peas

¼ cup crushed dry bread
  crumbs
1 tablespoon hot water
1 tablespoon grated
  Parmesan cheese
1 teaspoon parsley flakes
⅛ teaspoon thyme leaves
  Dash pepper

Serves 4

Remove stem ends of tomatoes and scoop out center
pulp and seeds. Place tomatoes in 8 × 8-in. baking dish; set aside.

In 1-qt. casserole combine bacon pieces, onion and celery. Cover.
Microwave at High 3 to 4 minutes, or until vegetables are tender.
Stir in peas, bread crumbs, water, cheese and seasonings.

Spoon stuffing into tomatoes. Cover dish with plastic wrap.
Microwave at High 2½ to 3½ minutes, or until tomatoes are heated
through, rotating dish ½ turn after half the time.

Scalloped Tomatoes

4 slices bacon
½ cup chopped celery
⅓ cup chopped onion
2 tablespoons butter or
  margarine
2½ tablespoons all-purpose
  flour
4 medium ripe tomatoes,
  peeled and cut
  into ½-in. cubes

1 cup dry bread cubes,
1½ teaspoons sugar
½ teaspoon salt
¼ teaspoon dry mustard
⅛ teaspoon pepper

Serves 4

Place bacon strips between double thickness of paper towels.
Microwave at High 3 to 4 minutes, or until crisp. Set aside to cool.

In 1 to 1½-qt. casserole combine celery, onion and butter. Cover.
Microwave at High 2 to 4 minutes, or until tender. Stir in flour. Add
tomatoes, bread cubes, sugar, seasonings and 3 bacon strips,
crumbled. Cover.

Microwave at High 4 to 6 minutes, or until thickened and bubbly,
stirring once or twice. Crumble remaining bacon strip and sprinkle
over casserole.

Variation:
Substitute 1 can (16 oz.) whole tomatoes, chopped, drained and ½
cup liquid reserved, for fresh. Follow directions above, adding
reserved liquid with tomatoes to bread cubes, sugar, seasonings
and bacon.

◄ Ratatouille

½ lb. eggplant, cut into
    ½-in. cubes
1 clove garlic, minced
1 small onion, sliced and
    separated into rings
1 small zucchini, thinly sliced
½ medium green pepper,
    cut into thin strips
1 stalk celery, chopped
1 tomato, cut into wedges
    Dash pepper
¼ teaspoon salt, optional
¼ teaspoon basil leaves
¼ teaspoon oregano leaves
⅛ teaspoon thyme leaves
1 tablespoon grated Parmesan
    cheese

Serves 6

Combine all ingredients in 2-qt.
casserole; cover. Microwave
at High 7 to 10 minutes, or
until eggplant is translucent,
stirring 2 or 3 times.

Per Serving:
  Calories: 33
  Sodium: 105 mg.
  Cholesterol: 3 mg.
  Exchanges: 1 vegetable

Stewed Tomatoes

3 cups hot water
4 tomatoes
¼ cup chopped onion
½ teaspoon savory leaves
¼ teaspoon basil leaves
½ teaspoon salt, optional
⅛ teaspoon pepper
1 tablespoon grated Parmesan
    cheese

Serves 4

Measure water into 2-qt. bowl or
casserole. Microwave at High 6
to 10 minutes, or until boiling.
Immerse tomatoes and let stand
1 to 2 minutes, or until skins slip
off easily. Peel. Cut each tomato
into 1-in. cubes. Combine
tomatoes and remaining
ingredients in 2-qt. casserole.
Microwave at High 5 to 7
minutes, or until tomatoes soften
and mixture is of sauce-like
consistency, stirring twice.

Per Serving:
  Calories: 34
  Sodium: 274 mg.
  Cholesterol: 4 mg.
  Exchanges: 1 vegetable

◄ Zucchini With Pimiento

2 cups thinly sliced zucchini
    (2 medium)
1 jar (2 oz.) pimiento, drained
    and diced
½ teaspoon salt, optional
½ teaspoon basil leaves
1 small onion, chopped
⅛ teaspoon garlic powder
⅛ teaspoon pepper
¼ teaspoon imitation butter
    flavor

Serves 4

In 2-qt. casserole mix together
all ingredients; cover. Microwave at High 6 to 7 minutes, or
until fork tender, stirring once.

Per Serving:
  Calories: 25
  Sodium: 254 mg.
  Cholesterol: 0
  Exchanges: 1 vegetable

Scalloped Onions With Cheese ▲

2 medium onions (1 lb.),
    peeled, thinly sliced and
    separated into rings
2 tablespoons water
2 tablespoons butter or
    margarine
2 tablespoons all-purpose
    flour

1 teaspoon parsley flakes
¼ teaspoon salt
¼ teaspoon dry mustard
⅛ teaspoon pepper
1 cup milk
½ cup shredded Cheddar
    cheese

Serves 4

In 2-qt. casserole combine onions and water. Cover. Microwave at
High 5 to 7½ minutes, or until tender, stirring after half the cooking
time. Set aside.

Place butter in 1-qt. casserole. Microwave at High 45 to 60
seconds, or until melted. Stir in flour and seasonings. Blend in milk.
Microwave at High 2½ to 3½ minutes, or until thickened, stirring
after 2 minutes and then every minute.

Drain onions. Stir into white sauce. Sprinkle cheese evenly over
top. Reduce power to 50% (Medium). Microwave 2 to 4 minutes,
or until cheese melts, rotating dish ½ turn after half the time.

Creamed Onions ▲

16 small onions, peeled, or 4
    medium onions, peeled
    and cut into quarters
2 tablespoons water
¾ cup dairy sour cream
¼ cup milk
½ teaspoon salt
    Dash nutmeg
    Dash pepper

Serves 4

In 1½-qt. casserole combine
onions and water. Cover.
Microwave at High 7 to 8
minutes, or until tender, stirring
gently once. Drain.

Combine remaining ingredients.
Pour sour cream mixture over
onions; toss gently to coat.
Reduce power to 50%
(Medium). Microwave,
uncovered, 1 to 2 minutes, or
until sauce is heated through.

Sweet-Sour Spinach ▲

1 lb. fresh spinach
4 slices bacon, cut into eighths
1 tablespoon all-purpose flour
1 tablespoon brown sugar
¼ teaspoon dry mustard
¼ teaspoon salt
   Dash pepper
½ cup half and half
1 tablespoon cider vinegar

Serves 4

Prepare spinach as directed, page 195. Drain; set aside. Microwave bacon in 1½-qt. covered casserole at High 3 to 4 minutes, or until crisp. Drain all but 1 tablespoon fat.

Stir in flour, sugar and seasonings. Blend in half and half. Microwave at High 1 to 1½ minutes, or until thickened; stir once. Stir in vinegar and spinach; toss. Microwave at High 1 to 2 minutes, or until heated.

Lettuce Braised in Stock ▲

¼ cup hot water
1 teaspoon instant chicken
   bouillon granules
4 cups shredded lettuce
1 small carrot, shredded
2 tablespoons chopped onion
2 tablespoons butter or
   margarine
½ teaspoon parsley flakes
⅛ teaspoon salt
   Dash white pepper

Serves 4

In small bowl or 1-cup measure, combine hot water and bouillon. Stir to dissolve.

Combine remaining ingredients in 1½ to 2-qt. casserole. Stir in bouillon. Cover. Microwave at High 2 to 4 minutes, or until lettuce is tender-crisp, stirring after half the cooking time.

Greens With Bacon ▲

4 slices bacon, cut into ¾-in.
   pieces
¼ cup chopped onion
½ teaspoon lemon juice
⅛ teaspoon salt
   Dash nutmeg
   Dash pepper
1 lb. fresh greens (collard,
   mustard or turnip), washed,
   drained and cut into
   1-in. strips

Serves 4

In 3-qt. casserole combine bacon and onion. Cover. Microwave at High 4 to 6 minutes, or until bacon is crisp, stirring after half the time.

Mix in lemon juice and seasonings. Add greens and toss to coat. Cover. Microwave at High 4 to 6 minutes, or until tender-crisp, stirring once.

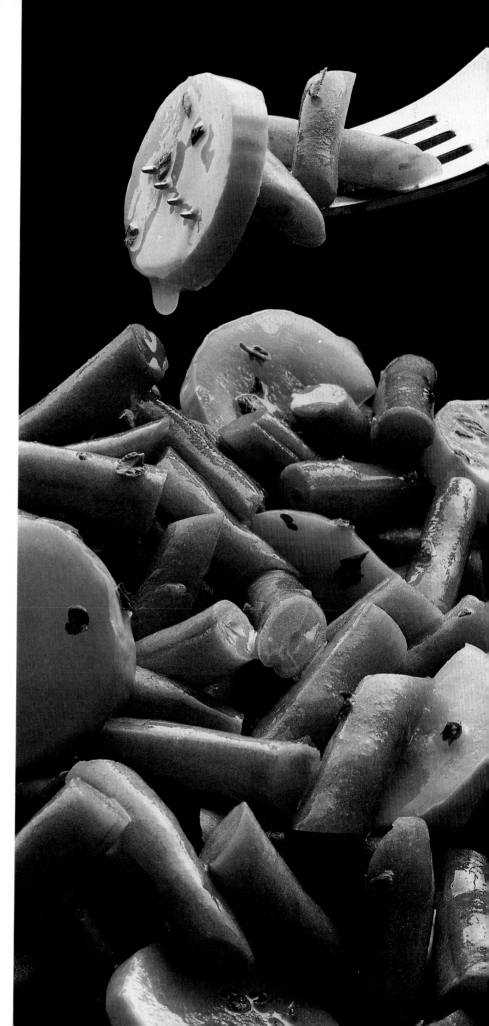

Summer Vegetable Combo

1 pkg. (10 oz.) frozen cut green
    beans
8 oz. crookneck squash, sliced
    ¼ inch thick
2 tablespoons water
2 tablespoons reduced-calorie
    margarine
½ teaspoon dried parsley flakes
¼ teaspoon onion powder
⅛ teaspoon dried oregano
    leaves
⅛ teaspoon garlic powder
    Dash pepper

6 servings

In 1½-quart casserole, combine
beans, squash and water. Cover.
Microwave at High for 7 to 11
minutes, or until vegetables are
tender-crisp, stirring twice. Set
vegetables aside.

In 1-cup measure, combine
remaining ingredients. Mix well.
Microwave at 70% (Medium
High) for 20 to 30 seconds, or
just until margarine melts. Drain
vegetables. Pour margarine
mixture over vegetables. Stir
to coat.

Per Serving:
Calories:	57
Protein:	2 g.
Carbohydrates:	7 g.
Fat:	5 g.
Cholesterol:	—
Sodium:	39 mg.
Calcium:	43 mg.
Exchanges:	1 vegetable, 1 fat

Stir-Fried Vegetables

The browning dish gives these combinations, which serve 3 to 4, the flavor and texture of stir-fries, but they are stirred only once. Before using, frozen vegetables should be microwaved in the package 2 to 3 minutes at High, or until they can be separated.

Corn, Peppers & Onions

1 pkg. (10-oz.) frozen corn, separated
⅓ cup ⅜-in. green pepper squares
⅓ cup ⅜-in. onion squares

Time: 4½ to 7½ minutes

Carrots & Celery

1 cup ⅛-in. thick carrot slices
1 cup ¼-in. thick celery slices

Time: 3½ to 5½ minutes

Broccoli & Cauliflowerets

1 to 1⅓ cups broccoli stems (cut in ½ if over 1-in. thick)
1 to 1⅓ cups cauliflowerets (large ones halved or quartered)
¼ cup sliced almonds, optional
1½ teaspoons soy sauce, optional

Time: 4 to 6½ minutes

Pea Pods, Mushrooms & Fresh Bean Sprouts ▲

1 pkg. (6-oz.) frozen pea pods, separated
1 cup ⅛-in. thick fresh mushroom slices
½ cup fresh bean sprouts or ½ cup canned bamboo shoots

Time: 3½ to 6½ minutes

How to Microwave Stir-Fried Vegetables

Preheat browning dish 1 to 2 minutes, depending on size.

Add 2 tablespoons butter or margarine and remaining ingredients. Cover.

Microwave at High, stirring after ½ the cooking time.

Italian Potatoes with Fennel ▲

3 tablespoons reduced-calorie
    Italian dressing
2 tablespoons sliced green
    onion
1 tablespoon snipped fresh
    parsley
⅛ teaspoon fennel seed,
    crushed

Dash pepper
2 medium white potatoes,
    sliced ¼ inch thick
1 tablespoon grated Parmesan
    cheese

4 servings

In 2-quart casserole, combine all ingredients, except potatoes and
Parmesan cheese. Stir. Add potatoes. Mix well. Cover. Microwave
at High for 9 to 12 minutes, or until tender, stirring twice. Let stand,
covered, for 4 minutes. Stir. Sprinkle with Parmesan cheese.

Per Serving:

Calories:	87	Cholesterol:	2 mg.
Protein:	2 g.	Sodium:	116 mg.
Carbohydrates:	17 g.	Calcium:	—
Fat:	1 g.	Exchanges:	1 bread

Tropical Yams

1¼ lbs. fresh yams or sweet
    potatoes
2 tablespoons frozen
    pineapple-orange juice
    concentrate
1 tablespoon reduced-calorie
    margarine

4 servings

Peel yams. Cut into ¼-inch
slices. In 1-quart casserole,
combine yams, pineapple-
orange juice concentrate and
margarine. Stir. Cover. Microwave at High for 10 to 13
minutes, or until tender, stirring
2 or 3 times. Let stand,
covered, for 2 minutes.

Per Serving:

Calories:	154
Protein:	2 g.
Carbohydrates:	29 g.
Fat:	4 g.
Cholesterol:	—
Sodium:	40 mg.
Calcium:	—
Exchanges:	2 bread, ½ fat

Baked Potatoes

The potato is an ideal microwave vegetable. Its high moisture content attracts microwave energy, and the natural tight covering holds in steam. The potato's uniform density helps it cook evenly. Times below are for medium size potatoes (5 to 7-oz.).

High Power

1 potato	3-5 min.
2 potatoes	5-7½ min.
3 potatoes	7-10 min.
4 potatoes	10½-12½ min.

How to Microwave Baked Potatoes

Prick well-scrubbed potatoes twice with a fork, so that some steam can escape during microwaving. Place a layer of paper towel on the oven floor to absorb moisture from trapped steam.

Arrange potatoes at least 1 inch apart so that microwave energy can penetrate from all sides.

Twice-Baked Potatoes

For each potato:	Optional:
1 to 2 tablespoons butter	Chopped chives
2 tablespoons milk or sour cream	Shredded cheese
Salt and pepper	Crumbled crisp bacon

After standing time, slice top from each potato; scoop out center. Set shells aside, and mash potatoes with butter and milk. Season; spoon into shells. Chives, cheese or bacon may be mixed into potatoes or used as a topping after reheating. To reheat potatoes before serving, microwave at High about 1 minute per potato. Add an extra ½ minute if potato has been refrigerated.

Turn potatoes over and rearrange them half way through the cooking time. This helps them cook more evenly.

Wrap potatoes in foil, shiny side in, or place them on a counter and cover with a casserole to hold in heat. They will still feel slightly firm, but will complete cooking during 5 to 10 minutes standing time. Potatoes will retain their heat about 45 minutes.

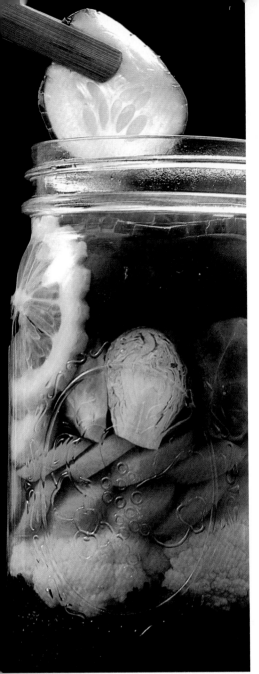

Pickles & Relishes

It's easy to microwave small batches of jellies, pickles and fruit syrups. Microwaving is cooler, cleaner, and faster than conventional methods, and small batches can provide more variety. These homemade specialties have true, natural flavor. They make welcome gifts when presented in an attractive bottle.

Pickles

These pickles are prepared in a quick pickling liquid, and are packed into sterilized jars after microwaving. They are not pressure- or water bath-canned so they require refrigeration.

◄ Antipasto Jar

Pickling Liquid:

1 cup water	1 tablespoon salt
½ cup cider vinegar	1 tablespoon vegetable oil

Three cups fresh vegetables: Use a combination of the following to equal 3 cups:

Broccoli flowerets and stalks, sliced ¼ in. thick

Brussels sprouts (¼ lb.), cut in half lengthwise

Sliced carrots, ¼-in. thick

Cauliflowerets

½ cup water

One cup fresh vegetables: Use a combination of the following to equal 1 cup:

Fresh whole mushrooms, 1-in. diameter

Green or ripe olives

Green pepper, cut into 1-in. pieces

Sliced cucumber

Garnish: Add one or more of the following:

1 lemon slice

1 bay leaf

1 sprig fresh dill, basil or oregano

Makes 1 quart

Follow photo directions, below.

How to Microwave Antipasto Jar

Mix pickling liquid in 4-cup measure. Microwave at High 3½ to 5½ minutes, or until boiling, stirring after half the time.

Combine desired 3 cups vegetables in 2-qt. casserole. Add ½ cup water. Cover.

Microwave at High 2 to 4 minutes, or until color of vegetables intensifies, stirring once.

Pickled Carrots

12 oz. fresh tiny whole carrots
¼ cup water

Pickling Liquid:
½ cup cider vinegar
⅓ cup sugar
½ to 1 teaspoon salt
⅛ teaspoon celery seed
⅛ teaspoon mustard seed
⅛ teaspoon dried crushed red
    pepper
4 whole cloves
4 whole peppercorns
2 small cloves garlic, peeled
1 bay leaf
1 stick cinnamon

Makes 1 pint

Wash and scrub or peel carrots; trim ends. Place in 1½-qt. casserole. Add water; cover. Microwave at High 3 to 4 minutes, or until tender-crisp, stirring after half the time. Place under cold running water until cool. Drain. Pack into sterilized 1-pint jar or two ½-pint jars. Set aside.

In 2-cup measure combine pickling liquid ingredients. Microwave at High 1 to 2 minutes, or until boiling, stirring after half the time to dissolve the sugar and salt. Pour over carrots in the jar. Cover. Refrigerate 1 week before serving. Store in refrigerator no longer than 1 month.

Place immediately under cold running water until cool. Drain. Add remaining 1 cup vegetables.

Pack vegetables into sterilized 1-qt. jar, layering if desired. Include choice of garnish.

Pour pickling liquid over vegetables. Cover. Refrigerate 2 to 3 days before serving. Store in refrigerator no longer than 1 month.

Watermelon Pickles

1 lb. watermelon rind
½ cup sugar
½ cup cider vinegar
1 tablespoon chopped
    crystallized ginger
2 teaspoons grated fresh
    orange peel or 1 teaspoon
    Dried Orange Peel, page
    285
4 whole cloves
1 stick cinnamon

Makes 1 pint

Trim dark green outer skin from
rind. Cut trimmed rind into 1-in.
chunks. (Yields 3 cups.) Place
chunks in 1½-qt. casserole.
Add sugar, tossing to coat.
Cover and let stand overnight.

Stir in vinegar, ginger, orange
peel and cloves. Add cinnamon.
Microwave, uncovered, at High
10 to 13 minutes, or until
chunks are transparent, stirring
every 3 minutes. Remove
cinnamon stick. Spoon into hot
sterilized 1-pint jar; cover.
Refrigerate 1 week before
serving. Store in refrigerator no
longer than 1 month.

Cabbage Relish

2½ cups shredded green or
    red cabbage
¾ cup chopped red onion
½ cup chopped green pepper
1 cup white vinegar
⅔ cup sugar
2 teaspoons salt
½ teaspoon celery seed
½ teaspoon mustard seed
¼ teaspoon ground turmeric

Makes 2 pints

In medium bowl combine
cabbage, red onion and green
pepper. Divide mixture equally
between two sterilized 1-pint
jars. Set aside.

In 4-cup measure combine
vinegar, sugar, salt, celery
seed, mustard seed and
turmeric. Microwave at High 2
to 4 minutes, or until boiling,
stirring after half the time to
dissolve sugar and salt. Divide
between the two jars; cover.
Refrigerate 1 week before
serving. Store in refrigerator no
longer than 1 month.

Corn Relish

3 cups frozen whole kernel
    corn
½ cup chopped green pepper
¼ cup chopped onion
2 tablespoons chopped
    pimiento, drained
1 cup white vinegar
⅔ cup sugar
1 teaspoon salt
1 teaspoon celery seed
½ teaspoon mustard seed
½ to ¾ teaspoon red pepper
    sauce

Makes 2 pints

In medium bowl combine corn,
green pepper, onion and
pimiento. Microwave at High 1½
to 2½ minutes, or until corn is
defrosted but cool to the touch,
stirring after half the time. Divide
equally between two sterilized
1-pint jars. Set aside.

In 4-cup measure combine
remaining ingredients. Microwave
at High 2 to 4 minutes, or until
boiling, stirring after half the
time to dissolve sugar and salt.
Divide mixture between the two
jars; cover. Refrigerate 1 week
before serving. Store in refrigerator no longer than 1 month.

Apple-Pear Chutney

- 2 medium apples, cored and chopped
- 2 medium pears, peeled, cored and chopped
- 1½ cups packed dark brown sugar
- 1 cup cider vinegar
- ¾ cup chopped onion
- ⅔ cup chopped green pepper
- ½ cup chopped dates
- 1 tablespoon chopped crystallized ginger
- 1 teaspoon salt
- 1 teaspoon dry mustard
- 4 whole cloves
- 4 whole allspice
- 2 bay leaves
- 1 stick cinnamon

Makes 2 pints

Combine apples, pears, brown sugar, vinegar, onion and green pepper. Process in food processor, turning motor on and off 4 to 6 times, or place in blender and process 10 to 15 seconds, or until chopped but not puréed. (Process in two batches, if necessary.) Place mixture in 2-qt. casserole. Stir in remaining ingredients.

Microwave at High 18 to 25 minutes, or until very thick, stirring 3 or 4 times. Cool to room temperature. Discard bay leaves and cinnamon stick.

Divide equally between two sterilized 1-pint jars; cover. Refrigerate 1 week before serving. Store in refrigerator no longer than 1 month.

NOTE: Use as a condiment for meat or curry dishes.

Transform Leftovers

Save watermelon rind for Watermelon Pickles, opposite. Use leftover cabbage in Cabbage Relish, opposite. When you fix a selection of raw vegetables for a relish or appetizer tray, set some aside to make an Antipasto Jar, page 216, the next day.

Salads

Turkey & Spinach Salad ▲

¾ lb. fresh spinach, trimmed
 and torn into bite-size
 pieces, about 6 cups
1 can (11 oz.) mandarin
 oranges, drained
1 cup fresh bean sprouts
8 oz. smoked turkey, cut into
 3 × ¼-inch strips
½ cup walnut halves
2 slices bacon, cut-up
 Vegetable oil
3 tablespoons cider vinegar
1 teaspoon freeze-dried chives
¼ teaspoon onion salt
¼ teaspoon dry mustard
 Dash pepper

6 to 8 servings

In large mixing bowl, layer
spinach, oranges, bean sprouts,
turkey and walnuts. Set aside.
Place bacon in 2-cup measure.
Microwave at High for 2½ to 3½
minutes, or until crisp, stirring
1 or 2 times. Remove bacon
with slotted spoon. Reserve
bacon fat. Add bacon to salad
mixture. Set aside. Add vegetable oil to bacon fat to equal
¼ cup. Stir in remaining ingredients. Microwave at High for
30 to 45 seconds, or until hot.
Stir to blend. Pour over salad.
Toss to coat.

Salmon Potato Salad

2 baking potatoes (8 oz. each)
 cut into ½-inch cubes
¼ cup sliced green onions
1 tablespoon snipped fresh
 parsley
1 tablespoon olive oil
½ teaspoon salt
¼ teaspoon dried dill weed
¼ teaspoon grated lemon peel

1 pkg. (10 oz.) frozen
 asparagus cuts
1 can (7½ oz.) salmon,
 drained and flaked
⅓ cup mayonnaise
2 tablespoons dairy sour
 cream
2 teaspoons Dijon mustard

4 servings

In 2-quart casserole, combine potatoes, onions, parsley, olive oil, salt,
dill and lemon peel. Cover. Microwave at High for 7 to 10 minutes,
or until potatoes are tender, stirring after every 3 minutes. Set aside.

Unwrap asparagus and place in 1-quart casserole. Cover. Microwave at High for 3 to 4 minutes, or until defrosted, stirring after half
the time to break apart. Drain. Add to potato mixture. Remove
bones and skin from salmon. Combine salmon with potato mixture.
Mix well. In small mixing bowl, blend mayonnaise, sour cream and
mustard. Spoon dressing over each serving of salad.

Hot Chicken Waldorf in Puff Pastry Shells ◄

1 can (6¾ oz.) chunk chicken, drained
⅔ cup chopped apple
½ cup shredded Swiss cheese
½ cup mayonnaise
2 tablespoons finely chopped celery
2 tablespoons sunflower nuts
1 tablespoon sliced green onion
1 teaspoon lemon juice
¼ teaspoon lemon pepper seasoning
6 baked individual pastry shells

6 servings

In 1-quart casserole, combine all ingredients, except pastry shells. Mix well. Microwave at High for 2½ to 4 minutes, or until mixture is hot and cheese melts, stirring twice. Spoon chicken mixture into puff pastry shells.

Hot Chicken Waldorf Sandwiches: Follow recipe above, except substitute 6 whole wheat hamburger buns, split, for pastry shells. Combine chicken mixture in small mixing bowl. Arrange bottom half of buns on paper towel-lined platter. Top each with about ⅓ cup chicken mixture. Microwave at High for 3 to 5 minutes, or until mixture is hot and cheese melts, rotating platter once. Top with remaining bun halves.

Tropical Chicken-Melon Salad

1 pkg. (7 oz.) uncooked spaghetti
2 slices bacon, cut-up
1 boneless whole chicken breast (8 to 10 oz.) skin removed, cut into ¾-inch cubes
1 small onion, thinly sliced

½ teaspoon dried marjoram leaves
½ teaspoon salt
⅓ cup mayonnaise
2 cups cubed cantaloupe, ¾-inch cubes
1 avocado, cut into ¾-inch cubes

4 to 6 servings

Cook spaghetti as directed on package. Drain. Set aside. Place bacon in 2-quart casserole. Microwave at High for 2½ to 3½ minutes, or until bacon is crisp, stirring 1 or 2 times. Remove bacon with slotted spoon. Set aside. In same casserole, combine bacon fat, chicken, onion, marjoram and salt. Mix well. Cover. Microwave at High for 3½ to 4 minutes, or until chicken is no longer pink, stirring after every 2 minutes. Drain. Reserve liquid. In small mixing bowl, combine reserved liquid, mayonnaise and bacon. Pour mayonnaise mixture over spaghetti. Toss to coat. Add cantaloupe to chicken mixture. Serve spaghetti topped with cantaloupe and chicken mixture. Top with avocado.

Wurst & German Potato Salad

1 cup water, divided
1½ teaspoons salt, divided
4 medium potatoes, peeled and cooked
4 slices bacon
½ cup chopped onion
¼ cup sugar
2 tablespoons flour
½ teaspoon celery seed
Dash pepper
½ cup cider vinegar
4 smoked bratwurst or knockwurst

Serves 4

How to Microwave Wurst & German Potato Salad

Combine ¼ cup water, ½ teaspoon salt and peeled, quartered potatoes. Cover. Microwave at High 9 to 12 minutes, or until fork tender, rearranging after half the cooking time. Drain and cut into chunks. Can be done the night before.

Place bacon on rack in 12×8-in. dish. Cover with paper towel. Microwave at High 3 to 4 minutes, or until crisp. Drain bacon on paper towels, reserving fat in dish.

Remove rack from dish. Add onion to bacon fat. Microwave 1½ to 2½ minutes, or until tender. Stir in sugar, flour, 1 teaspoon salt, celery seed and pepper.

Mix in ¾ cup water and vinegar. Microwave 5½ to 7 minutes, or until mixture thickens, stirring twice during cooking time. Crumble bacon into hot mixture.

Stir in potato chunks gently. Arrange wurst on top. Microwave 5½ to 7 minutes, or until wurst are hot, rearranging after half the cooking time.

Marinated Chicken ▶ & Bean Salad

1 pkg. (9 oz.) frozen artichoke hearts
1 boneless whole chicken breast (8 to 10 oz.) skin removed, cut into 1-inch cubes
½ cup chopped onion
1 clove garlic, minced
⅛ teaspoon dried crushed sage leaves
⅛ teaspoon dried thyme leaves
1 can (16 oz.) Great Northern beans, rinsed and drained
⅓ cup chopped red pepper
1 tablespoon snipped fresh parsley

Dressing:
3 tablespoons olive oil
2 tablespoons white wine vinegar
1 teaspoon salt
Dash cayenne

6 to 8 servings

Unwrap artichoke hearts and place in 2-quart casserole. Cover. Microwave at High for 3 to 4 minutes, or until slightly warm, stirring after half the time to break apart. Add chicken, onion, garlic, sage and thyme. Re-cover. Microwave at High for 4 to 6½ minutes, or until chicken is no longer pink, stirring twice. Drain. Place chicken mixture in large mixing bowl. Stir in beans, red pepper and parsley. In 1-cup measure, blend all dressing ingredients. Pour over chicken mixture. Toss to coat. Cover. Chill for at least 3 hours before serving.

Mediterranean Chicken Salad ▲

2½ to 3-lb. broiler-fryer chicken, cut into 4 pieces
1 teaspoon dried oregano leaves
½ teaspoon salt
¼ teaspoon pepper
½ cup red wine
2 cups peeled cubed eggplant, ½-inch cubes
½ cup chopped red onion
1 clove garlic, minced
2 medium tomatoes, seeded and chopped
⅓ cup sliced black olives

Dressing:
3 tablespoons olive oil
2 tablespoons lemon juice
1 tablespoon snipped fresh parsley
¾ teaspoon salt
½ teaspoon dried oregano leaves
¼ teaspoon sugar
¼ teaspoon pepper

6 servings

Arrange chicken in shallow 3-quart casserole with thickest portions toward outside of casserole. Sprinkle with oregano, salt and pepper. Pour wine over chicken. Cover. Microwave at High for 16 to 22 minutes, or until chicken near bone is no longer pink and juices run clear, turning chicken over after half the time. Remove chicken. Set aside.

Place 2 tablespoons cooking liquid from chicken in 2-quart casserole. Add eggplant, onion and garlic. Cover. Microwave at High for 5 to 7 minutes, or until eggplant is tender, stirring once. Remove chicken from bones. Cut into bite-size pieces. Add chicken, tomatoes and olives to eggplant mixture. In 1-cup measure, combine all dressing ingredients. Mix well. Pour over chicken and vegetables. Toss to coat. Cover. Chill for at least 3 hours before serving.

Tuna Niçoise

1 lb. new potatoes, thinly sliced
¼ cup olive oil
2 tablespoons red wine vinegar
1 tablespoon snipped fresh parsley
1 clove garlic, minced
½ teaspoon salt
¼ teaspoon dried thyme leaves
⅛ teaspoon pepper
1 pkg. (9 oz.) frozen whole green beans
6 to 8 cherry tomatoes, each cut into 4 pieces
¼ cup pitted black olives, cut in half
   Lettuce leaves
1 can (7 oz.) albacore tuna, drained

4 servings

In 2-quart casserole, combine potatoes, olive oil, vinegar, parsley, garlic, salt, thyme and pepper. Cover. Microwave at High for 7 to 13 minutes, or until tender, stirring after every 3 minutes. Set aside.

Unwrap beans and place in 1-quart casserole. Cover. Microwave at High for 4 to 5 minutes, or until beans are hot, stirring after half the time to break apart. Drain. Add to potato mixture. Re-cover. Chill for 3 to 4 hours. Stir in tomatoes and olives. Arrange lettuce on serving platter. Place flaked tuna in center of lettuce-lined platter. Spoon potato mixture around tuna.

Seafood Pasta Salad ▲

½ cup sliced carrot, ¼ inch thick
½ cup frozen peas
6 tablespoons Italian dressing, divided
¼ lb. bay scallops
¼ lb. extra-small shrimp, shelled and deveined

¼ teaspoon dried basil leaves
1 cup sliced fresh mushrooms
½ cup julienne zucchini (2 × ¼-inch strips)
1 pkg. (7 oz.) uncooked rotini pasta
½ teaspoon salt
⅛ teaspoon pepper

6 to 8 servings

In 1-quart casserole, combine carrot, peas and ¼ cup dressing. Cover. Microwave at High for 2 to 3 minutes, or until colors brighten, stirring once. Set aside. In 9-inch square baking dish, combine scallops and shrimp. Sprinkle with basil. Cover with plastic wrap. Microwave at 70% (Medium High) for 3 to 5 minutes, or until scallops and shrimp are opaque, stirring once or twice. Drain. Combine shrimp and scallops with carrot mixture. Stir in mushrooms and zucchini. Re-cover. Chill for 1 hour.

Cook rotini as directed on package. Rinse with cold water. Drain. Place in large mixing bowl. Mix in seafood and vegetables. In small bowl, blend remaining 2 tablespoons dressing, salt and pepper. Pour over salad. Toss to coat. Re-cover. Chill for at least 2 hours before serving.

Curried Broccoli & Shrimp Salad

2 cups fresh broccoli flowerets
½ cup shredded carrots
1 small onion, thinly sliced
1 clove garlic, minced
2 tablespoons vegetable oil
1 tablespoon honey
½ teaspoon curry powder
¼ teaspoon caraway seed
¼ teaspoon salt
⅛ teaspoon cayenne
1 lb. large shrimp, shelled and deveined
⅓ cup cocktail peanuts

4 servings

In 2-quart casserole, combine broccoli, carrots, onion and garlic. In small mixing bowl, combine oil, honey, curry powder, caraway, salt and cayenne. Pour over vegetables. Cover. Microwave at High for 5 to 6 minutes, or until vegetables are tender-crisp, stirring after half the time. Set aside.

Place shrimp in 1½-quart casserole. Cover. Microwave at 70% (Medium High) for 6 to 12 minutes, or until shrimp are opaque, stirring after every 2 minutes. Drain. Combine shrimp with vegetables. Re-cover. Chill for 3 to 4 hours, stirring once or twice. Stir in peanuts before serving.

Rice & Grains

◄ Wild Rice Medley

1½ cups uncooked wild rice
  5 cups hot water
  ½ cup chopped onion
  ½ cup finely chopped celery
  ¼ cup butter or margarine
  8 oz. fresh mushrooms, sliced
  1 tablespoon instant chicken
    bouillon granules

Serves 8

Rinse rice in wire strainer under cold running water. In 5-qt. casserole combine rice and hot water; cover. Microwave at High 30 to 35 minutes, or until rice is tender and fluffy, stirring every 10 minutes. Let rice stand, covered, 15 minutes.

In 2-qt. casserole combine onion, celery and butter; cover. Microwave at High 2 to 4 minutes, or until onion is tender-crisp. Stir in mushrooms and bouillon granules. Microwave at High 2 to 3 minutes, or until heated. Drain and rinse rice. Mix with vegetables; cover. Microwave at High 3 to 4 minutes, or until heated.

228

Long Grain Rice

⅔ cup uncooked long grain rice
½ teaspoon salt
1⅓ cups hot water
1 tablespoon butter or margarine

Serves 2

Combine all ingredients in 1-qt. casserole; cover. Microwave at High 3 minutes. Reduce power to 50% (Medium). Microwave 7 to 10 minutes, or until liquid is absorbed. Let stand 5 minutes.

Shrimp & Rice

2¾ cups hot water
¼ cup soy sauce
1½ cups uncooked long grain rice
1 tablespoon instant chicken bouillon granules
¼ cup chopped green onion
1 egg, beaten
1 can (4½ oz.) tiny shrimp, drained

Serves 6 to 8

In 3-qt. casserole combine water, soy sauce, rice and bouillon granules. Microwave, covered, at High 5 minutes. Reduce power to 50% (Medium). Microwave 16 to 21 minutes, or until liquid is absorbed. Stir in green onion. Let stand, covered, 5 minutes.

Mix in egg. Microwave at High 2 to 4 minutes, or until egg is set, stirring once. Stir in shrimp.

Advance preparation: Rice can stand, covered, 20 to 25 minutes. Rice can also be made early in the day and refrigerated. To serve, microwave, covered, at High 10 to 15 minutes, or until heated, stirring once or twice.

Saffron Rice

¼ cup chopped green pepper
1 large clove garlic, minced
1 tablespoon olive oil
¼ teaspoon ground saffron
3 cups hot water
1½ cups uncooked long grain rice

Serves 6 to 8

In 3-qt. casserole combine green pepper, garlic, olive oil and saffron. Microwave at High 2 minutes. Add water and rice.

Microwave, covered, at High 5 minutes. Reduce power to 50% (Medium). Microwave 12 to 17 minutes, or until rice is tender and liquid is absorbed. Let stand 5 to 10 minutes. Fluff with fork.

Parslied Rice

1 large onion, chopped
1 tablespoon olive oil or butter
¾ teaspoon dried basil leaves
¼ teaspoon dried thyme leaves
3 cups hot water
1½ cups uncooked long grain rice
¾ cup snipped fresh parsley
1½ teaspoons salt
¼ teaspoon pepper

Serves 6 to 8

Place onion, olive oil, basil and thyme in 3-qt. casserole. Microwave, covered, at High 2½ to 4 minutes, or until onion is tender. Stir in remaining ingredients; cover.

Microwave at High 5 minutes. Reduce power to 50% (Medium). Microwave 12 to 17 minutes, or until rice is tender and liquid is absorbed. Let stand 5 to 10 minutes. Fluff with fork.

Riz Indienne

½ cup chopped onion
2 tablespoons butter or margarine
3½ cups hot water
2 cups uncooked long grain rice
1 cup blanched almonds
1 cup raisins
2 tablespoons instant chicken bouillon granules
1 teaspoon salt
½ teaspoon pepper

Serves 6 to 8

Microwave onion and butter in 3-qt. casserole at High 2 to 4 minutes, or until onion is tender. Stir in remaining ingredients; cover. Microwave at High 8 minutes. Reduce power to 50% (Medium). Microwave 15 to 19 minutes, or until rice is tender and liquid is absorbed. Let stand, covered, 10 minutes. Fluff with fork.

Saffron Brown Rice

1 cup quick-cooking brown rice
1 cup hot water
½ cup dry white wine
1 small onion, chopped
2 tablespoons butter or margarine
1 teaspoon instant chicken bouillon granules
½ teaspoon salt
⅛ teaspoon ground saffron
Dash pepper

Serves 4

Combine all ingredients in 2-qt. casserole. Microwave, covered, at High 5 minutes. Reduce power to 50% (Medium). Microwave 7 to 12 minutes, or until liquid is absorbed. Let stand, covered, 5 minutes.

Rice & Grains Chart

Type	Amount	Utensil	Hot Water	Microwave Time at High	Procedure
Bulgur	1 cup	Med. mixing bowl	3 cups	5½ to 9 min.	Microwave water until boiling. Stir in bulgur. Let stand 30 minutes. Drain. Press to remove excess moisture.
Couscous	⅔ cup	1-qt. casserole	⅔ cup	2 to 3½ min.	Combine ingredients. Cover. Microwave until liquid is absorbed and couscous is tender. Let stand, covered, 3 to 5 minutes.
Cream of Wheat® Regular	2½ Tbls. 1/3 cup ⅔ cup	1-qt. casserole 2-qt. casserole 3-qt. casserole	1¼ cups 1¾ cups 3½ cups	4 to 6 min. 6 to 8 min 9 to 12 min.	Combine ingredients. Microwave, uncovered, until cereal is desired consistency, stirring 2 or 3 times.
Quick-cooking	2½ Tbls. 1/3 cup ⅔ cup	1-qt. casserole 2-qt. casserole 3-qt. casserole	¾ cup 1⅓ cups 2¾ cups	1½ to 3 min. 2½ to 4 min. 5 to 6½ min.	Combine ingredients. Microwave, uncovered, until cereal is desired consistency, stirring 2 or 3 times.
Grits, Quick-cooking	3 Tbls. ½ cup ¾ cup	1-qt. casserole 2-qt. casserole 3-qt. casserole	¾ cup 1½ cups 2¾ cups	2½ to 3 min. 3 to 3½ min. 6 to 8 min.	Combine ingredients. Microwave, uncovered, until grits are desired consistency, stirring 2 or 3 times.
Oats, Old-fashioned	1/3 cup ⅔ cup 1⅓ cups	1-qt. casserole 1½-qt. casserole 2-qt. casserole	¾ cup 1⅓ cups 2½ cups	4 to 6 min. 5 to 7 min. 7 to 10 min.	Combine ingredients. Microwave, uncovered, until cereal is desired consistency, stirring 2 or 3 times.
Quick-cooking	1/3 cup ⅔ cup 1⅓ cups	1-qt. casserole 1½-qt. casserole 2-qt. casserole	¾ cup 1½ cups 3 cups	2 to 4 min. 4 to 6 min. 6 to 8 min.	Combine ingredients. Microwave, uncovered, until cereal is desired consistency, stirring 2 or 3 times.
Rice, Long-grain Converted	1 cup	2-qt. casserole	2¼ cups	High 5 min., 50% (Med.) 15 to 22 min.	Combine ingredients. Cover. Microwave until liquid is absorbed and rice is tender. Let stand, covered, 5 minutes.
Long-grain White	1 cup	2-qt. casserole	2 cups	High 5 min., 50% (Med.) 12 to 15 min.	Combine ingredients. Cover. Microwave until liquid is absorbed and rice is tender. Let stand, covered, 5 minutes.
Brown	1¼ cups	3-qt. casserole	2⅓ cups	High 5 min., 50% (Med.) 35 to 45 min.	Combine ingredients. Cover. Microwave until liquid is absorbed and rice is tender. Let stand, covered, 5 minutes.
Wild	1 cup	3-qt. casserole	2¾ cups	High 5 min., 50% (Med.) 20 to 30 min.	Rinse rice. Drain. Combine ingredients. Cover. Microwave until rice is tender and kernels begin to open. Drain.

Sunny Couscous Cereal ▶

¾ cup water
¼ cup fresh orange juice
½ cup uncooked couscous
1 teaspoon grated orange peel
2 tablespoons finely chopped
  blanched almonds
1 tablespoon honey
1 tablespoon frozen apple juice
  concentrate
  Dash ground cinnamon

4 servings

In 1-quart casserole, combine all
ingredients. Cover. Microwave
at High for 5 to 6 minutes, or
until liquid is absorbed and
couscous is tender. Let stand,
covered, for 1 minute.

Per Serving:
Calories: 122
Protein: 3 g.
Carbohydrates: 23 g.
Fat: 2 g.
Cholesterol: —
Sodium: 1 mg.
Calcium: —
Exchanges: 1 bread, 1 fruit

Spiced Creamy Cereal

2 cups skim milk
⅓ cup regular cream of wheat
  cereal
2 tablespoons chopped dried
  apricots
⅛ teaspoon salt*
  Dash ground nutmeg
  Dash ground allspice

2 servings

In 2-quart casserole, combine
all ingredients. Microwave at
High for 6 to 8 minutes, or until
cereal thickens, stirring after
every 2 minutes.

*To reduce sodium omit salt.

Per Serving:
Calories: 78
Protein: 5 g.
Carbohydrates: 13 g.
Fat: —
Cholesterol: 5 mg.
Sodium: 171 mg.
Calcium: 196 mg.
Exchanges: 1 bread

Oatmeal with Prunes & Raisins

2½ cups hot water
1⅓ cups old-fashioned rolled
  oats
¼ cup instant nonfat
  dry milk powder
¼ cup chopped pitted prunes

2 tablespoons raisins
2 teaspoons dry natural
  butter-flavored mix
¼ teaspoon salt*
¼ teaspoon ground cinnamon

4 servings

In 2-quart casserole, combine all ingredients. Mix well. Microwave
at High for 8 to 10 minutes, or until desired consistency, stirring
after half the time.

*To reduce sodium omit salt.

Per Serving:
Calories: 172   Cholesterol: 1 mg.
Protein: 7 g.   Sodium: 582 mg.
Carbohydrates: 32 g.   Calcium: 80 mg.
Fat: —   Exchanges: 1½ bread, 1 fruit

Barley-Rice Pilaf ▲

⅓ cup quick-cooking barley
¼ cup uncooked brown rice
1⅔ cups hot water
1 cup sliced fresh mushrooms
¼ cup (¼-inch cubes) carrot
2 tablespoons snipped fresh
   parsley
1 clove garlic, minced
1 teaspoon lemon juice
½ teaspoon dried thyme
   leaves

6 servings

In 2-quart casserole, combine all ingredients. Mix well. Cover. Microwave at High for 5 minutes. Reduce power to 50% (Medium). Microwave for 35 to 45 minutes longer, or until liquid is absorbed and rice is tender. Let stand, covered, for 5 minutes.

Per Serving:
Calories:	62
Protein:	1.6 g.
Carbohydrates:	13.6 g.
Fat:	.3 g.
Cholesterol:	—
Sodium:	7 mg.
Calcium:	—
Exchanges:	1 bread

Barley & Black-eyed Peas

1 tablespoon reduced-calorie
   margarine
½ cup sliced carrot, ¼ inch
   thick
¼ cup sliced green onions
1 cup ready-to-serve
   low-sodium chicken broth

⅓ cup quick-cooking barley
1 tablespoon snipped fresh
   parsley
¼ teaspoon salt*
⅛ teaspoon pepper
1 can (16 oz.) black-eyed peas,
   rinsed and drained

4 servings

In 2-quart casserole, combine margarine, carrot and onions. Cover. Microwave at High for 3 to 6 minutes, or until tender, stirring after half the time. Add remaining ingredients, except black-eyed peas. Mix well. Re-cover. Microwave at High for 13 to 15 minutes longer, or until liquid is absorbed and the barley is tender. Stir in black-eyed peas. Re-cover. Microwave at High for 2 minutes, or until heated through.

*To reduce sodium omit salt.

Per Serving:
Calories:	177	Cholesterol:	—
Protein:	7 g.	Sodium:	456 mg.
Carbohydrates:	32 g.	Calcium:	—
Fat:	6 g.	Exchanges:	2 bread, 1 fat

Bulgur Pilaf

3 cups water
1 cup bulgur or cracked wheat
½ cup chopped carrot
¼ cup chopped onion
2 tablespoons snipped fresh
    parsley
1 clove garlic, minced
1 teaspoon dried chervil leaves
⅛ teaspoon pepper
2 tablespoons reduced-calorie
    margarine
1 cup frozen peas
1 tablespoon grated Parmesan
    cheese
¼ teaspoon salt*

8 servings

Place water in 4-cup measure. Microwave at High for 4 to 9 minutes, or until water boils. Place bulgur in medium mixing bowl. Add boiling water. Cover and let stand for 30 minutes to soften. Drain and press out excess moisture. Set aside.

In 2-quart casserole, combine carrot, onion, parsley, garlic, chervil, pepper and margarine. Cover. Microwave at High for 4 to 5 minutes, or until vegetables are tender, stirring after half the time. Add bulgur, peas, Parmesan cheese and salt. Mix well. Re-cover. Microwave at High for 2 to 4½ minutes longer, or until heated through.

*To reduce sodium omit salt.

Per Serving:
Calories:	141
Protein:	4 g.
Carbohydrates:	24 g.
Fat:	5 g.
Cholesterol:	—
Sodium:	121 mg.
Calcium:	18 mg.
Exchanges:	1½ bread, 1 fat

Tomato-Cheese Grits ▲

2 tablespoons reduced-calorie
    margarine
2 tablespoons sliced green
    onion
1 clove garlic, minced
¼ teaspoon salt*
⅛ teaspoon pepper

1¾ cups hot water
½ cup quick-cooking grits
1 medium tomato, seeded
    and chopped
¼ cup shredded Cheddar
    cheese

4 servings

In 2-quart casserole, combine margarine, onion and garlic. Microwave at High for 1½ to 2 minutes, or until tender. Add salt, pepper and water. Microwave at High for 3 to 6 minutes, or until water boils. Stir in grits and tomato. Microwave at High for 4 to 5 minutes, or until liquid is absorbed and grits are tender, stirring after half the time. Stir in Cheddar cheese.

*To reduce sodium omit salt.

Per Serving:
Calories:	96.5	Cholesterol:	7 mg.
Protein:	3 g.	Sodium:	360 mg.
Carbohydrates:	8 g.	Calcium:	55 mg.
Fat:	9 g.	Exchanges:	1 vegetable

Granola

3 cups old-fashioned rolled
  oats
½ cup shredded coconut
⅓ cup sliced almonds,
  chopped
⅔ cup honey
¼ cup packed dark brown
  sugar
¼ cup vegetable oil
1 teaspoon ground cinnamon
1 teaspoon vanilla
1 teaspoon molasses
½ cup raisins
⅓ cup chopped dried apples

Makes 6 cups

Granola Bars

6 cups Granola, left
½ cup butter or margarine
½ cup packed dark brown
  sugar
⅛ teaspoon salt
2 eggs, slightly beaten
¼ teaspoon almond extract

Makes 12 bars

Prepare granola as directed, except omit raisins. Set aside. Place butter in 2-cup measure or medium bowl. Microwave at High 45 seconds to 1½ minutes, or until melted. In medium bowl combine brown sugar, salt, eggs and almond extract. Beat in butter until combined. Stir in granola until coated. Press into greased 12 × 8-in. baking dish.

Microwave at High 6 to 9 minutes, or until firm to the touch, rotating dish ½ turn and pressing mixture with spatula every 2 minutes. Cut into twelve 4 × 2-in. bars. Cool completely before removing from dish. Store in refrigerator no longer than 1 week.

How to Microwave Granola

Mix rolled oats, shredded coconut and chopped almonds in large bowl. Set aside.

Combine remaining ingredients except raisins and apples in 8-cup measure. Microwave at High 2 to 3 minutes, or until boiling, stirring after each minute.

Pour honey mixture over oats, tossing to coat. Microwave at High 4½ to 7 minutes, or until mixture begins to stiffen and appear dry, stirring every 2 minutes. For crisper cereal, microwave 30 to 60 seconds longer, or until coconut begins to brown lightly.

Stir in raisins and apples. Allow mixture to cool about 1 to 1½ hours, stirring to break apart 1 or 2 times during cooling.

Breads

It's a myth that breads are fattening. The real culprit may be the high calorie spreads we put on them. These microwave breads are made with whole grains or other colorful ingredients and formulated to provide interesting flavor and texture when eaten "plain".

Four Grain Bread

1 cup whole wheat flour
½ cup rye flour
½ cup rolled oats
¼ cup corn meal
3 tablespoons light molasses
1 tablespoon vegetable oil
½ teaspoon salt
¼ cup warm water (105° to 115°)
1 cup boiling water
1 pkg. active dry yeast
1 to 1¼ cups white flour
 Skim milk
¼ cup wheat germ

Makes 24 slices
Serving size: 1 slice

Per Serving:
Calories:	70
Sodium:	42 mg.
Cholesterol:	0
Exchanges:	1 bread

How to Microwave Four Grain Bread

Blend whole wheat flour, rye flour, rolled oats, corn meal, molasses, oil, salt and boiling water in mixing bowl. Set aside.

Sprinkle yeast over warm water in 1-cup measure. Stir to dissolve. Stir into flour mixture.

Stir white flour gradually into mixture, adding just enough to make stiff dough.

Turn dough out on floured surface; with lightly greased hands, knead until smooth.

Knead by folding dough over toward you. Push with palms. Turn dough ¼ turn. Repeat, adding flour as needed.

Oil large bowl lightly. Place dough in bowl, turning to coat with oil. Cover loosely.

Let rise in warm place until light and doubled, about 45 to 90 minutes. Surface will be stretched and tight.

Test dough by pressing 2 fingers about ½ inch into it. If imprints remain, dough is doubled and risen.

Punch dough down; shape into ball. Turn dough out and cover with bowl. Let rest 15 minutes. Lightly oil 9-in. pie plate.

Shape dough into 18-in. strip. Brush with milk. Coat top and sides with wheat germ.

Sprinkle pie plate with remaining wheat germ. Shape dough, coated side up, into ring in pie plate. Pinch ends together.

Place lightly greased glass, open side up, in center of loaf. Let rise in warm place until doubled, 45 to 75 minutes.

Microwave at 50% (Medium) 6 minutes, rotating pie plate ½ turn after 3 minutes. Increase power to High.

Microwave 3 to 7 minutes, or until surface springs back when lightly touched, rotating pie plate once or twice.

Remove glass. Let stand 10 minutes. Transfer ring carefully to cooling rack.

Chewy Wheat Loaf

1 tablespoon lemon juice
  Skim milk
1 cup whole wheat flour
¼ cup brown sugar
1 teaspoon baking powder
1 teaspoon baking soda
¼ cup vegetable oil
2 eggs, slightly beaten
1 teaspoon cinnamon or
  pumpkin pie spice

Makes 24 slices
Serving size: 1 slice

In 1-cup measure combine
lemon juice and enough milk to
equal ½ cup. Stir.

Combine all remaining
ingredients in medium mixing
bowl. Stir in milk and lemon
juice. Beat at low speed of
electric mixer 1 minute. Line
9 × 5-in. loaf dish with wax
paper cut to fit bottom. Add
batter. Shield ends of loaf with
2½-in. wide strips of aluminum
foil, covering batter with 1½
inches and molding remainder
around handles of dish.

Microwave at 50% (Medium) 5
minutes, rotating dish once or
twice. Increase power to High.

Microwave 1½ to 4 minutes, or
until top of bread is firm to
touch and almost dry, with a
little moisture still visible. No
uncooked batter should be
visible through bottom of dish.

Let stand 3 minutes. Turn out of
pan. Cut into 24 slices.

Per Serving:
  Calories: 66
  Sodium: 60 mg.
  Cholesterol: 21 mg.
  Exchanges: ½ bread, ½ fat

Five Grain Quick Bread

½ cup all-purpose white flour
½ cup whole wheat flour
¾ cup 40% bran cereal
½ cup quick-cooking rolled oats
2 tablespoons wheat germ
¼ cup corn meal
2 teaspoons baking powder
2 tablespoons vegetable oil
3 tablespoons brown sugar
⅔ cup skim milk
2 eggs

Makes 24 slices
Serving size: 1 slice

Per Serving:
Calories:	51
Sodium:	66 mg.
Cholesterol:	23 mg.
Exchanges:	1 bread

How to Microwave Five Grain Quick Bread

Blend all ingredients in medium mixing bowl. Line bottom of 9 × 5-in. loaf dish with wax paper. Spoon batter into dish.

Shield ends of loaf with 2½-in. strips of foil, covering batter with 1½ inches and molding remainder around handles.

Microwave at 50% (Medium) 6 to 11 minutes, or until bread tests done, rotating dish ¼ turn every 2 to 3 minutes.

Test by touching top lightly; it should spring back.

Look through bottom of glass baking dish; no unbaked batter should appear.

Let stand on counter 5 minutes. Turn bread out. Remove wax paper. Cut into 24 slices.

◄ Wheat Biscuits

¾ cup whole wheat flour
¾ cup all-purpose white flour
2½ teaspoons baking powder
¼ teaspoon salt
3 tablespoons margarine or
   butter
½ cup skim milk
1 teaspoon poppy seeds
1 tablespoon wheat germ

Makes 10 biscuits
Serving size: 1 biscuit

In medium mixing bowl combine flours, baking powder and salt. Cut in margarine until particles are fine. Add milk and stir until dough clings together.

Knead on lightly floured surface 12 times. Pat out to ¾-in. thickness. Top with poppy seed and wheat germ. Cut into 1½-in. circles. Place biscuits ½ inch apart on paper towels. Microwave at High 1½ to 2 minutes, or until dry and puffy, rotating ¼ turn every 30 seconds.

Variation:

Substitute ¼ cup rye flour, ¼ cup whole wheat and 1 cup white flour for original flours.

Per Serving:
Calories: 100
Sodium: 164 mg.
Cholesterol: 0
Exchanges: 1 bread, ½ fat

Spoon Bread ▲

½ cup skim milk
½ cup water
⅓ cup corn meal
1 tablespoon margarine or
   butter
½ teaspoon baking powder
¼ teaspoon salt
1 egg, separated
1 egg white

Serves 8

In 1-cup measure combine milk and water.

In small bowl combine ¾ cup of milk mixture with corn meal. Microwave at High 2 to 3 minutes, or until very thick; stir with wire whip 2 or 3 times. Blend in remaining milk, margarine, baking powder, salt and egg yolk.

In medium bowl beat egg whites until soft peaks form. Fold corn meal mixture into egg whites. Pour into 9-in. round cake dish. Place on inverted saucer. Reduce power to 50% (Medium). Microwave 6 to 9 minutes, or until center is set, rotating dish 2 or 3 times.

Per Serving:
Calories: 56
Sodium: 92 mg.
Cholesterol: 39 mg.
Exchanges: ½ bread, ½ fat

Caraway Orange Rolls

1 cup all-bran cereal
1 tablespoon vegetable oil
2 tablespoons light molasses
1 teaspoon grated orange peel
1 to 1½ teaspoons caraway
    seed, divided
½ teaspoon salt
¾ cup boiling water

1 pkg. active dry yeast
¼ cup warm water (105°
    to 115°)
2 to 2½ cups all-purpose
    white flour
2 teaspoons wheat germ
1 to 2 teaspoons skim milk

Makes 24 rolls
Serving size: 1 roll

Per Serving:
Calories:	21	Cholesterol:	0
Sodium:	46 mg.	Exchanges:	½ bread

How to Microwave Caraway Orange Rolls

Blend bran, oil, molasses, orange peel, ½ to 1 teaspoon caraway seed, salt and boiling water in medium mixing bowl. Cool until just warm.

Dissolve yeast in warm water. Stir into bran mixture. Stir in flour to make stiff dough. On floured surface, knead until smooth, about 8 minutes, adding flour as needed.

Cover loosely. Let rise until light and doubled in size, about 45 minutes to 1¼ hours. Punch down dough.

Divide into 24 pieces. Shape into balls. In small bowl combine ½ teaspoon caraway seed and wheat germ. Dip tops of rolls in milk, then in wheat germ mixture.

Arrange on 2 paper towel-lined dinner plates or 9 to 10-in. pie plates. Cover loosely. Let rise in warm place until light and doubled in size, about 45 minutes to 1½ hours.

Microwave, 1 plate at a time, at 50% (Medium) 6 to 8 minutes, or until tops spring back when lightly touched, rotating ¼ turn every 2 minutes.

Vegetable Corn Muffins ▲

1 cup all-purpose white flour
½ cup cornmeal
1 tablespoon sugar
1 tablespoon baking powder
½ teaspoon salt
¾ teaspoon Italian seasoning
⅛ teaspoon garlic powder
2 eggs, beaten
1 tablespoon vegetable oil
½ cup corn, drained
⅓ cup skim milk
⅓ cup chopped green pepper
¼ cup finely chopped onion

Makes 12 muffins
Serving size: 1 muffin

Combine all ingredients in mixing bowl. Stir just until blended. Line each muffin or custard cup with two paper liners; fill half full. Microwave at High as directed below, or until top springs back when touched, rotating and rearranging after half the time.

1 muffin	¼ to ¾ minute
2 muffins	½ to 2 minutes
4 muffins	1 to 2½ minutes
6 muffins	2 to 4½ minutes

Per Serving:
Calories:	97
Sodium:	182 mg.
Cholesterol:	42 mg.
Exchanges:	1 bread, ½ fat

Carrot Bran Muffins ▲

1 cup 40% bran flakes
¾ cup skim milk
2 cups finely shredded carrot
1 cup whole wheat flour
2 tablespoons brown sugar
2 tablespoons vegetable oil
1 tablespoon lemon juice
1 teaspoon baking powder
½ teaspoon baking soda
¼ to ½ teaspoon cinnamon
¼ teaspoon salt
1 egg, slightly beaten

Makes 14 muffins
Serving size: 1 muffin

Combine bran, milk and carrot; let stand 5 minutes. Add remaining ingredients, stirring until particles are moistened. Line each muffin or custard cup with two paper liners; fill half full. Microwave at High as directed below, or until top springs back when touched, rotating and rearranging after half the time.

1 muffin	¼ to ¾ minute
2 muffins	½ to 2 minutes
4 muffins	1 to 2½ minutes
6 muffins	2 to 4½ minutes

Per Serving:
Calories:	86
Sodium:	87 mg.
Cholesterol:	18 mg.
Exchanges:	1 bread, ½ fat

Raisin Orange Muffins ▲

½ cup rolled oats
1 cup whole wheat flour
2 tablespoons vegetable oil
¼ cup sugar
2 teaspoons baking powder
¼ teaspoon salt
⅔ cup skim milk
2 eggs, slightly beaten
¼ cup raisins
½ teaspoon grated orange
  peel

Makes 12 muffins
Serving size: 1 muffin

Combine all ingredients in large mixing bowl. Stir just until particles are moistened. Line each muffin or custard cup with two paper liners; fill half full. Microwave at High as directed below, or until top springs back when touched, rotating and rearranging after half the time.

1 muffin	¼ to ¾ minute
2 muffins	½ to 2 minutes
4 muffins	1 to 2½ minutes
6 muffins	2 to 4½ minutes

Per Serving:
Calories:	113
Sodium:	100 mg.
Cholesterol:	42 mg.
Exchanges:	1 bread, 1 fat

Wheat Crackers

1 cup whole wheat flour
1 teaspoon caraway seed
¼ teaspoon salt
2 tablespoons margarine or
    butter
1 tablespoon vegetable oil
3 to 4 tablespoons water
    Corn meal or wheat germ

Makes 36 crackers
Serving size: 4 crackers

Per Serving:
Calories: 95
Sodium: 71 mg.
Cholesterol: 0
Exchanges: 1 bread, 1 fat

How to Microwave Wheat Crackers

Combine flour, caraway seed and salt in medium mixing bowl. With a pastry blender cut in margarine and oil until particles are fine.

Sprinkle water over mixture while tossing with fork until dough is just moist enough to hold together. Form dough into a ball.

Roll out on a floured pastry cloth to a 12 × 12-in. square. Prick generously with a fork. Cut into 36 squares.

Sprinkle large pie plate or microwave baking sheet with corn meal or wheat germ. Arrange half of crackers on baking sheet in circular pattern, placing 3 or 4 in center.

Microwave at High 2 to 3 minutes, or until dry and puffy, rotating twice. For crisper crackers, let cool on rack. Repeat with remaining crackers.

Desserts

Cakes & Frostings

With a microwave oven, you can have fresh, homemade cake whenever you want. Make the size that's right for you. There's no preheating, and no wasted energy if you bake one layer instead of two.

Cake Dishes. The cakes in this book can be microwaved in several different dish sizes and shapes. We suggest you use clear glass or plastic to help you check the bottom of the cake for doneness.

Ingredients. Shortening, butter and margarine are not interchangeable in cakes. Do not make substitutions. If you wish to use cake flour rather than all-purpose flour, increase the amount by 2 to 3 tablespoons for each cup of flour. It is usually safe to substitute flavoring ingredients, if you desire.

Browning. Microwave cakes do not brown. Once the cake is frosted, this difference is not apparent. However, the top can also be soft and sticky. To dry the top and make it easier to frost, sprinkle about 1 tablespoon graham cracker crumbs on each layer after baking.

How to Choose the Right Microwave Dish

One-layer recipe will make a 9-in. round, 8×8- or 10×6-in. cake, or 14 to 16 cupcakes.

Two-layer recipe will make two 9-in. round, 8×8- or 10×6-in. cakes, or 12×8-in. cake plus 4 to 8 cupcakes.

Ring or Bundt cakes are made from two-layer recipes in a 12- or 14-cup tube pan. If using 12-cup pan make 2 or 3 cupcakes.

How to Prepare Dishes

Layer cakes. For single layer cakes to be frosted and served from dish, no preparation is needed. For two-layer cakes, line bottoms with two circles of wax paper for easy removal. A few dabs of grease under paper will keep it from slipping when batter is spread.

Plain or fluted bundt cake. Grease dish well and coat with graham cracker crumbs. Shake out excess crumbs.

How to Mix Cakes and Fill Dishes

Place all cake ingredients in mixing bowl. Blend on lowest speed until dry particles are moistened. This prevents spatters when speed is increased.

Beat at medium or "cake" speed 2 minutes. With a hand mixer, use one of the higher speeds.

Scrape side of bowl occasionally while mixing. With a standard mixer, hold rubber spatula against side of bowl as it turns.

Clean beaters with spatula and stir this mixture into batter thoroughly. Any unblended batter will sink and make a hole in the bottom of the cake.

Spread batter in dishes, filling no more than ⅓ to ½ full. With a 12×8-in. dish, make 4 to 8 cupcakes. Some cakes make very full 9-in. round or 10×6-in. layers, so bake 2 to 4 cupcakes if necessary. For bundt cake, use a 14-cup dish.

How to Turn Out Cakes

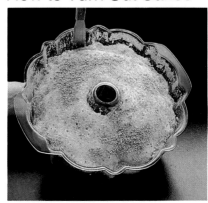

Loosen edges with flexible spatula. Loosen every flute and around the tube of bundt dish. Lift cake from bottom.

Top dish with wire rack; invert dish. If cake does not unmold, loosen edges again. Do not force cake out of dish.

Cut cakes served from pan with sharp knife. Remove pieces with small, flexible pancake turner. After the first piece, the rest will come out easily.

Cupcakes

Cupcakes are extremely easy and quick to microwave. You can make one in about half a minute. For fresh cupcakes daily, store batter in the refrigerator and use as needed. The one layer size cake recipe will make 14 to 16 cupcakes. Soda leavened batters can be refrigerated up to a week, and baking powder batters 3 to 4 days. No special pans are needed; cupcake liners and custard cups will do. Use two paper liners in each cup to absorb moisture during baking.

Cupcakes rise higher when microwaved, so use less batter than you would for conventional baking. For most batters, one third full is the right amount. Microwave a sample cupcake to test the amount of rising. Microwave muffin dishes have smaller cups, so use less batter in the liners than you do for custard cups.

Cupcake Chart

Quantity	High Power
1	25 to 30 seconds
2	¾ to 1¼ minutes
3*	1 to 1½ minutes
4*	1½ to 2 minutes
6*	2 to 3 minutes

*Rotate and rearrange after half the time.

How to Microwave Cupcakes

Place two paper cupcake liners in each 5 or 6 oz. custard cup or in microwave muffin dishes.

Fill each about ⅓ full. An old-fashioned ice cream scoop makes a good measure. Use less batter in muffin dishes.

Cut through batter with wooden pick to prevent large air spaces which can form because cupcakes bake quickly.

Arrange in ring in oven. Microwave at High, following chart. Rearrange or rotate after half the time as chart indicates.

Microwave until almost dry on top. Small moist spots will dry on standing. Overmicrowaving makes dry and tough cupcakes.

Remove cupcakes from cups as soon as they are microwaved. Let stand on wire cooling rack.

Ice Cream-Filled Cake

2 tablespoons sugar
1 pkg. (2-layer size) chocolate
   cake mix
1 qt. peppermint ice cream
½ cup chocolate chips
½ cup corn syrup
1 tablespoon half and half
½ teaspoon vanilla

Makes 1 ring cake

How to Microwave Ice Cream-Filled Cake

Grease 12- to 14-cup ring cake dish. Sprinkle with sugar. Prepare cake mix as directed on package. Pour into dish. Microwave at 50% (Medium) 12 minutes, rotating every 4 minutes. Increase power to High.

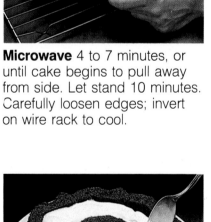

Microwave 4 to 7 minutes, or until cake begins to pull away from side. Let stand 10 minutes. Carefully loosen edges; invert on wire rack to cool.

Cut off top quarter of cooled cake; set aside. Remove center of cake by cutting ½ inch from inner and outer edge to within 1 inch from bottom.

Scoop out inside with spoon leaving 1 inch of cake on bottom. Refrigerate or freeze at least 1 hour.

Place ice cream in medium bowl. Microwave at 30% (Medium-Low) 30 to 60 seconds, or until softened. Spoon into cake. Replace top. Freeze at least 6 hours.

Combine chocolate chips and syrup in 1-qt. casserole. Microwave at High 30 to 60 seconds, or until chips melt. Stir in half and half and vanilla. Pour over cake before serving.

Festive Gelatin Cake ▲

2 cups all-purpose flour
1¼ cups sugar
1 tablespoon baking powder
1 teaspoon salt
1 teaspoon vanilla
⅔ cup shortening
⅔ cup milk

2 eggs
4 egg whites
1 cup water
1 pkg. (3 oz.) gelatin, any
   flavor
Fluffy Frosting, below

Makes two 8 × 8-in. cakes

Place all ingredients except water, gelatin and frosting in large bowl. Blend at low speed, scraping bowl constantly. Beat 2 minutes at medium speed, scraping bowl occasionally. Divide batter between two 8 × 8-in. baking dishes.

Microwave one dish at a time at 50% (Medium) 6 minutes, rotating twice. Increase power to High. Microwave 1 to 5 minutes or until top springs back when touched lightly. Let stand 10 minutes.

In 2-cup measure microwave water at High 1 to 3 minutes, or until boiling. Slowly add gelatin, stirring constantly. Pierce cakes at ¼-in. intervals with wooden pick. Pour half of gelatin mixture over each cake; cool. Frost with Fluffy Frosting. Refrigerate.

Fluffy Frosting

1 cup sugar
⅓ cup water
¼ teaspoon cream of tartar

⅛ teaspoon salt
2 egg whites
1 teaspoon vanilla

Frosts two 8 × 8-in. cakes

In 2-qt. casserole combine sugar, water, cream of tartar and salt; cover. Microwave at High 2 minutes. Stir. Microwave at High, uncovered, 1½ to 5 minutes, or until soft ball forms when small amount is dropped in cold water. Do not undercook.

Beat egg whites until stiff peaks form. Pour hot syrup slowly in a thin stream into beaten egg whites, beating constantly, until stiff and glossy. Add vanilla during last minute of beating.

Lemon Ring Cake

3 tablespoons graham
   cracker crumbs
2 cups all-purpose flour
1¼ cups sugar
2 teaspoons baking powder
1 teaspoon salt
4 eggs
⅔ cup shortening
½ cup milk
1 tablespoon grated lemon
   peel
1 teaspoon vanilla
4 drops yellow food coloring
¼ cup lemon juice
   Lemon Glaze, below

Makes 1 ring cake

Grease 10- or 12-cup ring cake dish. Coat with graham cracker crumbs. Place all ingredients except lemon juice and glaze in medium bowl. Blend at low speed of electric mixer 30 seconds, scraping bowl constantly. Add lemon juice. Beat at medium speed 2 minutes, scraping bowl occasionally. Spread in dish.

Microwave at 50% (Medium) 8 minutes, rotating ¼ turn every 2 minutes. Increase power to High. Microwave 3 to 8 minutes, or until wooden pick inserted in several places comes out clean, rotating 2 or 3 times during cooking. Let stand directly on counter 5 to 10 minutes. Remove from pan to cool. Drizzle with Lemon Glaze.

Lemon Glaze

1¼ cups powdered sugar
1 teaspoon grated lemon peel
2 tablespoons lemon juice
1 tablespoon butter or
   margarine
2 drops yellow food coloring

Frosts 1 ring cake

In medium bowl mix all ingredients until smooth.

Apple Cake ▶

1½ cups all-purpose flour
1¼ cups packed brown sugar
1½ teaspoons baking powder
1½ teaspoons ground
    cinnamon
 1 teaspoon baking soda
 ¼ teaspoon ground nutmeg
 ¼ teaspoon ground cloves
 2 cups peeled, finely
    shredded apple
 ¾ cup vegetable oil
 4 eggs
 ¼ cup finely chopped nuts
    Honey Frosting, below

Makes two 8 × 8-in. cakes

Place all ingredients except Honey Frosting in large bowl. Blend at low speed, scraping bowl constantly. Beat at medium speed 2 minutes, scraping bowl occasionally. Divide batter between two 8 × 8-in. baking dishes.

Place one dish at a time on inverted saucer in oven. Microwave at 50% (Medium) 6 minutes, rotating ¼ turn every 3 minutes. Increase power to High. Microwave 1 to 4 minutes, or until top springs back when touched lightly. Let stand directly on counter 5 to 10 minutes. Cool and frost.

Honey Frosting

½ cup packed brown sugar
½ cup butter or margarine
½ cup honey
 4 cups powdered sugar
 2 teaspoons vanilla
 1 to 2 tablespoons milk

Frosts two 8 × 8-in. cakes

In medium bowl combine brown sugar, butter and honey. Microwave at High 2 to 3 minutes, or until boiling, stirring after half the time. Boil 30 seconds longer.

Stir in powdered sugar and vanilla. Add milk, 1 tablespoon at a time, beating until smooth and of spreading consistency. Cool before serving.

Honey Cake

Cake:
 3 eggs, separated
 ⅓ cup honey
 3 tablespoons packed brown
    sugar
 2 tablespoons vegetable oil
 1 tablespoon water
 1 tablespoon grated orange
    peel
 1 teaspoon grated lemon peel
 ¾ cup all-purpose flour
 1 teaspoon ground cinnamon
 1 teaspoon ground allspice
 ¾ teaspoon baking powder
 ½ teaspoon ground cloves
 ¼ teaspoon baking soda
 ⅛ teaspoon salt

Topping:
 ⅓ cup honey
 ¼ cup butter or margarine
 1 tablespoon plus 1 teaspoon
    packed brown sugar
 ⅓ cup sliced almonds

Makes 1 cake

In deep bowl beat egg whites until stiff peaks form. In medium bowl beat egg yolks until frothy. Add honey, brown sugar, oil, water, orange peel and lemon peel. Beat until well blended. Mix in flour, cinnamon, allspice, baking powder, cloves, baking soda and salt. Fold batter into egg whites.

Pour into 8 × 5-in. loaf dish. Shield ends with foil. Place on inverted saucer in oven. Microwave at 50% (Medium) 3 minutes, rotating once. Remove shields. Microwave at 50% (Medium) 1 to 4 minutes, or until top springs back when lightly touched, rotating once or twice. Let stand on counter 5 minutes. Invert onto serving plate.

In small bowl or 2-cup measure combine topping ingredients except almonds. Microwave at High 1 to 4 minutes, or until butter melts, stirring once or twice. Stir to blend. Pierce top of cake with fork. Pour two-thirds of glaze slowly over cake. Sprinkle with almonds. Pour remaining glaze over cake.

Advance preparation: Honey Cake can be prepared 2 to 3 weeks in advance. Prepare cake as directed. Remove from pan but do not glaze; cool. Wrap, label and freeze no longer than 3 weeks. To serve, unwrap and place on serving plate. Microwave at 50% (Medium) 2 to 4 minutes, or until cake is defrosted and warm. Prepare glaze. Pour over cake as directed.

Easy German Chocolate Cake

½ cup butter or margarine, divided
⅔ cup packed brown sugar, divided
⅔ cup flaked coconut, divided
⅔ cup finely chopped pecans, divided
1½ cups all-purpose flour
1⅓ cups granulated sugar
¼ cup cocoa
1½ teaspoons baking powder
1 teaspoon salt
1 cup milk
⅔ cup shortening
3 eggs
1 teaspoon vanilla

Makes 2-layer cake

Cut wax paper to fit bottoms of two 9-in. round cake dishes. Place ¼ cup butter in each lined dish. Microwave, one dish at a time, at High 45 seconds to 1¼ minutes, or until butter is melted and bubbly. Mix ⅓ cup brown sugar, ⅓ cup coconut and ⅓ cup pecans into butter in each dish. Spread into an even layer. Set dishes aside.

Place remaining ingredients in large bowl. Blend at low speed of electric mixer, scraping bowl constantly. Beat 2 minutes at medium speed, scraping bowl occasionally. Divide and spread batter into cake dishes.

Place one dish on inverted saucer in oven. Reduce power to 50% (Medium). Microwave 6 minutes, rotating ½ turn after half the time. Increase power to High. Microwave 2 to 4 minutes, or until cake is light and springy to the touch, rotating dish once. Sides will just begin to pull away from dish. Let stand directly on counter 5 minutes. Invert onto serving plate. Remove wax paper. Spread any topping from wax paper onto cake top. Repeat with remaining cake. Invert onto wire rack. Cool. Place second layer on top of first layer with frosting side up.

254

Nectarine Upside-Down ► Gingerbread Cake

¼ cup butter or margarine
½ cup brown sugar
 1 tablespoon milk
 2 cups peeled, sliced fresh
   nectarines
 1 pkg. (14.5 oz.) gingerbread
   mix

Makes 8 × 8-in. cake

How to Microwave Nectarine Upside-Down Gingerbread Cake

Melt butter in 8 × 8-in. dish at High 1 to 1½ minutes. Blend in sugar and milk. Microwave at High 1½ to 2 minutes, or until slightly thickened and syrupy, stirring once or twice.

Arrange nectarine slices on top. Prepare gingerbread as directed on package. Spoon batter evenly over fruit.

Place dish on inverted saucer. Reduce power to 50% (Medium). Microwave 6 minutes, rotating ¼ turn every 2 minutes. Increase power to High.

Microwave 4 to 8 minutes, or until gingerbread springs back when lightly touched, rotating ¼ turn every 1 or 2 minutes.

Cool directly on countertop 5 minutes. Loosen edges well; turn out onto large platter.

Serve warm. If desired, top with whipped cream or ice cream.

Butter Pecan Frosting

3 tablespoons butter or
   margarine
¼ cup finely chopped pecans
1 to 2 tablespoons cream or milk
2 cups confectioners' sugar
½ teaspoon vanilla

> Frosts tops of 2 layers,
> 12×8-in. cake or
> 2½ doz. cupcakes

Microwave butter in small mixing
bowl at High 1 minute, or until
melted. Stir in pecans.
Microwave at High 2 to 4
minutes, or until browned,
stirring after 2 minutes. Add
remaining ingredients. Beat until
smooth and of spreading
consistency, adding few drops
milk, if necessary.

Browned Butter Frosting

3 tablespoons butter
   (not margarine)
2 cups confectioners' sugar
1 to 2 tablespoons cream or
   milk
¼ teaspoon vanilla

> Frosts tops of 2 layers,
> 12×8-in. cake, 24 cupcakes or
> 3 doz. cookies

Microwave butter in mixing bowl
at High 3 to 5 minutes, or until
browned, watching closely after
3 minutes. Stir in sugar. Blend in
cream and vanilla. Beat until
smooth and of spreading
consistency, adding a few drops
cream, if necessary.

Buttercream Frosting

2 tablespoons butter or
   margarine
2 tablespoons cream or milk
⅛ teaspoon salt
2 cups confectioners' sugar
½ teaspoon vanilla or rum
   flavoring

> Frosts tops of 2 layers,
> 12×8-in. cake, 24 cupcakes or
> 3 to 4 doz. cookies

In mixing bowl, combine butter,
cream and salt. Microwave at
50% (Medium) 1 to 2 minutes, or
until mixture is bubbling. Add
sugar and vanilla. Beat until
smooth and of spreading
consistency, adding few drops
cream, if necessary.

Variations:

Coffee Frosting: Add ½ teaspoon instant coffee to butter
mixture before microwaving.

Maple Frosting: Substitute ¼
teaspoon maple flavoring for
the vanilla.

Lemon Frosting

2 tablespoons butter or
   margarine
1 tablespoon cream or milk
1 tablespoon lemon juice
1 teaspoon grated lemon peel
⅛ teaspoon salt
2 cups confectioners' sugar
½ teaspoon vanilla
2 or 3 drops yellow food
   coloring

Frosts tops of 2 layers,
12×8-in. cake, 24 cupcakes or,
3 to 4 doz. cookies

In mixing bowl combine butter,
cream, juice, peel and salt.
Microwave at 50% (Medium) 1 to
2 minutes, or until bubbling. Add
sugar, vanilla and coloring. Beat
until smooth and of spreading
consistency, adding few drops
cream, if necessary.

Variation:

Orange Frosting: Substitute 2
tablespoons orange juice for
cream and lemon juice and
orange peel for lemon peel.

Peanut Butter Frosting

2 tablespoons butter or
   margarine
2 tablespoons peanut butter
2 tablespoons cream or milk
⅛ teaspoon salt
2 cups confectioners' sugar
½ teaspoon vanilla

Frosts tops of 2 layers,
12×8-in. cake, 24 cupcakes or,
3 to 4 doz. cookies

In mixing bowl combine butter,
peanut butter, cream and salt.
Microwave at 50% (Medium) 1 to
2 minutes, or until mixture is
bubbling. Add sugar and vanilla.
Beat until smooth and of
spreading consistency, adding
few drops cream, if necessary.
Sprinkle frosted cake with finely
chopped peanuts if desired.

Cherry Nut Frosting

2 tablespoons butter or
   margarine
1 tablespoon cream or milk
1 tablespoon cherry juice
⅛ teaspoon salt
2 cups confectioners' sugar
2 tablespoons chopped
   maraschino cherries
2 tablespoons chopped nuts
½ teaspoon vanilla

Frosts tops of 2 layers,
12×8-in. cake, 24 cupcakes or,
3 to 4 doz. cookies

In mixing bowl combine butter,
cream, juice and salt.
Microwave at 50% (Medium) 1 to
2 minutes, or until mixture is
boiling. Add sugar, cherries,
nuts and vanilla. Beat until
smooth and of spreading
consistency, adding few drops
cream, if necessary.

Butterscotch Frosting

3 tablespoons butter or
   margarine
3 tablespoons milk
⅓ cup packed brown sugar
⅛ teaspoon salt
2 cups confectioners' sugar
½ teaspoon vanilla

> Frosts tops of 2 layers,
> 12×8-in. cake or
> 24 cupcakes

In medium mixing bowl,
combine butter, milk, sugar and
salt. Microwave at High 1½ to 4
minutes, or until mixture comes
to a boil, stirring after half the
time. Boil 30 seconds. Add
confectioners' sugar and vanilla.
Beat until smooth and of
spreading consistency, adding
few drops milk, if necessary.

Chocolate Frosting

1 oz. unsweetened chocolate*
   (pre-melted or squares)
2 tablespoons butter or
   margarine
3 tablespoons milk

2 cups confectioners' sugar
½ teaspoon vanilla or
   mint flavoring
⅛ teaspoon salt

> Frosts tops of 2 layers,
> 12×8-in. cake or 24 cupcakes

In small mixing bowl, combine chocolate, butter and milk. Microwave at 50% (Medium) 3 to 4 minutes, or until chocolate is soft and
mixture is thick, stirring after half the time. Stir in remaining ingredients. Let stand 5 to 10 minutes. Beat until smooth and of spreading
consistency, 1 to 3 minutes, adding few drops milk, if necessary.

*If recipe is cut in half use the full amount of chocolate.

Variations:

Choco-Cherry Frosting: Substitute maraschino cherry juice for half
the milk and add 9 maraschino cherries, cut fine, with the sugar.

Chocolate Peanut Frosting: Add 3 tablespoons peanut butter to
chocolate mixture before microwaving. Sprinkle frosted cake with
finely chopped peanuts, if desired.

Chocolate Mallow Frosting: Just before frosting cake, stir in 1½
cups miniature marshmallows. (If frosting a layer cake, remove ¾
cup frosting before adding marshmallows; use to frost the sides.)

Cocoa Frosting: Substitute 3 tablespoons cocoa for chocolate and
increase butter to ¼ cup.

How to Make the Right Amount of Frosting

Recipes in this chapter frost the tops of two 9-in. round, 8×8- or 10×6-in. layers, a 12×8-in. cake, 2 to 3 dozen cupcakes or 3 to 4 dozen cookies.

Double the amounts of all the ingredients if you want to frost and fill a two-layer cake, or 3 dozen cupcakes.

Cut ingredients in half to frost tops of 9-in. round, 8×8- or 12×8-in. cake, 1 to 2 dozen cupcakes or 2 to 3 dozen cookies.

Lemon Filling

⅓ cup sugar
1½ tablespoons cornstarch
   Pinch salt
¾ cup water
1 egg yolk, beaten
1 tablespoon butter or margarine
2 teaspoons grated lemon peel
3 tablespoons lemon juice

    Makes about 1¼ cups

In 4-cup measure or small mixing bowl, combine sugar, cornstarch and salt. Gradually stir in water. Microwave at High 3 to 4 minutes, or until very thick, stirring after 2 minutes, then every minute. Mix a little hot mixture into egg yolk. Blend into remaining sugar mixture. Microwave at 50% (Medium) 1 minute. Stir in butter, peel and lemon juice until smooth. Cover; cool slightly.

Vanilla Cream Filling

¼ cup sugar
2 tablespoons cornstarch
   Pinch salt
1¼ cups milk
2 egg yolks, beaten
1 tablespoon butter or margarine
1 teaspoon vanilla

    Makes about 1½ cups

In 4-cup measure or small mixing bowl, combine sugar, cornstarch and salt. Gradually stir in milk. Microwave at High 4 to 7 minutes, or until very thick, stirring after 2 minutes, then every minute. Mix a little hot mixture into egg yolks. Blend into remaining milk mixture. Microwave at 50% (Medium) 1 minute. Stir in butter until smooth. Cover; cool slightly. Stir in vanilla.

Variation:

Chocolate Filling: Increase sugar to ⅓ cup and add 1 oz. unsweetened chocolate to milk mixture before microwaving. If cooked filling is not smooth, beat with rotary beater.

Pies

Microwaved pastry is exceptionally tender, flaky and puffy, but it does not brown. Add a few drops of food coloring, or brush pastry with egg yolk before microwaving.

Crumb crusts take only a few minutes to prepare, and are microwaved just long enough to firm up.

Banana Cream Pie

1 9-in. microwaved crumb
    crust or pastry shell
1 small pkg. pudding mix
    (vanilla, chocolate,
    butterscotch)
2 bananas

Makes 1 9-in. pie

Prepare pudding mix. Cool slightly. Slice 2 bananas into pie crust. Top with pudding. Cool. Garnish with whipped cream, if desired.

Graham Cracker Crust

5 tablespoons butter or
    margarine
1⅓ cups fine graham cracker
    crumbs
2 tablespoons white or
    brown sugar

Makes 9 or 10-in. crumb shell

Cookie Crumb Crust

Use finely crushed vanilla wafers, ginger snaps or chocolate wafers. Decrease butter to ¼ cup and omit sugar.

How to Microwave a Crumb Crust

Melt butter in a 9 or 10-in. pie plate at High, ¾ to 1 minute. Stir in crumbs and sugar until well moistened. Remove 2 tablespoons crumb mixture for garnish, if desired.

Press crumbs firmly and evenly against bottom and sides of plate. Microwave 1½ minutes, rotating ½ turn after 1 minute. Cool.

Microwave pastry shells before filling. Remove frozen pastry shells to glass pie plate. Before pricking, defrost 1½ to 2½ minutes at 50% power.

One Crust Pastry Shell

⅓ cup shortening
 1 to 2 tablespoons room temperature butter or margarine
 1 cup all purpose flour
½ teaspoon salt
 3 tablespoons cold water
 3 to 4 drops yellow food coloring

Makes 9 or 10-in. pastry shell

Cut shortening and butter into flour and salt with a pastry blender until particles resemble coarse crumbs.

Combine water and food coloring. Sprinkle over pastry while stirring with fork, until dough is just moist enough to hold together.

Form into ball. Flatten to ½-in. Roll out on floured pastry cloth to scant ⅛-in. thick circle, 2-in. larger than inverted 9 or 10-in. pie plate.

Fit loosely into pie plate. Trim overhang to ½-in. Fold edge to form standing rim and flute.

How to Microwave a Pastry Shell

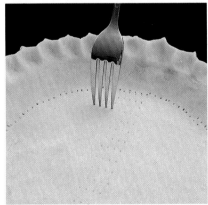

Prick crust with a fork at ⅛-in. intervals at bend of dish and ½-in. apart on bottom and sides of dish.

Microwave at High 6 to 7 minutes, rotating dish ½ turn after 3 minutes.

Check bottom of crust for doneness. It should be dry and opaque. A few brown spots may appear.

Lemon Pie

1 9-in. microwaved crumb crust
   or pastry shell, page 260
1 cup sugar
4 tablespoons cornstarch

¼ teaspoon salt
1¾ cup water, divided
3 egg yolks, slightly beaten

Serve lemon pie cool, topped with whipped cream.

2 tablespoons butter or
   margarine
1 tablespoon grated lemon peel
⅔ cup lemon juice

makes 1 9-in. pie

Combine sugar, cornstarch, salt and ¼ cup water in a 1½-qt. casserole. Microwave remaining water at High 2 to 3 minutes until boiling.

Stir into sugar mixture. Microwave 4 to 6 minutes until very thick. Stir every 2 minutes. Mix a little hot mixture into egg yolks.

Blend yolks well into sugar mixture. Microwave 1 minute. Stir in butter, peel and juice. Cool slightly and turn into pie shell.

French Apple Pie

1 microwaved 9-in. pastry shell, with high fluted edge, page 261

Filling:
- 5 to 6 cups peeled, sliced apples
- 1 tablespoon lemon juice
- ½ cup sugar
- 2 tablespoons flour
- ½ teaspoon cinnamon or ¼ teaspoon nutmeg

Topping:
- ¼ cup butter or margarine
- ½ cup flour
- ¼ cup brown or granulated sugar
- ½ teaspoon nutmeg

Makes 1 9-in. pie

How to Microwave French Apple Pie

Toss filling ingredients together. Pile high in pastry shell. Cut butter into other topping ingredients until crumbly. Sprinkle evenly over filling.

Place wax paper under plate while microwaving. Microwave at High 8 minutes. Rotate ½ turn. Microwave 6 to 10 minutes until apples are tender.

Fruit Pie ▶

- 1 9-in. microwaved pastry or crumb crust, page 261
- 1 can (21-oz.) cherry or other pie filling

Makes 1 9-in. pie

Spread filling in pie shell. Microwave at High 7 to 10 minutes, rotating dish after 4 minutes until filling is hot and bubbly. Decorate with Pastry Cut Outs or reserved crumbs.

Pastry Cut Outs. Roll out leftover pastry to ⅛-in. thickness. Cut into 6 pieces with cookie cutter. Sprinkle with mixture of 1 teaspoon sugar and ⅛ teaspoon cinnamon. Arrange in ring on microwave baking sheet or wax paper. Microwave at High 2 to 4 minutes until dry and puffy, rotating after 2 minutes. Use to garnish fruit pies.

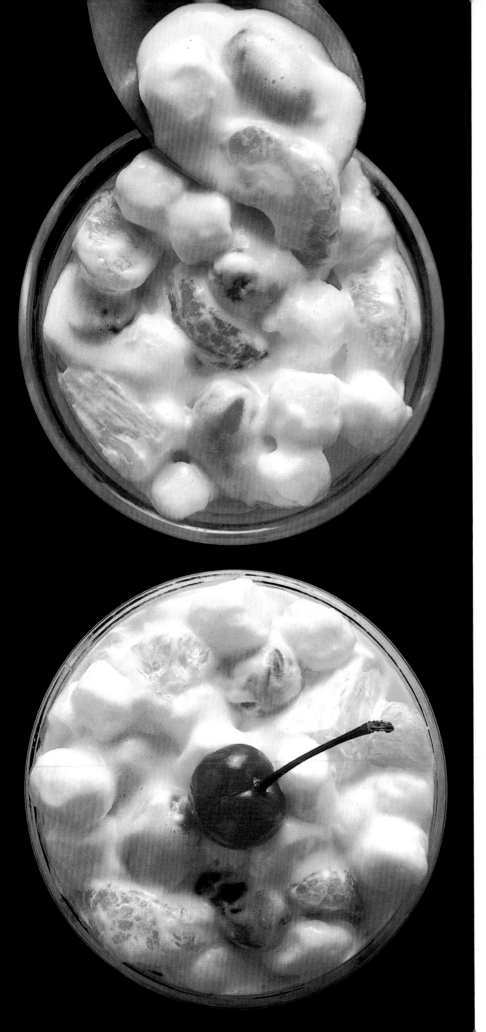

Refrigerator Desserts

Refrigerator desserts must be made in advance, so they're good choices for occasions when you want to avoid last minute cooking. Many can be stored several days.

Some refrigerator desserts are baked, cooled and chilled before serving. Others go into the refrigerator soft and firm up after several hours.

Easy Overnight Fruit Salad Dessert

    1 package (3 to 3⅝ oz.) vanilla
        pudding and pie filling
1¾ cups milk
    1 can (11 oz.) mandarin
        oranges, well drained
    1 can (20 oz.) pineapple
        chunks, well drained
    2 cups seedless grapes,
        banana slices* or apple
        chunks
    2 cups miniature
        marshmallows
    1 cup whipping cream,
        whipped, or 2 cups
        whipped cream substitute
    Maraschino cherries or
        strawberries

Makes 10 to 12 servings

Place pudding mix in 4-cup measure or 1½-qt. mixing bowl. Stir in about ⅓ cup milk until smooth, then add remaining milk. Microwave at High 3 minutes; stir. Microwave 1 to 4 minutes, stirring every minute, or until mixture boils. Refrigerate until cold.

In large bowl, combine pudding, fruit and marshmallows. Fold in whipped cream. Refrigerate at least 8 hours or overnight. Garnish with cherries or strawberries.

*If bananas are used, add at serving time.

Cherry Lemon Tarts ▲

24 cupcake liners
  2 tablespoons butter or
    margarine
  1 cup graham cracker crumbs
  2 tablespoons sugar
  1 can (14 oz.) sweetened
    condensed milk
  2 eggs
  1 tablespoon grated lemon
    peel
⅓ cup lemon juice
  1 can (21 oz.) cherry pie filling

Makes 12 servings

Place 2 liners in each 5- or 6-oz. custard cup.* In small bowl, microwave butter at High 45 to 60 seconds, or until melted. Stir in crumbs and sugar. Place 1 rounded tablespoonful crumb mixture in each liner. Press down firmly with small glass. Blend remaining ingredients except pie filling until thickened. Place 2 tablespoons in each cup. Arrange 6 cups in ring in oven.

Microwave at 50% (Medium) 2 to 5 minutes, or just until each bubbles in 1 or 2 spots, rotating after half the time. Remove tarts as they appear done. Cool and serve topped with pie filling. (Extra pie filling can be warmed and served over ice cream.)

*To re-use custard cups, transfer baked tarts to muffin pan to cool. If less than 6 are microwaved at a time, allow 20 to 30 seconds per cup.

Creamy Orange Squares ▶

1 recipe gingersnap or
  chocolate Cookie Crumb
  Crust, page 260
1 package (3 to 3⅝ oz.) vanilla
  pudding and pie filling
2 cups milk
1 package (3 oz.) orange gelatin
1 cup boiling water
1 can (11 oz.) mandarin
  oranges, well drained
1 cup whipping cream,
  whipped, or 2 cups whipped
  cream substitute

Makes 8 or 9 servings

Press all but ¼ cup crumbs in bottom of 8×8- or 9×9-in. baking dish. Microwave at High 1½ minutes, rotating after half the time.

Place pudding mix in 4-cup measure or 1½-qt. mixing bowl. Stir in about ⅓ cup milk until smooth, then add remaining milk. Microwave at High 3 minutes; stir. Microwave 2 to 6 minutes, stirring every minute, or until mixture boils; set aside. Dissolve gelatin in boiling water; stir into pudding with oranges. Refrigerate until thickened but not set.

Fold orange mixture into whipped cream. Spoon over crumb crust. Sprinkle with reserved crumbs. Refrigerate at least 4 hours, or until set.

NOTE: May be served as a fruit salad dessert without the crust.

Make Ahead
Lemon-Blueberry Dessert
pictured at right

3 eggs, separated
½ cup sugar, divided
1 tablespoon grated lemon peel
¼ cup lemon juice
⅓ cup butter or margarine
2½ cups graham cracker crumbs, divided
1 can (21 oz.) blueberry pie filling
2 cups sweetened whipped cream or prepared whipped topping

Makes two 9-in. desserts

Variation:
Double Lemon Dessert:
Substitute 1 can (21 oz.) lemon pie filling for blueberry filling.

Apricot Ring
pictured page 246

1 can (16 oz.) apricots, drained and 3 tablespoons juice reserved
3 eggs, separated
½ cup sugar
Dash salt
¼ cup apricot preserves
2 tablespoons lemon juice
2 cups sweetened whipped cream or prepared whipped topping

To serve:
1 can (8 oz.) apricots, drained

Serves 6 to 8

Purée apricots in blender or food processor. Set aside. In medium bowl beat egg yolks, sugar and salt until thick and lemon-colored. Blend in preserves, lemon juice and reserved apricot juice. Microwave at 50% (Medium) 5 to 7 minutes, or until thick, stirring 1 or 2 times. Mix in puréed apricots. Cool.

Beat egg whites until stiff peaks form. Fold apricot mixture into egg whites, then fold into whipped cream. Pour into 8-cup ring mold. Wrap, label and freeze no longer than 1 month.

To serve, unwrap and dip mold into hot water for 15 to 30 seconds. Loosen edges with knife. Unmold on plate. Garnish with apricots.

How to Microwave Make Ahead Lemon-Blueberry Dessert

Blend egg yolks, ¼ cup sugar, lemon peel and lemon juice in small bowl. Microwave at 50% (Medium) 3 to 5 minutes, or until thick, stirring 2 or 3 times during cooking. Cool.

Line two 9-in. round cake dishes with foil. Place butter in medium bowl. Microwave at High 45 to 60 seconds, or until butter melts. Stir in 2 cups crumbs until moist.

Press half of crumbs evenly and firmly in bottom of each prepared dish. Gently spoon half of pie filling into each crust, taking care not to lift crumbs. Set aside.

Beat egg whites until foamy. Beat in remaining ¼ cup sugar, 1 tablespoon at a time, until soft peaks form. Fold whipped cream into cooled lemon mixture, then fold into beaten egg whites.

Spread half over pie filling in each dish. Sprinkle each with remaining ½ cup graham cracker crumbs. Freeze until firm. Remove from dishes with foil liner. Wrap, label and freeze no longer than 2 weeks.

To serve, unwrap one package and place in 9-in. round cake dish. Microwave at 30% (Medium-Low) 1½ to 3½ minutes, or until wooden pick can be easily inserted in center, taking care not to melt edge. Let stand 10 to 15 minutes.

Banana Custard Pudding   Butterscotch Custard Pudding   Chocolate Custard Pudding

Puddings & Custards

Nutritious puddings and custards help supply the family's daily requirement of milk and eggs in an appealing form. For a party, serve them in a parfait or wine glass and top or layer with fruit or a dessert sauce.

Microwaving makes puddings and custards easy to make. It eliminates much of the stirring, and you can cook in a 4-cup measure.

Vanilla Custard Pudding or Cream Pie Filling

½ cup sugar
2 tablespoons cornstarch
1 tablespoon flour
¼ teaspoon salt
2 cups milk

3 or 4 egg yolks, slightly beaten*
2 tablespoons butter or margarine, optional
1 teaspoon vanilla

Makes 6 servings

In 2- or 2½-qt. mixing bowl or casserole, combine sugar, cornstarch, flour and salt. Stir in milk. Microwave at High 7 to 10 minutes, or until thickened, stirring every 3 minutes.

Stir about ½ cup mixture into yolks. Return to mixture in casserole, stirring well. Microwave 1 to 2 minutes, or until thick. Stir in butter. Cool slightly and stir in vanilla. Cover to prevent skin from forming.

*2 whole eggs may be used. Increase flour to 2 tablespoons. For a pie filling use egg yolks, the filling makes a firm cut with soft sides. If a stiffer filling is desired, increase flour to 2 tablespoons. Use egg whites to make a meringue top.

Strawberry 'n Cream Pudding   Coffee Pecan Custard Pudding   Eggnog Custard Pudding

Variations:

Butterscotch Custard Pudding: Substitute packed brown sugar for granulated sugar. If desired, stir in ¼ cup chopped pecans with vanilla.

Banana Custard Pudding: Fold 2 sliced bananas into vanilla or chocolate pudding with vanilla.

Chocolate Custard Pudding: Increase sugar to ⅔ cup and add 2 ounces unsweetened chocolate to milk mixture. (Chocolate will melt when pudding is stirred. If not smooth, beat with rotary beater before adding yolks.)

Date Nut Custard Pudding: Use half brown sugar and add ½ cup cut-up dates before microwaving. Stir in ¼ cup chopped nuts with vanilla.

Coconut Custard Pudding: Stir ½ cup flaked coconut into mixture before microwaving. Add ¼ teaspoon almond extract with vanilla. (For pie, sprinkle meringue with coconut.)

Strawberry 'n Cream Pudding: Prepare Strawberry Sauce, page 275, and layer with Vanilla Custard Pudding in sherbet or parfait glasses.

Coffee Pecan Custard Pudding: Use half brown sugar and add 2 teaspoons powdered instant coffee to mixture before microwaving. Stir in ⅓ cup chopped pecans with vanilla.

Eggnog Custard Pudding: Use 4 egg yolks. Stir in 2 teaspoons rum flavoring and ¼ teaspoon nutmeg with vanilla. Serve topped with whipped cream and sprinkled with nutmeg.

Calorie Counter: Decrease sugar to ⅓ cup. Use skim milk and omit butter.

Crêpes

1 cup all-purpose flour
1½ cups buttermilk or
    skim milk
1 egg, slightly beaten
¼ teaspoon salt, optional
    Vegetable oil

               Makes 18 crêpes

Blend flour, milk, egg, and salt. Heat lightly oiled 6-in. skillet on conventional range. Pour 2 tablespoons batter in skillet; cook until golden brown on bottom. Turn over. Brown other side. Repeat with remaining batter. Use in one of the following crêpe recipes.

NOTE: Leftover crêpes may be frozen between 2 layers of wax paper.

Per Serving:
Calories: 31
Sodium: 25 mg.
Cholesterol: 15 mg.
Exchanges: ½ bread, ½ fat

◄ Apple Crêpes

8 crêpes, above
¼ cup orange juice
1 teaspoon cornstarch
⅛ teaspoon ground allspice
2 cups unpeeled, chopped
    apples, ¼-in. pieces
2 tablespoons vanilla low fat
    yogurt
⅛ teaspoon orange extract

                  Serves 8

In 1-qt. casserole combine orange juice, cornstarch and allspice. Stir in apples; cover. Microwave at High 7 to 9 minutes, or until apples soften and sauce thickens, stirring once or twice. Place 1 tablespoon mixture on each crêpe; roll up around filling.

In small bowl combine yogurt and extract. Top each crêpe with ¾ teaspoon mixture.

Per Serving:
Calories: 49
Sodium: 25 mg.
Cholesterol: 15 mg.
Exchanges: ½ fruit, ½ bread,
           ½ fat

Banana Crêpes ▲

8 crêpes, opposite
1 cup diet cream soda
2 teaspoons cornstarch
½ teaspoon ginger
1 teaspoon cinnamon
3 ripe bananas, cut into ½-in. chunks
¼ cup vanilla low fat yogurt
Dash cinnamon
Dash nutmeg

Serves 8

In 1-qt. casserole blend soda, cornstarch, ginger and 1 teaspoon cinnamon. Stir in bananas. Microwave at High 3½ to 6½ minutes, or until thickened, stirring 2 or 3 times.

Place 3 tablespoons of banana mixture on each crêpe; roll up around filling.

In small bowl blend yogurt, dash of cinnamon and dash of nutmeg. Top each crêpe with 1½ teaspoons of yogurt mixture.

Per Serving:
Calories: 91
Sodium: 29 mg.
Cholesterol: 15 mg.
Exchanges: 1½ fruit, ½ bread, ½ fat

Raspberry Cheese ▲ Crêpes

8 crêpes, opposite
1 cup low fat cottage cheese
⅓ cup low sugar red raspberry jam
¾ teaspoon vanilla extract
¼ teaspoon cinnamon
⅛ teaspoon nutmeg
2 tablespoons low sugar red raspberry jam

Serves 8

In small mixing bowl combine cottage cheese, ⅓ cup jam, vanilla, cinnamon and nutmeg. Microwave at 50% (Medium) 1 to 2½ minutes, or until mixture is heated and jam dissolves, stirring once or twice. Place 1½ tablespoons filling on each crêpe; roll up around filling. Microwave remaining jam at High 45 seconds to 1¼ minutes, or until melted. Drizzle ¾ teaspoon over each crêpe.

Per Serving:
Calories: 69
Sodium: 95 mg.
Cholesterol: 18 mg.
Exchanges: ½ bread, ½ low fat meat, ½ fat

Mocha Crêpes ▲

8 crêpes, opposite
1 envelope (1 oz.) low calorie chocolate pudding mix
1 cup skim milk
½ cup water
1½ teaspoons instant coffee
¼ cup plus 8 teaspoons prepared low calorie whipped topping

Serves 8

In 1-qt. measure blend pudding mix, milk, water and coffee. Microwave at High 3 to 7 minutes, or until bubbly and slightly thickened, stirring every 2 minutes with wire whip. Place plastic wrap directly on pudding to avoid skin formation. Cool to room temperature. Blend in ¼ cup whipped topping.

Place 2 tablespoons pudding mixture on each crêpe; roll up around filling. Top each crêpe with 1½ to 2 teaspoons pudding mixture and 1 teaspoon whipped topping.

Per Serving:
Calories: 78
Sodium: 43 mg.
Cholesterol: 15 mg.
Exchanges: 1 fruit, ½ bread, ½ fat

Fruit Desserts

Fruit desserts are refreshing, nutritious and low in calories. Because of its speed, microwaving enhances the fresh flavor and texture of fruits.

Fruits microwave quickly, and continue to cook a few minutes after removal from the oven. They should be just fork-tender with a slightly firm, fresh texture.

While fresh fruits are available all year 'round, most of them have peak seasons when their quality and price are best. Fruits in season are naturally sweet and need little or no additional sugar.

Some fruits turn brown when peeled and sliced. Prepare them just before serving time, or sprinkle them with lemon juice.

Bananas Royale ▲

3 or 4 medium bananas, peeled*
2 tablespoons butter or margarine
¼ cup packed brown sugar
¼ teaspoon nutmeg
¼ teaspoon cinnamon
¼ cup whipping cream
1 teaspoon rum flavoring or 2 tablespoons rum
Ice cream

Makes 6 servings

Slice bananas in half lengthwise, then crosswise once. Place butter in 2-qt. casserole. Microwave at High about 30 seconds, or until melted. Stir in sugar, spices and cream. Microwave at High 1½ to 2 minutes, or until slightly thickened; blend well. Add bananas, turning to coat with sauce. Microwave at High 30 seconds. Stir in rum. Serve immediately over ice cream. (To flame, omit rum and follow directions right.)

* Bananas should be very firm and slightly green. If too ripe, they cook to pieces very quickly.

Cherries Jubilee

1 can (16 oz.) pitted dark sweet cherries*
¼ cup sugar
2 teaspoons cornstarch
1 quart vanilla ice cream

Makes 6 to 8 servings

Drain cherries, reserving juice. In 1½-qt. casserole or microwave-proof serving bowl, combine sugar and cornstarch. Gradually stir in cherry juice. Microwave at High 2 to 4 minutes, or until clear and slightly thickened, stirring every minute. Stir in cherries. Microwave at High 30 seconds. Serve hot over ice cream.

*For less sauce, use ¼ cup cherry juice and decrease sugar to 3 tablespoons and cornstarch to 1 teaspoon. Microwave 1 to 1½ minutes.

Flame desserts. Place 2 to 4 tablespoons brandy in small dish. Microwave at High 15 to 20 seconds to warm. Pour into ladle; ignite and pour over dessert.

Peaches & Sour Cream

1 can (29 oz.) peach halves,
 drained
4 to 6 tablespoons brown sugar
 Cinnamon
1 cup dairy sour cream
 Nutmeg

Make 5 or 6 servings

Place peaches around edge of
large pie plate or 9-in. round
baking dish. Place ½ tablespoon sugar in center of each.
Sprinkle with cinnamon. Microwave at High 3 to 6 minutes, or
until sugar bubbles, rotating ¼
turn every minute. Top each half
with spoonful of sour cream.
Sprinkle with nutmeg.
Refrigerate at least 8 hours or
overnight, covering after cool.

Chocolate Bananas

10 wooden skewers
 5 firm bananas, peeled and
 halved crosswise
 1 cup chocolate chips
 3 tablespoons shortening

Makes 10 servings

Insert skewers in cut ends of
bananas. Freeze at least 2
hours. Just before serving, place
chips and shortening in small
mixing bowl. Microwave at 50%
(Medium) 2½ to 4 minutes, or
until most of the chips are shiny
and soft; blend well. Dip frozen
bananas in chocolate to coat or
spoon chocolate over bananas,
allowing excess to drip off. Serve
immediately. (Remelt chocolate
mixture if necessary.) Wrap and
freeze leftover coated bananas.

Dessert Sauces

Butterscotch Topping

1 cup packed brown sugar
2 tablespoons flour
¼ cup milk
2 tablespoons corn syrup
¼ cup butter or margarine
  Dash of nutmeg, optional

Makes about 1½ cups

In 1½-qt. mixing bowl, combine brown sugar and flour. Stir in milk and syrup, then butter. Microwave at High 2 to 4 minutes, or until mixture boils; stir well. Microwave 3½ minutes. Stir in nutmeg. Serve warm.

Easy Caramel Sauce

28 caramel candies (½ lb.)
  ¼ cup half & half or milk

Makes about 1 cup

Combine ingredients in 2-cup measure or small bowl. Microwave at High 2 to 4 minutes, or until melted, stirring every minute. Serve warm or cold.

Hot Fudge Topping

½ cup granulated sugar
½ cup packed brown sugar
3 tablespoons cocoa
2 tablespoons flour
⅛ teaspoon salt
⅔ cup milk
2 tablespoons light corn syrup
1 tablespoon butter or
  margarine
½ teaspoon vanilla

Makes about 1½ cups

In 4-cup measure or small bowl, combine sugars, cocoa, flour and salt. Stir in milk and syrup, then butter. Microwave at High 2 to 4 minutes, or until mixture boils; stir well. Microwave 2 to 5 minutes, or until desired thickness and a rich chocolate color, stirring every 1½ minutes. Stir in vanilla. Serve hot or at room temperature.

Sauces dress up many desserts: ice cream, pudding, gingerbread, fresh fruit, even leftover cake. Microwaving eliminates scorching, constant stirring and messy clean up.

Microwave sauces take only minutes to make. Hot sauces can be made just before serving or as early as the day before. Store them in the refrigerator and reheat the amount needed. To reheat a cup or more, microwave 1 minute, then add 30 seconds at a time, stirring every 30 seconds, until sauce is as warm as desired. Smaller amounts may need only 30 seconds.

Praline Sauce

½ cup packed brown sugar
½ cup butter or margarine
2 tablespoons water

Makes about ¾ cup

Place ingredients in 4-cup measure or small bowl. Microwave at High 1 to 2 minutes, or until butter is almost melted. Stir with rubber spatula or wire whisk, until smooth. Microwave 1½ to 2½ minutes, or until mixture boils 1 minute. Serve warm. Good topped with Cinnamon-sugared Walnuts, page 281.

Variation:

Spun Sugar Topping: Decrease water to 1 tablespoon. Boil 2 minutes. Drizzle in thin stream over ice cream or cold desserts.

NOTE: To reheat leftover sauce, add 1 to 3 teaspoons water.

Quick Chocolate Sundae or Fondue Sauce

1 cup semi-sweet or milk
  chocolate chips
1 cup miniature marshmallows
¼ cup milk

Makes about 1 cup

Combine ingredients in 4-cup measure or small bowl. Microwave at High 2½ to 4½ minutes, or until mixture comes to full boil and is thick and smooth, stirring well every minute. If sauce is too thick, stir in more milk. Serve warm.

For Fondue Sauce: Serve with chunks or wedges of apples, bananas, pears, pineapple, angel food or sponge cake, or large marshmallows.

Strawberry Sauce

2 teaspoons cornstarch
1 package (10-oz.) frozen,
  sweetened strawberries,
  thawed*
1 tablespoon lemon juice
  Red food coloring, optional

Makes about 1⅓ cups

In 4-cup measure or small bowl, combine cornstarch and strawberry juice. Stir in strawberries. Microwave at High 2 to 5 minutes, or until clear and thickened, stirring every minute. Stir in lemon juice and food coloring. Serve warm or cold.

*Other frozen fruit may be substituted for the strawberries.

Candies

Both short-cut and old-fashioned cooked candies microwave easily with a minimum of stirring. Since candy syrups boil hard and can become very hot, use a large container which can withstand high temperatures. A bowl which has a handle is convenient. If a recipe calls for covering, use plastic wrap when a cover is not available.

Do not use a conventional candy thermometer in the microwave oven. Special microwave candy thermometers are available. If you do not have one, follow the cold water tests in the recipes.

Mallow Fudge

1 can (5⅔ oz.) evaporated milk
½ cup butter or margarine
2 cups sugar
1 jar (7 oz.) marshmallow creme

2 cups semisweet chocolate chips
½ cup chopped nuts, optional

Makes about 36 pieces

In 3-qt. casserole, combine milk, butter and sugar. Microwave at High 9 to 12 minutes, or until soft ball forms when small amount is dropped in cold water, stirring every 3 minutes.

Remove cover from creme. Microwave in jar at 50% (Medium) 30 seconds, or until softened. Stir into sugar mixture with chips and nuts until well blended. Pour into buttered or wax paper-lined 9×9-in. pan or dish. Let stand or refrigerate until firm. Cut into 1½-in. squares.

Chocolate Cobblestones

1 lb. chocolate confectioners' or
   candy coating
2 tablespoons shortening
1 cup salted peanuts
2 cups miniature marshmallows

Makes about 1½ lbs.
(36 pieces)

If candy coating is in solid piece,
break into squares. Place in
single layer in 2-qt. casserole
with shortening. Microwave at
50% (Medium) 3 to 5 minutes, or
until pieces are soft, stirring after
3 minutes.

Stir in peanuts, then marshmallows, using as few strokes as
possible. Spread on wax paper
to 9-in. square. Let stand until
firm. Cut into 1½-in. squares.

Nut Yummies

1 lb. vanilla confectioners' or
   candy coating
¼ cup milk

1½ cups salted peanuts
¾ lb. chocolate candy coating

Makes about 3 dozen

If vanilla candy coating is in solid piece, break into squares. Place in
single layer in 2-qt. casserole. Microwave at 50% (Medium) 3 to 5
minutes, or until soft, stirring after 3 minutes. Stir in milk and peanuts.
Drop by rounded measuring teaspoonfuls onto wax paper,
flattening each to ¼- to ½-in., if necessary. Let stand until firm.

Break chocolate candy coating into squares; place in small mixing
bowl. Microwave as directed above for white candy coating. (If too
thick, add 1 tablespoon shortening.) Dip each piece candy into
chocolate coating to cover completely, using 1 or 2 forks. Let stand
on wax paper until firm.

Sponge Candy

1 cup sugar
1 cup dark corn syrup
1 tablespoon vinegar
1 tablespoon soda

Makes about 1 lb.

NOTE: Sponge Candy is a hard candy best made when humidity is low. Pieces can be dipped into melted chocolate.

How to Microwave Sponge Candy

Combine sugar, syrup and vinegar, in 2-qt. mixing bowl or casserole. Cover and microwave at High 3 minutes; stir well.

Microwave uncovered at High 4½ to 10 minutes, until thickened (300°F.). Test by dropping small amount in cold water.

Remove threads from water. If threads bend, microwave a little longer. Candy is done if threads are very brittle.

Quickly stir in soda; mix well. Mixture will foam up as soda is stirred in.

Pour into buttered foil-lined 8×8- or 9×9-in. baking dish, allowing mixture to spread itself.

Let stand until firm. Remove from dish and break into pieces.

Caramel Nut Rolls

½ lb. caramel candies
   (about 28)
¼ cup butter or margarine
2 tablespoons half & half or
   milk
1½ cups confectioners' sugar
1 cup salted peanuts
2 cups miniature
   marshmallows
1 cup flaked coconut

Makes about 2 lbs.
(48 pieces)

In 2-qt. casserole or mixing
bowl, place caramels, butter and
half & half. Microwave at 50%
(Medium) 3 to 5 minutes, or until
melted and smooth, stirring after
2 minutes, then every minute.

Stir in sugar until smooth, then
peanuts. Stir in marshmallows,
using as few strokes as possible.
Sprinkle 2 large sheets of wax
paper with coconut. Spoon half
the caramel mixture in strip on
each sheet. Shape into 10- or
12-in. rolls, using wax paper to
help shape; coat well with
coconut. Wrap and refrigerate.
To serve, cut into ½-in. slices.

Light Caramels

2 cups sugar
¾ cup light corn syrup
¼ cup butter or margarine
1¾ cups whipping cream,
   divided
Pinch salt
1 teaspoon vanilla
1 cup chopped walnuts or
   other nuts, optional

Makes about 2 lbs. (36 pieces)

In 3-qt. casserole, combine
sugar, syrup, butter, 1 cup
cream and salt. Microwave at
High 10 minutes, stirring twice.
Gradually stir in ¾ cup cream.
Microwave 15 to 19 minutes, or
until hard ball forms (250°F.)
when small amount is dropped in
cold water. Stir every 3 or 4 minutes the first 15 minutes, then
every 1 or 2 minutes. (When cooked, mixture will be caramel color.)

Stir in vanilla and nuts. Pour into
buttered foil-lined 8×8-in. pan.
Let stand until firm. Remove from
pan. Cut into 1-in. squares. Wrap
in plastic wrap.

NOTE: If mixture separates while
cooking, beat until smooth with
wire whisk or rotary beater.

279

10-Minute Peanut Brittle

1 cup sugar
½ cup light corn syrup
⅛ teaspoon salt
1 to 1½ cups roasted, salted
    peanuts

1 tablespoon butter or
    margarine
1 teaspoon vanilla
1 teaspoon soda

Makes 1 pound

Very-Thin Peanut Brittle
Cool mixture on cookie sheet 3
to 5 minutes. Lift from sheet
and pull or stretch mixture to
desired thinness.

How to Microwave Peanut Brittle

Combine sugar, syrup and
salt in 2-qt. casserole or
mixing bowl. Microwave at
High 5 minutes.

Stir in peanuts. Microwave 2 to 5
minutes, stirring after 2 and 4
minutes, until syrup and peanuts
are lightly browned.

Stir in butter, vanilla and soda
until light and foamy. Spread
to ¼-in. thickness on large,
well-buttered cookie sheet.

Bark Candy

1 pound confectioners' or
    candy coating (vanilla,
    chocolate, butterscotch or
    caramel)
1 cup of any of the following:
    roasted, salted nuts
    (unblanched almonds,
    peanuts, walnuts, pecans
    or mixed nuts) sunflower
    seeds or soya nuts, raisins

Makes approx. 1¼ pounds

If candy coating is in a solid
piece, break into squares.
Place in a single layer in a
2-qt. casserole. Microwave at
50% power (Medium) 3 to 5
minutes, until pieces are soft,
stirring after 3 minutes.

Add nuts, seeds or raisins. Stir
until candy coating is smooth
and completely melted.

Spread on wax paper to ¼-in.
thickness. Cool until hard, then
break into pieces.

Granola Crunch

½ cup butter or margarine
¾ cup packed brown sugar
¼ cup honey
¼ cup water
1 teaspoon salt
½ teaspoon cinnamon
3 cups old-fashioned oats
1 cup sunflower seed or almond
  slices
1 cup wheat germ
1 cup flaked coconut, optional*

Makes 2 lbs.

In 2½- or 3-qt. casserole, combine butter, sugar, honey, water, salt and cinnamon. Microwave at High 5 to 8 minutes, or until slightly thickened, stirring after 4 to 6 minutes.

Stir in remaining ingredients. Reduce power to 50% (Medium). Microwave 8 to 12 minutes, or until rich golden brown, stirring after 3 to 6 minutes, then every 2 minutes. Spread on buttered cookie sheet, pressing down lightly with pancake turner. Let stand until firm. Break into small pieces and store in airtight container.

*Raisins may be substituted; stir in after microwaving.

Cinnamon-sugared Walnuts

½ cup sugar
½ cup packed brown sugar
½ cup water
½ teaspoon cinnamon
½ teaspoon vanilla
2 cups walnut halves or other
  nuts

Makes 3 cups
(scant lb.)

In 3-qt. mixing bowl or casserole, combine sugars, water and cinnamon. Cover and microwave at High 3 minutes; stir well. Microwave uncovered 5 to 8 minutes, or until soft ball forms when small amount is dropped in cold water.*

Stir in vanilla and walnuts until coating sugars. Spread on wax paper. Let stand until firm. Store in airtight container.

*If mixture boils near top of dish, open oven door occasionally to slow down boiling.

Glazed Corn & Nut Clusters

1 cup butter or margarine
½ cup light corn syrup
1¼ cups sugar
2 quarts salted popped corn
1½ to 2 cups nuts*
1 teaspoon vanilla

Makes 12 cups

In 2- or 2½-qt. mixing bowl or casserole, combine butter, syrup and sugar. Microwave at High 9 to 15 minutes, or until brittle threads form when small amount is dropped in cold water, stirring every 3 minutes.

In buttered 5-qt. (or larger) container, combine corn and nuts. Stir vanilla into cooked syrup and immediately pour over corn mixture. Stir with meat fork until well coated. Spread mixture in single layer on 2 large sheets of wax paper. Let stand until firm. Break into small pieces and store in airtight container.

*Use walnut or pecan halves, whole almonds, salted peanuts or a combination.

Fruits, Peels & Nuts

Fruits & Peels

The microwave oven cooks fresh or dried fruits quickly for true fruit taste, and also aids in everyday preparations like peeling and juicing. Use lemon and orange rinds to prepare your own extracts and dried or candied peels.

Airtight Jars

Save pimiento jars and spice bottles for microwave dried fruit peels and citrus extracts. Instant coffee or tea jars make good containers for candied peels.

◄ **Peel Tomatoes, Peaches, Nectarines & Apricots.** Place 4 cups water in large bowl or 3-qt. casserole. Cover with plastic wrap or glass lid. Microwave at High 8 to 11 minutes, or until boiling. Place three fruits in water. Let stand 1 to 1½ minutes. Remove fruit to bowl of cold water. Skin will then peel easily. Do only three pieces at a time. For additional fruit, return water to boiling and repeat procedure. For one or two fruits, place 1 cup water in small bowl or 2-cup measure. Microwave, covered, at High 2 to 3 minutes, or until boiling. Do only one piece at a time. Proceed as directed above.

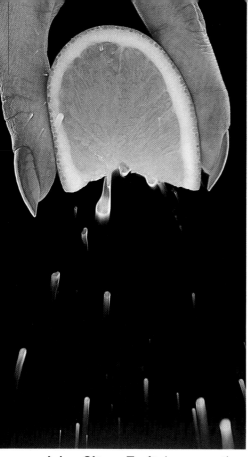

Juice Citrus Fruit. Increase the amount of juice from fresh oranges, grapefruit, lemons or limes. Before cutting and squeezing, microwave at High 20 to 35 seconds, or until slightly warm to the touch.

Plump Dried Fruit. Place 1 cup dried fruit (raisins, apricots, prunes or mixed dried fruit) in small bowl. Sprinkle with 1 tablespoon water. Cover with plastic wrap. Microwave at High 30 to 60 seconds, or until plumped and softened, stirring after half the time. Let stand, covered, 2 to 3 minutes. Drain any remaining liquid.

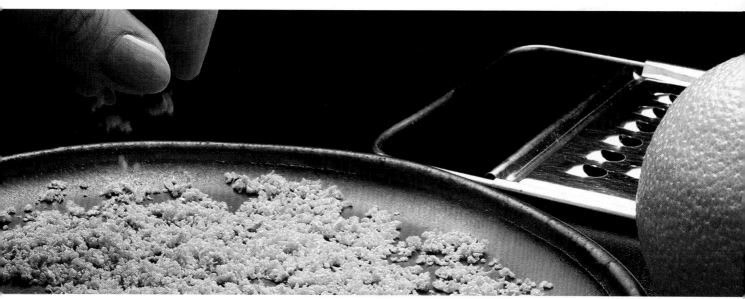

Dried Orange & Lemon Peel. Sprinkle grated peel from one medium orange or two small lemons (about 2 tablespoons) evenly in single layer on plate. Microwave at High 2 to 4 minutes, or until dry to the touch, turning plate and lifting and tossing peel with fingers after each minute. Let stand about 2 hours, or until completely cooled and brittle.

Store in small airtight container no longer than 2 months.

NOTE: ½ teaspoon dried peel is equivalent to 1 teaspoon grated fresh peel.

◄ Lemon or Orange Extract

1 lemon or orange
½ cup vodka

Makes ½ cup

Remove peel from lemon with vegetable peeler or zester. Do not include white membrane. Place peel in 4-oz. bottle. Add vodka. Microwave at High 30 to 45 seconds, or until bottle is warm to the touch. Cap bottle. Let stand at room temperature about 2 weeks before using.

Stewed Fruit

1 cup dried fruit (prunes, apricots, apples or mixed dried fruit)
½ cup water

Makes 1 cup

Place dried fruit in 1½-qt. casserole; sprinkle with water. Cover. Microwave at High 2 to 4 minutes, or until water boils, stirring after each minute. Let stand, covered, 5 minutes. Stir before serving. Sprinkle with cinnamon, if desired.

Candied Pineapple ▲

1 cup sugar
1 can (20 oz.) pineapple slices, packed in own juice, drained and ⅓ cup juice reserved
2 tablespoons light corn syrup
Sugar

Makes 10 slices

In 3-qt. casserole combine 1 cup sugar, ⅓ cup reserved pineapple juice and the corn syrup. Arrange five pineapple slices in single layer over sugar mixture. Microwave at High 8 to 12 minutes, or until sugar dissolves and slices are glossy and transparent on edges, turning over and rearranging every 4 minutes. Remove slices to wire rack to cool. They will become more transparent as they stand.

Add remaining slices to hot syrup. Microwave as directed above. Cool. When slices have cooled completely, coat with sugar. Cover with wax paper and let stand on wire rack at least 24 hours to dry. Re-coat with sugar. Slices will be slightly sticky. Store in airtight container with wax paper between layers no longer than 2 weeks.

Candied Peel

   3 large oranges
   1 lemon
6⅓ cups water, divided
  ⅔ cup granulated sugar
  ¼ cup powdered sugar

Makes 1 cup

How to Microwave Candied Peel

Remove peel from oranges and lemon with vegetable peeler or zester. Do not include the white membrane of the fruit.

Combine 2 cups water and the strips of peel in 4-cup measure or medium bowl. Microwave at High 4 to 6 minutes, or until water boils. Drain.

Repeat process 2 more times, boiling all the peel in 2 cups of water each time. Rinse peel. Drain on paper towels; pat dry.

Combine ⅓ cup water and the granulated sugar in 3-qt. casserole. Stir in peel. Microwave at High 6 to 8 minutes, or until sugar dissolves and peel is glossy and transparent, stirring every 2 minutes.

Remove peel with slotted spoon to rack. Cool. Sift powdered sugar over peel. Let cool completely. Store in airtight container no longer than 1 month.

Serve as a dipper for chocolate fondue, or add one strip of peel to cup of coffee or hot chocolate to flavor the drink.

Nuts & Seeds

Turn to your microwave oven whenever you need to shell or toast nuts for baking, garnishing or snacking. Even chestnuts and Brazil nuts shell easily after microwaving. Toasting nuts and seed enhances their flavor.

◄ **Shelled Nuts.** Shell nuts which are difficult to remove whole when cracked. In medium bowl or 2-qt. casserole combine 8 ounces of unshelled walnuts, pecans, Brazil nuts, filberts or almonds and 1 cup water. Cover with plastic wrap. Microwave at High 2½ to 4 minutes, or until water boils. Let stand 1 minute; drain. Spread on paper towels to cool. Crack shells and remove nutmeats. Shells will contain hot water, so open them carefully.

Peeled Chestnuts. Start with ¼ pound (about 1 cup) of nuts. Make a horizontal cut through shell of each chestnut without cutting nutmeat. Cut should extend across width of rounded side and just past edges of flat side. Place chestnuts in 4-cup measure or 1-qt. casserole. Pour in 1 cup water. Cover with plastic wrap or glass lid. Microwave at High 2½ to 4 minutes, or until water boils. Boil 1 minute. Let stand 5 to 10 minutes.

Remove nuts one at a time from water. Peel shell and inner skin. Spread on paper towel to cool. Set aside any which do not peel easily; boil again.

Blanched Almonds. Place 1 cup water in 1-qt. casserole; cover. Microwave at High 2 to 3½ minutes, or until boiling. Add 1 cup unblanched whole shelled almonds. Microwave, uncovered, at High 1 minute. Drain. Slip skins off. Spread on paper towels to dry.

Toasted Almonds. Place 1 tablespoon butter or margarine in 9-in. pie plate. Microwave at High 30 to 45 seconds, or until melted. Stir in ½ cup blanched whole almonds or ¼ cup slivered or sliced almonds, tossing to coat. Microwave at High 3 to 7 minutes (whole) or 3½ to 4½ minutes (slivered or sliced), or until light golden brown, stirring every 2 minutes. Let stand 5 minutes. Almonds will continue to toast after they are removed from oven. Use as a garnish for vegetables or main dishes.

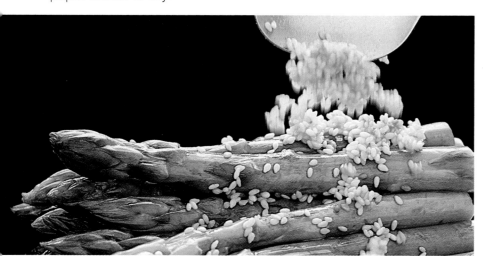

Toasted Sesame Seed. Place 1 tablespoon butter or margarine in 1-cup measure. Microwave at High 30 to 45 seconds, or until melted. Stir in 2 tablespoons sesame seed. Microwave at High 3 to 4½ minutes, or until light golden brown, stirring after each minute. Let stand 2 to 3 minutes. Seed will continue to toast after it is removed from oven. Drain seed on paper towel-lined plate. Sprinkle over cooked vegetables.

Toasted Coconut. Sprinkle ½ cup grated fresh coconut in thin layer in 9-in. pie plate. Microwave at 70% (Medium-High) 3 to 4 minutes, or until light brown, tossing with fork after each minute. Let cool. Store in airtight container no longer than 1 month. Serve with curry dishes or use as a dessert garnish.

Popcorn

Popping corn in the microwave is fast and easy and requires little clean-up. Because it uses little or no oil, microwave popcorn is a light snack.

Fresh popcorn is low in moisture. To get the best yield of popped kernels, maintain low moisture by storing in an airtight jar in a dry, cool place.

Microwave popcorn poppers are essential equipment. Do not try to microwave popcorn in a brown paper bag; it could catch on fire. For amounts of popcorn and cooking times, follow the instructions for your popper. Don't overcook. Listen; corn is done as soon as it stops popping. Discard any unpopped kernels.

The popcorn snacks on these pages can be made with corn you pop yourself, or from bagged popped corn purchased from the supermarket. Leftover or purchased popcorn can also be rewarmed and refreshed in the microwave oven.

Cheese Popcorn ▲

8 cups popped popcorn
¼ cup plus 2 tablespoons butter or margarine
¼ cup grated American cheese food
¼ cup grated Parmesan cheese
Seasoned salt

Makes 8 cups

Place popcorn in large bowl. Set aside. Place butter in 2-cup measure. Microwave at High 45 seconds to 1¼ minutes, or until melted and bubbly. Stir in cheeses. Drizzle over popcorn. Toss to coat. Sprinkle with seasoned salt to taste.

Variation:

Substitute ¼ cup grated Romano cheese for the grated American cheese food.

Rewarm Popped Popcorn

Place 4 to 8 cups in large bowl. Microwave at High 45 seconds to 1½ minutes, or until popcorn is warm to the touch, tossing every 30 seconds. Do not overheat.

Caramel Corn

3 tablespoons butter or
    margarine
¾ cup packed brown sugar
⅓ cup shelled raw peanuts
3 tablespoons dark corn syrup
½ teaspoon vanilla
¼ teaspoon baking soda
    Dash salt
5 cups popped popcorn

Makes 5 cups

NOTE: Soft Crack Stage: Syrup
separates into hard but not
brittle threads when dropped
into cold water.

How to Microwave Caramel Corn

Place butter in 8-cup measure
or large bowl. Microwave at High
30 to 45 seconds, or until melted.

Stir in brown sugar, peanuts
and corn syrup. Insert microwave candy thermometer.

Microwave at High 3 to 4
minutes, or until mixture reaches
280°F. (soft crack stage).

Mix in vanilla, baking soda and
salt. Place prepared popcorn in
large bowl.

Pour hot mixture quickly over
popcorn, stirring to coat. Microwave popcorn at High 2 minutes, stirring after half the time.

Stir again. Cool about 30
minutes, stirring occasionally to
break apart.

Convenience Foods

Many convenience foods now include microwave instructions on the packages. Most of them can be microwaved to serving temperature in far less time than it takes conventionally. Even foods which you finish in a conventional oven become more convenient when you microwave-defrost them first.

How to Microwave TV Dinners High Power, 7½-11 min.

Remove foil-lined lid from tray. Place dessert in custard cup and set aside. Remove any bread.

Cover tray with wax paper and place in oven. Microwave at High for ½ the total time.

Turn main course over; stir vegetables. Microwave remaining time. Microwave dessert 20 to 30 seconds, or cook in toaster oven.

How to Microwave Family-Size Entreés High Power, 8-10 min. per lb.

Preheat browning grill 5 minutes at High. Loosen lid from foil pan. If lid is foil-lined, replace it with wax paper cut to same size.

Place pan on grill. Be sure wax paper does not touch grill. Microwave at High, rotating pan ½ turn after ½ the cooking time.

Heat from grill defrosts bottom of food, making it unnecessary to remove from foil pan. After heating let stand, covered, 5 minutes or as package directs.

How to Defrost Orange Juice or Lemonade

Remove one metal lid from 6-oz. can of frozen orange juice. Place upright in oven. Microwave at High ½ to 1½ minutes.

Concentrate should be softened but not warm. Pour into container and stir in cold water as directed on package.

How to Microwave Fully-Cooked Fried Chicken   High Power, 1 lb., 9-11 min.; 2 lb., 15-17 min.

Separate chicken pieces and arrange on roasting rack in single layer with meatiest portions to outside of dish.

Cover with paper towel. Microwave at High for ½ the time. Rearrange pieces, but do not turn over. Cover.

Microwave remaining time. Remove to plate lined with paper towels. Cover with paper towel and let stand 2 to 3 minutes to crisp.

How to Defrost Frozen Bread Dough

Measure 1 to 1½ cups water into a 12×8-in. baking dish. Microwave at High until boiling. Heavily grease an 8×4 or 9×5-in. loaf dish. Butter frozen dough on all sides.

Place in loaf dish set in hot water. Cover with wax paper. Microwave at 50% power (Medium) 2 minutes, rotating ¼ turn every minute. Turn dough over.

Microwave and rotate 2 minutes more. Let stand 10 minutes. Dough should be defrosted and slightly warm. If not, microwave and rotate, 1 minute at a time, until ready.

How to Defrost Frozen 2-Crust Pies and Pot Pies   50% Power (Medium), 5½-9 min. per lb.

Remove pie from metal pan to a suitable glass pie plate, inverted 1½-qt. casserole lid or an individual casserole.

Microwave at 50% power (Medium), rotating after ½ the time. Pie is defrosted when a wooden pick can be inserted in center.

Bake conventionally as directed on package for ½ to ⅔ suggested time. Do not defrost 1-crust custard pies before baking.

How to Defrost Cakes and Brownies   30% Power (Low), 1½-3½ min. per lb.

Remove cake or brownies from foil pan. Place on plate lined with paper towel.

Microwave at 30% power (Low), rotating after ½ the time. Lower power level is necessary or frosting will melt. Watch whipped cream frosting carefully.

Test by inserting a wooden pick into center of cake or brownies. Pick should meet little or no resistance.

How to Defrost Cream Pies   30% Power (Low), ¾-2 min. per lb.

Remove pie from foil pan to plate or pie dish. Microwave at 30% Power (Low).

Test by inserting wooden pick in center of pie. It should meet no resistance. Let stand 5 minutes, if needed, to complete defrosting.

How to Microwave Frozen Vegetables in Box or Poly Bag

Place frozen vegetables in 1-qt. casserole with 2 tablespoons water. Cover.

Microwave at High as directed in chart, on pages 194-195, until vegetables are heated and tender-crisp, stirring once.

Let stand, covered, 2 to 3 minutes to equalize heat and complete cooking.

How to Microwave Frozen Vegetables in Pouch

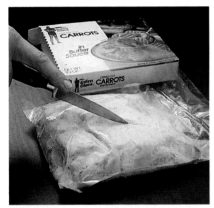

Flex pouch to break apart vegetables. Cut large "X" in one side of pouch.

Place cut side down in 1-qt. casserole or serving dish.

Microwave at High as directed in chart, opposite, until center of pouch is hot to touch. Empty vegetables into dish; stir.

How to Microwave Frozen Stir-Fry Vegetables

Preheat microwave browning dish at High 3 minutes. Spread vegetables in dish.

Pour 1 tablespoon vegetable oil over vegetables and sprinkle with seasonings from packet.

Stir quickly to coat pieces. Cover. Microwave at High as directed on package, until vegetables are heated and tender-crisp.

Baby Food

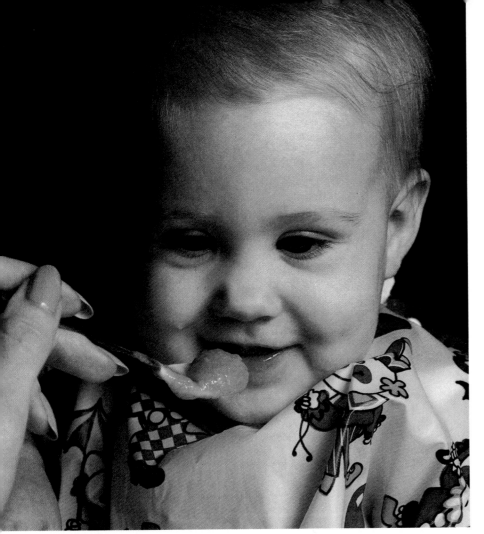

Microwaving vegetables and fruits for baby has the same advantages it does for adults. It's faster and needs less water than conventional cooking, so more nutrients are retained. The taste and color are fresh. Homemade baby food has no added salt, sugar or preservatives. Freeze it in single servings for quick defrosting in the microwave.

Formula and commercial baby food can also be warmed in the microwave oven. It takes just a few seconds.

How to Freeze & Defrost Homemade Baby Food

Freeze baby food in ¼-cup or ½-cup quantities in freezer bags or small jars. Or, place 2 tablespoons baby food in each section of ice cube tray. Freeze until solid; place cubes in freezer bag and seal. Label and freeze no longer than 6 months.

Defrost food in small bowl. Microwave as directed in chart, right, until warm, stirring and breaking apart with a fork after half the time. Test temperature before feeding baby.

Don't Overheat

Baby food and formula should be warmed, not heated. A safe temperature of 80° to 90°F. will feel slightly warm when a few drops of formula are sprinkled on the inner wrist.

Defrosting Baby Food Chart

Amount	Microwave Time at High
2 tablespoons (1 cube)	20 - 40 sec.
¼ cup (2 cubes)	45 - 60 sec.
½ cup (4 cubes)	1 - 2 min.

Cooking Vegetables for Homemade Baby Food Chart

Cook vegetables as directed. To purée cooked vegetables for baby food, follow directions, below.

Item	Amount	Cooked Yield	Microwave Time at High	Procedure
Sweet Potato (7 to 8 oz. each)	2	1½ cups	5 - 9 minutes	Pierce potatoes with fork. Place on paper towel. Rearrange after half the time. Peel and quarter.
Acorn Squash (1 lb.)	1	1 cup	5 - 7 minutes	Cut in half. Scoop out seeds and fibers. Wrap each half in plastic wrap. Rearrange after half the time. Scoop out pulp.
Carrots 1 lb.	6 medium	2 cups	7 - 9 minutes	Peel and slice ¼-in. thick. Place in 2-qt. casserole with ¼ cup water; cover. Stir every 2 minutes. Let stand, covered, about 5 minutes.
Frozen Loose-Pack Vegetables	1 cup	1 cup	4 - 6½ minutes	Place in 22-oz. casserole. Add 2 teaspoons water; cover. Stir 2 or 3 times.

Puréed Baby Food From Fresh Vegetables. Microwave vegetable as directed in chart, above. Place cooked vegetable in blender. Add ½ cup water. (Except acorn squash; use ¼ cup water.) Blend about 1 minute, or until puréed. If thinner consistency is desired, add up to an additional ¼ cup water.

Variation:
Puréed Baby Food From Frozen Vegetables. Microwave frozen vegetables as directed in chart, above. Place vegetables, cooking liquid and 3 to 5 tablespoons additional water in blender. Blend about 1 minute, or until puréed.

Applesauce. Peel and core four cooking apples. Chop finely. Place in 2-qt. casserole. Add ½ cup water; cover. Microwave at High 10 to 13 minutes, or until tender, stirring 1 or 2 times. Place in blender. Add 2 tablespoons sugar, if desired. Blend about 30 seconds, or until puréed. Makes about 2 cups.

Convenience Baby Food Chart

Item	Amount	Microwave Time at High: Room Temp.	Microwave Time at High: Refrigerated	Procedure
Baby Food Jars 3½ to 4¾ oz. or half of 7½ to 7¾ oz.	1 jar	15 - 30 sec.	30 - 40 sec.	Transfer food from jar to serving dish. Stir and check temperature after half the minimum time. Do not overheat. If necessary, continue microwaving. When microwaving two or more jars at a time, check temperature after minimum time and remove any food that is warm. Check temperature before feeding baby.
	2 jars	30 - 40 sec.	1 - 1¼ min.	
	3 jars	40 - 60 sec.	1¼ - 1½ min.	
Baby Formula	4 oz.	15 - 20 sec.	25 - 40 sec.	Use dishwasher-safe plastic or glass bottles for baby formula. Do not use bottles with plastic liners. The liners can melt in the microwave oven. Microwave, without cap and nipple, until warm. To test temperature, attach nipple and cap; shake bottle to distribute heat. Sprinkle few drops on inner wrist.
	6 oz.	20 - 30 sec.	30 - 45 sec.	
	8 oz.	30 sec.	45 - 60 sec.	

Kids' Stuff

Lollipops

1 cup sugar
½ cup light corn syrup
¼ cup water
¼ teaspoon orange, lemon,
    peppermint, or lime extract
    Food coloring (orange,
    yellow, red or green)
12 wooden popsicle sticks or
    lollipop sticks

            Makes 12 lollipops

NOTE: Hard Crack Stage: Syrup
separates into hard, brittle threads
when dropped into cold water.

How to Microwave Lollipops

Mix sugar, corn syrup and water
in 8-cup measure. Use wet pastry
brush to wash sugar crystals
from sides of measure. Insert
microwave candy thermometer.

Microwave at High 9 to 12½
minutes, or until mixture reaches
310°F. (hard crack stage), stirring every 2 minutes. Stir in desired extract and food coloring.

Pour over sticks arranged on
buttered foil, or pour into lollipop
molds, below. Let stand about 1
hour, or until hard. Wrap in plastic
wrap. Store in a cool, dry place.

How to Make Lollipop Molds

Cut 1 inch off top of twelve 9-oz.
wax-coated paper drinking
cups.

Grease inside of top portion of
cup. Punch small hole in side of
mold; insert stick.

Place molds on buttered foil. Fill
as directed, above.

Graham Cracker Cookies

1 cup all-purpose flour
½ cup whole wheat flour
2 tablespoons sugar
½ teaspoon baking soda
¼ teaspoon salt
¼ teaspoon ground cinnamon
¼ cup shortening

1 tablespoon butter or
   margarine
2 tablespoons plus 1
   teaspoon water
1 tablespoon honey
1 tablespoon molasses
½ teaspoon vanilla

Makes 3 to 3½ dozen cookies

In medium bowl combine flours, sugar, baking soda, salt and cinnamon. Cut in shortening and butter until particles resemble small peas. In small bowl combine water, honey, molasses and vanilla. Sprinkle over dry mixture, tossing with fork until particles cling together and resemble small peas. Form into a ball. Cover with plastic wrap. Refrigerate at least 1 hour.

Divide dough in half. Roll out half the dough to ⅛-in. thickness between two sheets of wax paper. Cut with cookie cutters. Prick with fork. Line 10-in. plate with wax paper. Arrange 12 cookies around edge of plate. Microwave at High 1 to 2 minutes, or until dry and firm to the touch, rotating every 30 seconds. Cool on wire rack. Cookies will crisp as they cool. Repeat with remaining dough.

Edible Ornaments

1 tablespoon butter or
   margarine
1 cup miniature marshmallows
3 shredded wheat biscuits,
   crushed
   Jelly beans, red hot candies
   or black gumdrops, optional

Makes 4 to 6 ornaments

Place butter in medium bowl. Microwave at High 30 to 45 seconds, or until melted. Add marshmallows, stirring to coat. Microwave at High 30 to 60 seconds, or until marshmallows puff and mixture can be stirred smooth. Stir in crushed cereal.

Shape into Easter nests and fill with colored jelly beans; or shape into Christmas wreaths and decorate with red hot candies; or shape into snowmen and decorate with black gumdrops and red hot candies.

Microwaving is a good way for children to learn to cook. It's safe because the oven doesn't get hot. In the excitement of sampling their results, children can forget to turn off a conventional oven or surface burner; the microwave oven turns off automatically, so less adult supervision is needed.

The speed and simplicity of microwave cooking appeal to children, who like to make uncomplicated foods which are done fast; otherwise they may become discouraged or lose interest. These nutritious snacks are so easy the children can cook and clean up themselves.

Hamburger. Place one ¼-lb. hamburger patty on microwave roasting rack. Cover with wax paper. Microwave at High 1 minute. Turn over; cover. Microwave 30 seconds to 1½ minutes, or until meat is no longer pink. Let stand 1 to 2 minutes.

For two patties, microwave first side 1½ minutes; turn. Microwave second side 1 to 2½ minutes.

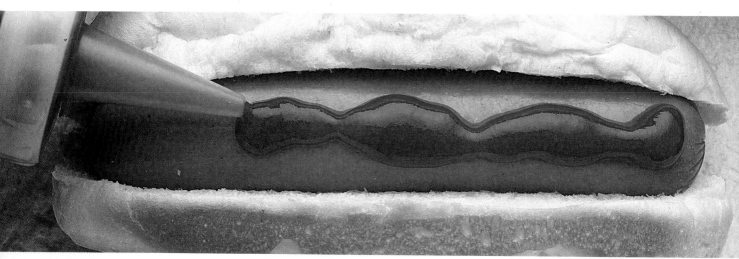

Hot Dog. Place one or two hot dogs in bun. Wrap each in paper towel. Microwave one at High 30 to 45 seconds, or two 45 seconds to 1¼ minutes, or until buns are warm to the touch, rearranging and rotating after half the time.

Pizza Crackers

4 saltine crackers
   Bottled pizza sauce
1 slice (¾ oz.) mozzarella
   cheese, quartered
4 thin slices pepperoni,
   optional

Serves 1

Spread crackers with pizza sauce. Top each with a cheese quarter and a slice of pepperoni. Place on paper plate. Microwave at 50% (Medium) 30 to 60 seconds, or until cheese melts, rotating plate after 30 seconds.

Mini S'More Snacks

2 Graham Cracker Cookies,
   page 301, or 2 graham
   cracker squares
1 square of a milk chocolate
   candy bar (1.45 oz.), or
   6 chocolate chips
3 miniature marshmallows

Serves 1

Prepare Graham Cracker Cookies as directed. Place one cookie or cracker on paper napkin or paper plate. Top with chocolate square or chips and marshmallows. Microwave at High 15 to 30 seconds, or until marshmallows just start to puff. Top with second cookie.

Easy Fruit & Gelatin

1 can (17 oz.) fruit cocktail,
   packed in its own juice
⅓ cup water
1 box (3 oz.) fruit-flavored
   gelatin
1 cup cold water

Serves 4

In 1½-qt. casserole combine fruit and juice with ⅓ cup water. Microwave at High 4 to 7 minutes, or until boiling, stirring after half the time. Mix in gelatin, stirring until dissolved. Stir in 1 cup cold water. Chill until set.

Miscellaneous Tips

Discover some of the microwave shortcuts and simple techniques you can use to make cooking easier. Soften an underripe avocado when there isn't time to let nature do it, or ease opening of fresh clams and oysters. Add a pretty top crust to a microwaved pie, or speed conventional cooking by using the microwave to scald milk or rehydrate dried beans.

Scald Milk. Place ½ cup milk in 1-cup measure. Microwave at High 1 to 1½ minutes, or until thin film forms over top of milk and tiny bubbles form at edge of cup (about 175°F.).

For 1 cup milk, place in 2-cup measure; microwave at High 2 to 2¾ minutes.

Soften Avocados. Use your microwave to soften underripe avocados, then use them in your favorite recipe. Microwave avocados at High 1 minute. Cool completely before slicing or mashing.

Warm Chow Mein Noodles. Before serving, place about 1 cup noodles at a time on serving plate. Microwave at High 1 to 1½ minutes, or until bottom center of plate is warm to the touch.

Drier Baked Potatoes. For drier skins on microwave baked potatoes, stand pierced potatoes on end in muffin cups.

Soften Acorn Squash. Soften acorn squash to ease cutting. Microwave 1-lb. squash at High 1½ minutes, or until just warm to the touch. Halve and remove seeds. Place butter and brown sugar in cavity. Add nuts, if desired. Cover each half with plastic wrap. Microwave at High 6 to 10 minutes, or until tender.

Hard-Cook Eggs. To hard-cook eggs for chopping and adding to salads or casseroles, crack one egg into small, lightly greased bowl or custard cup. Prick yolk with wooden pick. Cover with plastic wrap. Microwave at 50% (Medium) 1¾ to 2 minutes, or until white is set and yolk is almost set. Let stand, covered, 1 minute to complete cooking.

Bacon-Basted Meats & Poultry. When microwaving roasts or whole poultry with very little natural fat cover, place strips of bacon over top of meat and secure with wooden picks. The bacon shields meat, attracts energy evenly and allows some browning while basting and flavoring the meat.

Warm Brandy. Place 2 ounces of brandy in snifter. Microwave at High 15 seconds to warm.

Rehydrate Dried Beans. Dried beans don't need to be soaked in water overnight. Place 1 lb. dried beans with 8 cups water in 5-qt. casserole; cover tightly. Microwave at High 8 to 10 minutes, or until boiling. Let stand, covered, 1 hour. Continue as directed in your favorite recipe.

Easy Tea. Heat water for brewing tea right in the teapot. Be sure teapot does not have any metal parts. Measure about 4 cups water into teapot; cover. Microwave at High 8 to 10 minutes, or until boiling. Add tea.

Two-Crust Pies. To give a microwaved one-crust pie a two-crust appearance, prepare a lattice top as directed, below, or prepare pastry cut-outs.

To make cut-outs, roll excess dough to ⅛-in. thickness and cut with cookie cutters. Or, cut out one 6- to 7-in. circle and prick with fork to mark six wedges.

Transfer pieces to wax paper, arranging pieces in ring.

Sprinkle with ground cinnamon and sugar. Microwave at High 2 to 4 minutes, or until dry and puffy, rotating after each minute. Place cut-outs on top of prepared pie.

How to Microwave Lattice Top

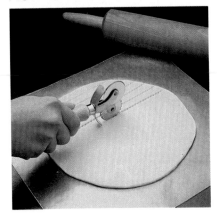

Roll excess pastry into 8-in. circle on wax paper. Cut into ten or twelve ½-in. wide strips.

Weave strips to form lattice on wax paper. Microwave at High 2 to 4 minutes, or until dry and puffy, rotating after each minute.

Remove lattice top from wax paper while warm. Place on top of the prepared pie.

Croutons. Prepare croutons to use in salads or to top casseroles. Cut enough white, wheat, rye or other bread into ½-in. cubes to measure 4 cups. Spread cubes in 12 × 8-in. baking dish. Microwave at High 4 to 5 minutes, or until dry to the touch, stirring every 2 minutes. Let stand until cool.

Variations:
Herb-Seasoned Croutons:
Microwave 1 tablespoon butter or margarine at High 30 to 45 seconds, or until melted. Stir in 1 teaspoon dried parsley flakes, ½ teaspoon poultry seasoning, and ⅛ teaspoon salt. Toss cubed bread in seasoned butter. Microwave as directed.

Italian-Seasoned Croutons:
Microwave 1 tablespoon butter or margarine at High 30 to 45 seconds, or until melted. Mix in 1 tablespoon grated Parmesan or Romano cheese, 1 teaspoon dried parsley flakes, ⅛ teaspoon salt, and ⅛ teaspoon garlic powder. Toss cubed bread in seasoned butter. Microwave as directed.

Bread Crumbs. Prepare bread crumbs to use for coating, toppings or as an ingredient in recipes. Microwave Croutons as directed, above. After cooling, crush in blender or place cubes in plastic bag and crush with rolling pin.

Variation:
Seasoned Bread Crumbs: Prepare Herb-Seasoned or Italian-Seasoned Croutons as directed, above. Crush.

Re-crisp Snack Foods. Stale snack foods such as potato chips, pretzels or popcorn can be re-crisped. Place 2 to 3 cups in small napkin-lined bowl or nonmetallic basket. Microwave, uncovered, at High 15 to 60 seconds, or until food is warm to the touch. Cool.

► **Elevating to Aid Cooking.** If any area in breads and quiches remains uncooked after recommended cooking time, elevate dish on inverted saucer and continue microwaving at 1-minute intervals. This will expose more of the uncooked area to microwave energy and aids in cooking.

Cakes and quick breads may have uncooked batter on the bottom center. Microwave until wooden pick inserted in center comes out clean.

Custard pies and quiches may sometimes have uncooked area on the top center. Microwave until knife inserted in center comes out clean.

How to Open Fresh Oysters & Clams

Clean oysters or clams. Soak in cold water at least 3 hours. Arrange six oysters at a time in 9-in. round cake dish or 2-qt. casserole. Cover with plastic wrap or lid.

Microwave at High 45 seconds, or until shells have just opened. Remove all opened shells and continue microwaving any unopened oysters, checking every 15 seconds.

Insert knife between shells near hinge and open. Use knife to cut muscle away from shell. To cook oysters or clams, microwave another 30 to 60 seconds, or until firm.

308

Drain Ground Beef. Microwave and drain ground beef at the same time. Crumble 1 lb. ground beef into dishwasher-safe plastic colander with no metal parts. Place colander in 2-qt. casserole or deep bowl. Microwave at High 4 to 6 minutes, or until meat is no longer pink, stirring with fork to break apart every 2 minutes.

Frozen Vegetable Pouches. If possible, flex pouch to break apart vegetables. Cut a large "X" in one side of pouch. Place 9- or 10-oz. pouch, cut side down, in serving dish. Microwave at High 5 to 8 minutes, or until heated. Lift opposite corners of pouch to protect your hands from steam as vegetable is released into dish. Stir.

Frozen Vegetables in Box. To defrost a 10-oz. package of frozen vegetables for use in a recipe, remove paper wrapping; place box on oven floor. Microwave at High 4 minutes, or until box is warm to the touch, turning after half the time. Let stand to complete defrosting. Drain. Add to recipe.

Cooking bags provide an easy clean-up method for roasting. When using cooking bags, tie loosely with string or rubber band to allow steam to escape. Do not use twist ties.

Leftover Rice. Freeze leftover rice in 1- or 2-cup quantities. Store no longer than 6 months. To defrost, place rice in casserole indicated in chart, below; cover. Microwave at High as directed, until hot, breaking apart and stirring once.

Amt.	Casserole Size	Microwave Time
1 cup	15-oz.	2 - 3 min.
2 cups	1-qt.	4 - 8 min.

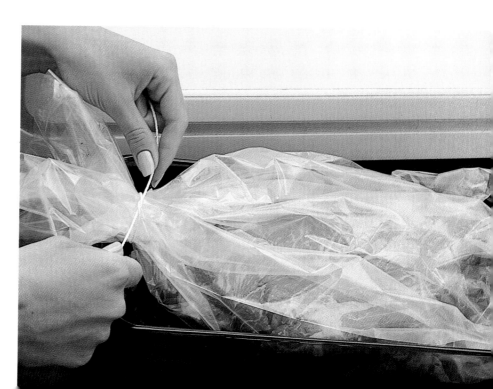

◀ **Oshibori Towels.** Fold four dampened washcloths and place in non-metallic basket or shallow dish. Microwave at High 1 to 2 minutes, or until warm to the touch. Offer to guests before and after dining.

For scented washcloths, place lemon peel, studded with 4 whole cloves, in each washcloth. Microwave as directed. Remove lemon before using.

Warm Compress. Place one dampened washcloth in oven. Microwave at High 15 to 30 seconds, or until warm to the touch. Use as compress.

Easy Ironing of Linens. To make ironing of linens, tablecloths and napkins easy, sprinkle lightly with water. Place in 1-gallon plastic garbage bag. Twist end to close loosely. Microwave at High 1 minute, or until warm to the touch. Iron.

Hot Towels

Carefully check towels after microwaving. They may become very warm.

▲ **Oven Refresher.** For a quick oven refresher, place ½ cup water in 4-cup measure or bowl. Add one of the following fresheners. Microwave, uncovered, at High 1 to 2 minutes, or until boiling. Microwave 1 minute longer. Oven and kitchen will smell fresh and clean.

Fresheners:
· 2 slices fresh lemon, orange or lime
· 1 tablespoon lemon juice
· ¼ teaspoon ground cinnamon
· 8 whole cloves and 8 whole allspice
· 1 teaspoon baking soda

Easy Oven Cleaning. Place dampened dishcloth in oven. Microwave at High 15 to 30 seconds, or until warm but not hot. Wipe up spills or cooked-on foods in oven cavity with warm cloth.

A Note on Dietary Exchange Information

The exchange system has become a popular and useful tool for dieters in planning their daily food consumption. It combines calorie counting and basic food groupings to make weight management and getting good nutrition easier. The exchange values of many recipes in this book have been calculated so you will know how different dishes fit into your diet.

Foods are divided into six groups, or Exchanges. They are grouped by comparable calorie and nutrient values — such as meats and fish in one group, fruits in another. Foods in any one group can be exchanged with any other food in the same group, following serving-size guidelines you can find in any exchange-based diet book. It takes all six groups working together to supply all the nutrients needed for a balanced diet.

Special diets will require a given number of exchanges from the six groups to total the desired number of calories needed per day to maintain, gain, or lose weight. Instead of counting calories, you count exchanges. They are outlined below.

Exchange Chart

FRUIT EXCHANGES:	One Fruit Exchange contains 40 calories and 10 grams of carbohydrate, plus vitamins, minerals and fiber.
MILK EXCHANGES:	One Milk Exchange contains 80 calories, 12 grams of carbohydrate, 8 grams of protein, a trace of fat, calcium, and other minerals and vitamins.
VEGETABLE EXCHANGES:	One Vegetable Exchange contains 25 calories, about 5 grams of carbohydrate, 2 grams of protein, and vitamins and minerals. (Note that corn, lima and dried beans, squashes and pumpkin, peas, potatoes, rice and barley are grouped in the Bread Exchange. Avocados are grouped in the Fat Exchange.)
BREAD EXCHANGES:	One Bread Exchange contains 70 calories, 15 grams of carbohydrate, 2 grams of protein and minerals. (Includes breads, cereals and starchy vegetables.)
FAT EXCHANGES:	One Fat Exchange contains 45 calories and 5 grams of fat. (Includes animal and vegetable fats; margarine, butter, cream and cream cheese; nuts; olives; salad dressings; bacon and salt pork.)
MEAT EXCHANGES:	Foods grouped as Meat Exchanges are classified according to their relative fat content. (Includes meats, fish, cheese and peanut butter.)
	One Low-Fat Meat Exchange contains 55 calories, 7 grams of protein and 3 grams of fat. One Medium-Fat Meat Exchange contains 78 calories, 7 grams of protein and 5.5 grams of fat. One High-Fat Meat Exchange contains 100 calories, 7 grams of protein and 8 grams of fat. Many Meat Exchange foods contain iron, zinc and B-complex vitamins.
FREE FOODS:	Free Foods have 20 calories or less per serving; they provide negligible nourishment. (Includes seasonings, condiments, broths, certain raw vegetables, coffee, tea and diet soft drinks.)

Herbs & Spices Chart

Spice	Meat	Poultry	Fish & Seafood	Eggs & Cheese	Vegetables	Sauces	Desserts
Allspice	Ham Meatballs Meat Loaf Pot Roast Spare Ribs Stew	Chicken Fricassee	Steamed Fish		Carrots Eggplant Potato Soup Spinach Squash Turnips	Barbecue Cranberry Tomato	Fruitcake Fruits Mince Pie Pumpkin Pie Steamed Pudding
Basil	Beef Lamb Pork Veal	Chicken	Crab Shrimp Steamed Fish Tuna	Creamed Eggs Omelets Scrambled Eggs Soufflés	Bean Soup Eggplant Green Beans Tomatoes Wax Beans Potato Soup	Spaghetti Tomato	
Bay Leaf	Soups Stews Tongue	Chicken Chicken Soup Chicken Stew	Shrimp		Artichokes Beets Green Beans Tomatoes	Gravies Marinades	
Caraway Seed	Pork		Fish Seafood Stew	Cottage Cheese	Cabbage Potatoes Sauerkraut	Cheese	
Celery Seed	Stews		Fish	Cheese Dishes	Cabbage Cauliflower Onions Potato Salad Tomatoes		
Chili Powder	Beef Stew Chili Tamales	Barbecued Chicken Chicken	Shrimp	Fondue Scrambled Eggs	Cauliflower Lima Beans Onions Pea Soup	Cheese Seafood	
Cinnamon	Beef Stew Ham Pork	Stewed Chicken	Shrimp		Carrots Onions Spinach Squash Sweet Potatoes	Apple	Apples Fruit Compotes Puddings
Cloves	Ham Soups Stews Tongue	Creamed Chicken	Fish		Bean Soup Beets Carrots Onions Squash	Tomato	Apples Gingerbread Pears
Coriander	Curries Meatballs Meat Loaf Sausage	Curries	Curries				Apple Pie Peach Pie Rice Pudding
Cumin	Chili Curry Sausage Soups Stews		Curries	Egg Dishes Cheese Dishes	Sauerkraut Tomatoes		
Dill Seed Dill Weed	Beef Lamb Pork Soups Stews Veal	Chicken	Salmon Shellfish	Cottage Cheese Deviled Eggs	Beans Cabbage Carrots Cauliflower Lentils Peas Potatoes	Cocktail Sauce Fish	

Spice	Meat	Poultry	Fish & Seafood	Eggs & Cheese	Vegetables	Sauces	Desserts
Ginger	Beef Pork Pot Roast	Roast Chicken Stir Fries	Fish	Macaroni & Cheese	Baked Beans Beets Carrots Squash Sweet Potatoes		Gingerbread Pears Puddings Steamed Fruit
Mace & Nutmeg	Meatballs Meat Loaf Pot Roast Stews Veal Soups	Chicken Fricassee	Fish Oysters Shrimp Creole	Quiche Lorraine	Artichokes Brussels Sprouts Cabbage Onions Spinach	Cheese Fish Mushroom Spaghetti	Apple Pie Custard Pumpkin Pie
Marjoram	Beef Lamb Liver Meatballs Meat Loaf Pork Stews Veal	Chicken Salad Roast Chicken Soups Stuffings Turkey	Crab Salmon	Cheese Soufflé Omelets Scrambled Eggs	Celery Eggplant Green Beans Lima Beans Onion Soup Potatoes Spinach Zucchini		
Oregano	Chili Hamburger Liver Pot Roast Soups Stews Veal	Chicken	Fish Shellfish		Broccoli Cabbage Eggplant Lentils Onions Tomatoes Onions Zucchini	Mushroom Spaghetti	
Parsley	Meat Loaf Pot Roast Soups Stews	Stuffings	Fish Fillets Lobster	Cottage Cheese Scrambled Eggs	Beans Carrots Cauliflower Eggplant Mushrooms Peas Potatoes Tomatoes	Spaghetti	
Rosemary	Beef Lamb Pork Veal	Roast Chicken Roast Turkey Stuffings	Fish Fillets	Egg Dishes Cheese Dishes	Eggplant Mushrooms Onions		
Sage	Ham Pork Sausage Veal	Roast Chicken Roast Turkey Soups Stuffings	Fish	Cheese Dishes Cottage Cheese Egg Dishes	Brussels Sprouts Egg Plant Green Beans Lima Beans Squash Tomatoes	Cheese	
Tarragon	Beef Veal	Chicken	Fish Fillets Lobster	Egg Dishes	Beets Spinach	Fish	
Thyme	Beef Lamb Pork Soups Stews	Chicken Stuffings	Clam Chowder Oysters Tuna	Omelets Scrambled Eggs Soufflés	Carrots Eggplant Green Beans Onions Peas Tomatoes		

Index

Don't Stop with *The Joy of Microwaving!*

The Joy of Microwaving is just the beginning of what you can do with your microwave. The Microwave Cooking Library has 12 specialized cookbooks that can help you make even more of the foods you like best and introduce you to some new favorites. Whether your specialty is quick meals, one certain course or low calorie menus, or if you just want to learn more about the many ways to use your microwave — you'll find more books tailored to your special interests and favorite foods. Each cookbook is illustrated with over 250 color photographs offering step-by-step instructions for easy, foolproof microwaving. You'll find them at your local book store. Or use the handy order blank for home delivery.

I want to expand my microwave library. Please send me the following cookbooks priced at only $14.95 for each hardcover copy. Prices are subject to change.

☐ **Basic Microwaving**
0-671-61069-4

☐ **Microwaving Baking & Desserts**
0-671-61075-9

☐ **Microwave Cooking: Adapting Conventional Recipes**
0-671-61074-0

☐ **Microwave Cooking: From the Freezer**
0-671-61066-X

☐ **Microwave Meals in 30 Minutes**
0-671-61072-4

☐ **Microwaving Convenience Foods**
0-671-61076-7

☐ **Microwaving for One & Two**
0-671-61070-8

☐ **Microwaving Light & Healthy**
0-671-61967-5

☐ **Microwaving Meats**
0-671-61077-5

☐ **Microwaving on a Diet**
0-671-61068-6

☐ **Microwaving Poultry & Seafood**
0-671-62268-4

☐ **101 Microwaving Secrets**
0-671-61073-2

Enclosed is my ☐ check ☐ money order. Or, please charge my ☐ MasterCard ☐ Visa. I've included $1.50 postage and handling for the first book and $1.00 each additional. Please add appropriate sales tax regardless of payment method.

Name _____

Address _____

City _____ State _____ Zip _____

Account # ☐☐☐☐☐☐☐☐☐☐☐☐☐☐☐☐ Expir. date ☐☐☐☐

Signature _____

PRENTICE HALL PRESS • A Division of Simon & Schuster, Inc. • Dept. VM • 200 Old Tappan Road • Old Tappan, NJ 07675

G-779-0